Secession
The Morality of Political Divorce from Fort Sumter to Lithuania and Quebec

Allen Buchanan

Westview Press

BOULDER • SAN FRANCISCO • OXFORD

Copyright © 1991 by Westview Press, Inc.

Published in 1991 in the United States of America by Westview Press, Inc., 5500 Central Avenue, Boulder, Colorado 80301, and in the United Kingdom by Westview Press, 36 Lonsdale Road, Summertown, Oxford OX2 7EW

Library of Congress Cataloging-in-Publication Data
Buchanan, Allen E., 1948–
  Secession : the morality of political divorce from Fort Sumter to
Lithuania and Quebec / by Allen Buchanan.
    p. cm.
  Includes bibliographical references and index.
  ISBN 0-8133-1132-2.—ISBN 0-8133-1133-0 (pbk.).
  1. Political obligation—Moral and ethical aspects. 2. Secession—
Moral and ethical aspects. I. Title.
JC329.5.B83 1991
320'.01'1—dc20   91-13396
                                                                          CIP

Printed and bound in the United States of America

The paper used in this publication meets the requirements
of the American National Standard for Permanence of Paper
for Printed Library Materials Z39.48-1984.

10   9   8   7   6

Contents

Preface

Perhaps no other question of political philosophy, or of international law, pregnant with such unutterable calamities, has ever been so partially and superficially examined as the right of secession.

—Albert Taylor Bledsoe

These lines were penned in 1866 in a book that attempted to prove that an implicit constitutional right to secede existed in the United States at the time of Southern secession.[1] They are as true today as they were then. From Quebec to Lithuania to the Ukraine to Azerbaijan, new secessionist movements are springing up and old ones are rejuvenating, with no end in sight; and the stakes are high. Yet official pronouncements, media coverage, and the discourse of ordinary citizens about these extraordinary events all suffer from superficiality and confusion, while the leading figures of political philosophy, past and present, are virtually mute on the issue of secession.

Neither Plato, Hobbes, Locke, Rousseau, Hegel, Marx, nor Mill devoted any serious attention to secession. It is true, of course, that the topic was hotly debated by statesmen-political philosophers such as Webster and Calhoun in America in the period preceding and during the Civil War.[2] However, as will become clear later, the peculiarities of the American situation greatly narrowed the focus of thinking on secession; and even within those confines, no adequate, systematic analysis of secession emerged.

One especially striking feature of current debate over secession is its overtly *moral* character. Even those who usually take a certain perverse pride in posturing as moral skeptics or *realpolitikers* inevitably speak the language of right (and rights) and wrong when it comes to secession. Gorbachev says that American indignation at his resistance to Lithuanian secession is hypocrisy, coming from a country that reveres Lincoln for crushing its own secessionist movement. Quebecois claim a moral right to an autonomous society. Many Western observers condemn secessionist talk by Azerbaijanis or Ghurzhis, saying that these peoples want autonomy so they will be free to commit atrocities against Armenians and others. The question is not whether the debate about secession will be framed in moral terms. Rather, it is this: Can a coherent and illuminating moral framework for grappling with the real world problems of secession be developed?

Some purport to abstain from the moral debate, dismissing moral judgments about secession and other major political conflicts as naive, declaring with a smug, world-weary sigh that naked power, as always, will decide the issue. The cynic assumes either that there is no such thing as moral reasoning and that there are no moral *judgments*, but only subjective tastes parading as judgments, or that moral beliefs are motivationally impotent, that only the lust for power determines behavior in the political realm. Such pessimistic conclusions about the morality of secession, I shall argue, are exaggerated. It *is* possible to think coherently about the morality of secession, and some positions on secession are more reasonable from a moral point of view than others. Systematic moral reflection can provide substantive guidance. This book aims to do just that. Whether it succeeds in doing so the reader can determine only after reading it.

But at the outset I would remind the cynic that his assumption that moral judgments play no role in determining what individuals and nations really do is highly improbable in light of one very simple fact: Even the most ruthless perpetrators of injustices, and especially those scoundrels who have been among the most skillful manipulators of motivation, have invariably recognized the importance of providing moral justifications for their actions. From Julius Caesar's attempt to justify the invasion of Gaul as a purely defensive measure to Adolf Hitler's claim that conquest is the prerogative of the master race, tyrants as well as defenders of freedom have tried to justify their policies morally.

Now, if what people believe about what is right or wrong has no effect on their behavior, the struggle for the high moral ground that invariably pervades the world of international as well as domestic politics, and that is waged everyday in conflicts over secession, would make no sense. If one acknowledges that moral beliefs do influence behavior and also grants the rather modest claim that some moral beliefs are more justified than others, one is already in a position to appreciate and participate in an attempt to think about the morality of secession in a clear-headed, sensitive, and systematic way.

In more optimistic moments I am tempted to say that the first three chapters of this book present a moral *theory* of secession and that the fourth then uses the moral theory to develop a *theory* of the constitutional right to secede. In one sense this is quite accurate: Sometimes moral philosophers use the term 'theory' in a relatively unambitious way to refer to any serious and at least minimally successful attempt to think self-consciously and self-critically, in a systematic, consistent, and principled way, about what we ought or ought not to do in some area of human activity where hard choices must be made. At the very least, the concept of a theory can serve as a guiding ideal for our investigation—a standard of rigor, completeness, and insight the pursuit of which, even if ultimately unsuccessful, can spur us on to do the best of which we are capable.

The notion of theory has another advantage: The proper evaluation of a theory is always, ultimately, *comparative*. In general, when we try to decide whether or not to accept a theory, the appropriate question is not "Does it explain all the data or solve all the problems?" but, rather, "Is it the best theory available?" In judging the moral views on secession presented here (whether one honors them with the title 'theory' or not), the fundamental question is not whether they solve all or even most of the moral dilemmas of secession, but whether they improve significantly upon the current prevalent ways of thinking about the issue. In the end, the only way to refute a theory conclusively is to advance a better theory.

Nonetheless, this use of the term is risky, especially in interdisciplinary contexts, because, for some, 'theory' has much grander connotations. Perhaps a prudent compromise would be to say that this book offers a *moral framework* for thinking about secession that provides consistent and reasoned guidance for some of the many hard choices we confront concerning secession and that this framework can serve as the beginning of a theory of secession (in the more ambitious sense). However, if even the term 'framework' suggests more *completeness* and *finality* than is warranted here, a still more humble characterization of the enterprise might be: *Moral reflections on secession.*

Contemporary scholarship on international law does contain opposing views on whether or under what conditions there is a legal right to secede; and, at times, almost in spite of themselves, international lawyers take moral positions. Yet they do so without anything like a systematic examination of the moral issues and often without any clear distinction between moral and legal questions. To my knowledge, the reflections contained here are the closest thing to a moral theory of secession currently available. That will change quickly, I have no doubt. In some ways this state of affairs is liberating: One bold or foolish enough can plunge right in and try to grapple with the problems without being crushed beneath the paralyzing weight of a mountain of previous thinking to be sifted through. (Thus the pioneer striving for a truly systematic moral theory of secession might be tempted to say: "If I have not seen very far, it is because I stood on the shoulders of midgets!") At the same time, the risks of making a fool (or, as this is a moral issue, a knave) of oneself are correspondingly greater. When the contemplation of these risks oppresses me, I console myself with the hope that this volume will be classified—and judged—as an early work on the moral theory of secession!

Though an early work, it is not simply a reaction to the current spate of secessionist movements in the Soviet Union or to the resurgence of secessionist sentiment in Quebec or elsewhere. My own interest in secession predates these events. At most, the current headlines on secession prompted me to undertake sooner rather than later something I had intended to do for many years. My interest in secession stems from three seemingly unrelated sources: my sense of the profound tragedy of the American Civil War, my interest in and personal experience of the struggle for human rights in South Africa, and my ambivalent love of liberalism as the least bad political philosophy among the alternatives.

Reflection on the origins of the American Civil War have convinced me that the only sound moral justification for resisting Southern secession was the liberation of blacks. For as we shall see, it is hard to fathom how just the need to "preserve the Union" could justify the staggering destruction of human life and property that ensued. (One in every four Southern men of military age died in the conflict, and the number of *Union* soldiers who fell in the series of battles from the Wilderness to Cold Harbor, from May to June in the last year of the war, nearly equaled the total number of Americans who died in Vietnam; moreover, two-thirds of the South's wealth, *excluding* property in slaves, was destroyed in the war.[3])

The true tragedy of the American Civil War is not simply that the losses were so great, but that the only goal which could have justified them was not fully attained: Slavery was abolished, but the task of liberating black Americans was left unfinished. Not until the Civil Rights Act of 1964 and the 1965 Voting Rights Act—one hundred years after the fighting had ceased—did blacks in the South secure some of the most fundamental civil rights. Thus in one sense the South won the Civil War: Southern whites preserved their domination over blacks, developing new forms of institutional racism that reached a crescendo in the Jim Crow Laws, after the institution of slavery was swept away by the war.[4]

Any sensitive student of the American Civil War is bound to be struck by the fact that on both sides there was a profound moral ambiguity concerning *what the war was really being fought for.* And it is hard not to believe that this lack of moral clarity infected the peace, reinforcing other factors that led to a failure of nerve in completing the task of black liberation. Because many, perhaps most, Northerners believed that the primary if not the exclusive war aim was to preserve the Union (and that, as Lincoln actually said, abolition of slavery was justified only as a means toward that end[5]), it is not surprising that the commitment to improving the condition of blacks waned once the crisis of disunion was past. My sense is that most Americans to this day have not squarely faced the moral issues raised by Southern secession.

For good or for ill, the vividness of the issues of the American Civil War is fading with each successive generation, even in the South. By contrast, the second source of my interest in secession is a social revolution now in progress: the battle against apartheid. I have been privileged to bear witness to this heroic struggle for black liberation. In 1988 I traveled extensively in South Africa, speaking to diverse individuals and groups on the role of appeals to justice in the social revolution occurring in that beautiful and tragic country and attempting to defend the liberal emphasis on individual rights against those on the left and on the right who would denigrate them.

That visit impressed upon me the tremendous ethnic and political diversity of South Africa. Throughout numerous discussions of the prospects for constitutional reform and eventually for a postapartheid constitution, two questions kept surfacing: Will a constitutional framework of exclusively individual rights suffice, or should group rights of some sort be included; and will there be one South Africa or will the process of social revolution result in fragmentation? These two questions intersect in a third: Should a constitution for postapartheid South Africa include a right to secede? Some South Africans (black and white) with whom I spoke were willing to explore the latter query. Others thought that even talking about secession ran the risk of weakening the solidarity essential for the success of the struggle against apartheid.

The third source of my interest in secession is my long-standing effort to understand liberalism and to ascertain its strengths and weaknesses. By 'liberalism' I mean something in a sense quite simple, though at the same time quite general and inclusive: that core of the Western tradition in political philosophy which is committed first and foremost to the basic individual civil and political rights that find expression in the great documents of the French and American revolutions. (This understanding of liberalism, I should emphasize, is much more basic than a number of political philosophies that present themselves under that title; and it is not to be identified with any of its more particular variations, such as the antiwelfare, police-and-nightwatchman state "liberalism" that is known in America as libertarianism. Indeed 'liberalism', as I shall use that term, is itself noncommittal as to the extent of the proper distributive or redistributive functions of the state.) It had puzzled me that liberalism, a political philosophy that preeminently values self-determination and prizes diversity and that views the state as a human creation to serve human needs, not a deity or an unalterable fact of nature, should have so little to say about secession. Moreover, in assessing the criticisms of liberalism advanced by those contemporary thinkers who call themselves communitarians,[6] I had begun to think more critically about what they take to be liberalism's exclusive concern with individual rights and to wonder whether it might have room for group rights of some kind, including perhaps a right to secede. Recent political events have made the question of whether liberalism can accommodate a right to secede all the more pertinent: In many cases, secessionist movements, especially in the Soviet Union, are riding the crest of what appears to be—or at least purports to be—a liberal revolution.

My problem, therefore, was not lack of interest, but rather, how to translate this interest into a systematic and fruitful inquiry into the morality of secession and the idea of a constitutional right to secede. Here a conflict of roles soon emerged. On the one hand, I hoped to adopt the traditional philosophical posture of gadfly—to criticize prevalent ways of thinking about the issues, ruthlessly exposing hidden assumptions, answering one question with two or more, further complicating the difficult and making strange the familiar. Since Socrates, the gadfly has been a valuable, if exasperating, contributor to society.

On the other hand, work I had done over the years in so-called applied ethics, particularly in the ethics of health care, had convinced me that philosophers can play a more constructive role—that the tools of moral philosophy, if properly employed, can actually provide some guidance in the world of action. But the attempt to engage in genuine action-guiding, that is, *normative* ethics, while at the same time preserving the rigor and ruthless self-criticism of the traditional philosophical gadfly, is exceedingly difficult. At times the result approaches schizophrenia—or rather, not just a split in the mind, but in the heart as well.

More precisely, the conflict is this. On the one hand, any proffered moral guidance on a topic like secession must satisfy two conditions: It must be reasonably concrete, and it must justify its recommendations by arguments that are widely accessible, not just convincing to colleagues who happen to share one's own deep philosophical views. That is, one must say something of normative significance about the issues without first solving all the fundamental problems of moral theory to the satisfaction of professional moral philosophers. The only sane approach to doing this is to begin with widely shared moral principles and values and to attempt to develop new and useful guidance by carefully formulating and refining them, articulating their interconnections and implications, and modifying and improving or even discarding some of them where necessary. The principles in question are gleaned from common-sense morality, from points of agreement among the major ethical traditions, both religious and secular, and from the most stable and fruitful core of the law, especially the common law, understood as an institutional embodiment of techniques of practical reasoning for dealing with conflicts of interest, developed and refined over many generations.[7]

On the other hand, for the philosophical gadfly, none of this is enough. He will demand something more ambitious, more foundational, and more intellectually self-sufficient. Why rely at all upon ethical or legal traditions; or, more to the point, why rely upon one tradition rather than any other? Surely an adequate view on secession must be derived from adequate theories of distributive justice and of political obligation and, ultimately, from an adequate metaethical theory—a theory that explains the nature of moral discourse and provides an account of what ultimately makes a moral judgment or principle valid.

When giving an informal presentation of my work on secession to a small group of philosophers and political scientists, I was confronted by such demands in extreme, almost caricature, form. One philosopher (a logician, not a moral philosopher) asked me to formulate my "theory" of secession by filling in the blank, "Secession is morally justified if and only if ____," with a list of necessary and sufficient conditions, 1, 2, 3, etc. My somewhat grumpy reply was that I doubt if anyone could plausibly fill in the blanks for almost any hard moral issue. For example, is it really reasonable to think that one could say "killing another human being is morally justified if and only if 1, 2, 3"? Often the most one can reasonably aim for is to supply some of the necessary conditions and some of the sufficient conditions.

A political scientist in the same group expressed undisguised indignation that my treatment of the topic failed to make clear which (single!) fundamental moral decision rule I was relying on. Was it utilitarianism (maximize overall utility), or was it the maximin principle (choose the option that has the least bad worst outcome), or the libertarian principle of private property rights, or what? My response to this demand was not so much irritation as astonishment. I believe that most moral philosophers now agree that there is no single over-arching principle (and certainly none of the above!) that is a plausible basis for all moral decisions. Further, the same worries about the arbitrariness of starting points that lead the philosopher as gadfly to be suspicious of initial reliance on common-sense moral principles apply as well to grand "fundamental" principles. None has been shown to be uniquely rational or uniquely appropriate in any way.

So for three distinct reasons I begin *in medias res*—in the midst of what I believe to be some of the most widely held and least controversial moral views—rather than attempting to develop a foundational ethical theory and then to apply it to secession. First, neither I nor anyone else possesses a fully developed, uniquely valid moral theory in the ambitious sense (or at least not one that is substantive and concrete enough to tell us much of interest about secession). Second, even if such a theory were available, it would be inaccessible—and, I am confident, quite uninteresting—to the majority of those who are interested in real-world struggles about secession and who may play some role in deciding those contests. Finally, I am especially concerned with the relationship between liberalism and secession, both because of my own predilections for that view and because it is liberal ideas that are currently sweeping across the international political landscape. Hence it makes a good deal of sense to rely, at least initially, on substantive moral beliefs and styles of argument that are part of the broadly liberal tradition in ethics, politics, and law.

Some, no doubt, will charge me with liberal bias. More specifically, they may assume that my use of styles of argument characteristic of liberalism commits me to *individualism*, opposition to which unifies an otherwise diverse collection of schools of thought from Marxism to communitarianism to deconstructionism and critical theory. In addition to their opposition to liberal individualism, what unites these quite different views is their remarkable unclarity about what individualism is, their failure to articulate a plausible alternative to it, and the lack of any convincing argument to show precisely how the liberal emphasis on individual civil and political rights is necessarily linked to the kind or kinds of "individualism" that are objectionable.[8]

Instead of attempting to defend liberalism, however, I want to emphasize that this book can be seen as a fundamental *criticism* of liberalism in at least three respects. First, I make a case here for certain group or collective rights, including a right to secede —and liberalism, as it is ordinarily understood, and not just by those who criticize it for its "individualism" but by some of its champions as well, is said to recognize only individual rights. Second, I argue that the grounds for justified opposition to political authority are broader than liberalism usually admits: Revolution or secession can be justified as efforts to relieve injustices other than those consisting of the violation of individual rights. In particular, I show in Chapter 2 that a group may be justified in opposing the state with force if that group is the victim of discriminatory redistribution —that is, if the state's economic policies or taxation schemes systematically work to the disadvantage of that group and for the benefit of others, in the absence of any sound moral justification for this difference in treatment. Third, I argue that under certain conditions a group is justified in seceding if doing so is necessary for the preservation of its distinctive culture or form of communal life. Each of these conclusions is a sharp departure from what is often taken to be a central feature of liberal individualism: the exclusive preoccupation with individual rights and a corresponding failure to appreciate the importance of community or group membership for the individual's well-being and very identity.

Hence if I am to be convincingly convicted of the charge of "individualism," that will take some showing. My critic would have to specify the sense in which the view developed in this book is individualistic *and* what it is about this (at best rather attenuated) individualism that is defective. More specifically, she would need to show that there is some incoherence or other flaw in the idea of a moral-political framework that includes both individual rights and collective rights. In Chapters 2 and 5 I provide a positive defense of the mixed approach, arguing that the most plausible account of what rights are makes it clear that there are both individual and group rights. There I also argue that an "individualistic" justification can be given for group rights, but that the relevant notion of individualism is wholly innocuous and affirms, rather than denies, the value and centrality of community in people's lives.

I prefer to think of this volume as making a case for significantly modifying liberalism, for pruning back its excessively individualistic elements. But I have no strong objection if some should see it instead as a rejection of liberalism, so long as they understand that it is not a repudiation of the individual rights associated with that theory but, rather, an attempt to supplement them.

This is not to say, however, that what follows is neutral with regard to disputes between liberalism and antiliberal stances. Even though I offer fundamental criticisms of some elements of liberalism, at least in some of its forms, the framework of arguments and values I utilize is clearly closer to liberalism than to any competing position. I make no apologies for this, because I believe that liberalism, with all its flaws, provides greater resources for systematic and sensitive normative guidance in thinking about political institutions than do its rivals, whose attraction more often than not lies in their vagueness and steadfast refusal to take clear positions on concrete issues.

Within these limitations, I have attempted to strike a reasonable balance between the two conflicting philosophical roles. A sure sign that I have not entirely neglected either the gadfly or the practical guide is that some of what I say will be unsatisfying to both of their constituencies. I accept that fate, asking only that the reader acknowledge that the task at hand is inescapably one of compromise between the two perspectives.

Allen Buchanan

Notes

1. Albert Taylor Bledsoe, *Is Jeff Davis a Traitor?* (New York: Innis & Company, 1866), p. 1.

2. John Stuart Mill, in *On Representative Government*, includes a very brief discussion of "nationality" (or, as we would say, nationalism), but nothing like a systematic consideration of moral arguments for and against secession. See Mill, "On Representative Government," in *John Stuart Mill: Three Essays*, with an introduction by Richard Wollheim (Oxford: Oxford University Press, 1975), pp. 380–388.

3. For a powerful statement of the magnitude of the destruction wreaked during the American Civil War, see James M. McPherson, *The Battle Cry of Freedom* (Oxford: Oxford University Press, 1988), pp. 485–486, 730–731, 807–819, and 854–856. For detailed accounts of the major battles in Virginia in the spring and summer of 1864, see Noah André Trudeau, *Bloody Roads South* (New York: Fawcett Columbine, 1989) and Shelby Foote, *The Civil War: A Narrative*, vol. 3, *Red River to Appomatox* (New York: Vintage Books, Random House, 1986).

4. C. Vann Woodward, *The Strange Career of Jim Crow*, 3d rev. ed. (New York: Oxford University Press, 1974).

5. Abraham Lincoln, *Speeches and Writings*, vol. 2, edited by Don E. Fehrenbach (New York: Literary Classics of America, 1989), pp. 357–358.

6. Allen Buchanan, "Assessing the Communitarian Critique of Liberalism," *Ethics*, vol. 99, no. 4, July 1989, pp. 852–882.

7. One important reason for a guarded confidence in relying on the common law as a model for types of arguments is its (qualified) success in providing a stable, enduring alternative to violence as a way of coping with conflicts of interest —an alternative that emphasizes both the equal standing of all persons and procedural fairness. But of equal if not greater importance are two other considerations. First, the common law is an *argumentative* and hence inherently *self-critical* institution. Even if it does not (as Justice Holmes said) "work itself pure," it can work itself purer. In its doctrine of precedent the common law does give a prominent place to authority, in a sense; but it is the authority of *principles*, principles that are framed, and subjected to criticism, as *reasons* for acting. Second, this system has developed within the context of a type of society that has been increasingly characterized by freedom of expression, of belief, and of association. Other things being equal, we have more reason to rely upon an institution that has evolved under free conditions and in response to free criticism.

8. See Buchanan, "Assessing the Communitarian Critique of Liberalism," especially pp. 852–865, 878–881. See also Will Kymlicka, "Liberal Individualism and Liberal Neutrality," *Ethics*, vol. 99, no. 4, July 1989, pp. 883–905.

Acknowledgments

One of the most enjoyable aspects of writing this book was the opportunity it provided for discussing a fascinating, neglected, and politically current topic with a large number of extraordinarily intelligent people. I have profited immeasurably from the generosity of numerous individuals and from strong institutional support as well.

I am especially indebted to Spencer Carr, James Fishkin, Dale Jamieson, Will Kymlicka, Christopher Morris, and David Schmidtz, who expended a great deal of labor in providing me with exceptionally insightful, constructive comments on the entire manuscript of the book. In addition, the following individuals volunteered valuable comments on parts of the book or on the initial paper on secession with which the project began ("Towards a Theory of Secession," *Ethics*, vol. 101, no. 2, January 1991, pp. 322–342): Peter Aranson, Richard Arneson, Hugo Bedau, James Buchanan, Lea Brilymayer, Thomas Christiano, Jules Coleman, Norman Daniels, William Dennis, Jacqueline Dunaway, Nancy Goldberg, Jean Hampton, Hurst Hannum, Michael Hechter, Robert Hessen, Howard Klepper, Russell Schafer-Landau, Don Lenihan, Eric Mack, Jeffrey Paul, Stephen Perry, John Rawls, Jennifer Roback, Holly Smith, Richard Teichgraeber, Gordon Tullock, Christopher (Kit) Wellman, and Robert A. Williams, Jr. I am also grateful to Kenneth Cust, Nancy Goldberg, and Howard Klepper for their excellent work as research assistants.

In the summer of 1990 I was able to work exclusively and intensively on this book at the Center for Social Philosophy and Policy at Bowling Green State University as a Summer Research Professor. I also received valuable research support from the Earhart Foundation. By sponsoring a symposium entitled "Liberalism, Federalism, and the Question of Secession" in Tucson in December 1990, the Liberty Fund, Incorporated, enabled me to share my work on the topic with a number of excellent thinkers from a variety of disciplines.

I am also deeply indebted to Jack R. Cole, Vice President for Academic Affairs and Provost; Holly Smith, Vice Provost; Lee Sigelman, Dean of the Faculty of Social and Behavioral Sciences; and Ronald Milo, Head of the

Department of Philosophy of the University of Arizona, for allowing me a temporary leave from my teaching responsibilities to complete this project.

My heartfelt thanks also go to Lois Day and Ann Hickman, who helped with many revisions and prepared the manuscript for publication, and to Matthew Held and Spencer Carr of Westview Press, whose excellent editorial skills and warm enthusiasm made my work so much easier.

A. B.

1

The Problems of Secession

I would save the Union. . . . My paramount object in this struggle *is* to save the Union, and is not either to save or to destroy slavery. If I could save the Union without freeing *any* slave I would do it, and if I could save the Union by freeing some and leaving others alone I would also do that. What I do about slavery, and the colored race, I do because I believe it helps to save the Union.
—Abraham Lincoln[1]

I. The Practical Need for a Theory of Secession

When we ponder Lincoln's statement that he was concerned above all to save the Union, our sense of awe in the face of his moral grandeur should be tempered by consternation at his willingness to preserve a human artifice, a political union not yet a hundred years old, no matter what the cost in death and destruction, and even if it meant making a bargain with those who owned other human beings. We cannot evade the disturbing question: Had slavery not been at issue, how could Lincoln's behavior be justified? And how could the abolition of slavery, which was not even a Northern war aim until the end of the conflict, serve to justify commencing the war to keep the South in the Union in the first place?

Most Americans probably cannot but think of our Civil War as a war to end slavery. Perhaps we lack Lincoln's cool ability to separate ruthlessly the issue of slavery from that of secession. Slavery is such an abomination that the mere contemplation of it tends to swamp the pure secession issue.

Today we are confronted with the issue of secession in a quite different context—indeed in a number of different contexts. In recent months in Eastern and Central Europe and in the Soviet Union, demands for political and economic reforms have in some cases escalated to demands for secession, or at least for official recognition of a right to secede—in the Baltic Republics, in Yugoslavia, in the Ukraine, and in Soviet Georgia and Armenia. In South Africa, there is debate about whether a postapartheid federalism will be able to accommodate that country's remarkable racial, ethnic, and tribal diversity, and whether a new constitution should recognize a right to secede.[2] And as these words are being written, the Province of Quebec seems closer to secession from Canada than ever before.

Some see this astonishing rash of secession movements as the expression of an unpredicted and profoundly disturbing resurgence of *nationalism*, which many regard as one of the most dangerous phenomena of the modern era. If the nationalist imperative is that each ethnic group, each "people," is entitled to its own state, then it is a recipe for virtually limitless upheaval, an exhortation to break apart the vast majority of existing states, given that most if not all began as empires and include a plurality of ethnic groups or peoples within their present boundaries.[3]

To say that the proliferation of secessionist movements may have disturbing consequences for international order and peace is to indulge in serious understatement. It was remarked (by Churchill, I believe), in reference to earlier separatist movements that triggered World War I, that the Balkans produce more violence than they can consume domestically. Similarly, the fate of current secessionist movements in distant countries can have momentous effects on the domestic politics of nations that are culturally and geographically far removed. Secession can shatter old alliances, stimulate the forging of new ones, tip balances of power, create refugee populations, and disrupt international commerce. It can also result in great loss of human life. And regardless of whether it acts or refrains from acting, each state takes a stand on each secessionist movement—if only by recognizing or not recognizing the independence of the seceding group.

Thus, there is an urgent need—a practical necessity—for an adequate *theory* of secession. Or rather, for two theories, one positive or explanatory, the other normative or action-guiding. And, clearly, the two must fit together. The normative theory's guidance for action must be informed by a sound understanding of the real-world phenomena of secession.

An adequate explanatory or positive theory of secession would answer the following questions:

- Who tries to secede and under what conditions?
- When is a demand for a right to secede merely a strategic bluff to extract gains while remaining within the political union?
- Under what conditions and by whom are secessionist movements likely to be resisted, and by what means?
- Which types of secessionist movements are likely to succeed, and under what conditions?
- Under what conditions are secessionist movements likely to receive recognition and/or support from other countries?
- To what extent is nationalism, understood as the desire for ethnic political self-determination, the prime motivational force in secessionist movements? (Other candidates for key motivational factors include the

sense of being victims of historical injustices, the desire to end what is perceived to be current economic discrimination on ethnic grounds, and so on.)

- Can secession as an instance of collective action be adequately explained using standard economic models of rationality, or is participation in secessionist movements at least in significant part nonrational or irrational?
- Under what conditions does opposition to the state result in an attempt to secede rather than in revolution?

At present there is no positive theory of secession capable of providing plausible answers even to most, much less all, of these important questions.[4] Yet it is fair to say that the situation is far more primitive with respect to normative theorizing. And the questions a normative theory of secession must answer are, if anything, even more perplexing.

- On what grounds and under what conditions is secession morally justified?
- What methods for achieving secession are morally justified?
- Under what conditions and for what reasons is it morally justified to resist secession, and by what methods?
- Under what conditions may or ought a country to recognize and/or actively support a secessionist movement in another country, and what methods may it use to do so?
- Under what conditions may or ought a country to aid those who resist secession, and by what means?

In addition to these basic moral questions, an adequate normative theory of secession would have to include principled responses to a number of moral-legal issues.

- Should there be a constitutional right to secede? (At present only the Soviet Constitution contains such a right.) For what sorts of political associations, and under what conditions, is a right to secede appropriate? If a constitution is to include a right to secede, what should its scope and limits be, and what sorts of procedures are appropriate for its exercise?
- Is existing international law adequate in its treatment of secession? (If not, how might it be improved in this regard? For example, should provisions be made for international tribunals to mediate disputes between secessionists and the government of the state from which they seek to secede as to whether secession is justified and whether appropriate procedures for exercising a right to secede are being followed?)

Given the practical urgency and theoretical interest of secession, the lack of a normative theory of secession in the central works of political philosophy is puzzling. It is remarkable that the topic of secession receives no serious consideration by the leading figures in the history of political philosophy. The same holds true for contemporary political philosophy, with a few limited exceptions. Although secession has not yet become a serious topic of discussion in the resurgence of political philosophy stimulated (at least in part) by the appearance of John Rawls's *A Theory of Justice* in 1971, very recently a few brief references have been made to the possibility of secession as a means of accommodating the deep pluralism of modern societies. In one case an effort has been made to begin the task of drawing the implications concerning secession of one particular theory of political obligation.[5] However, a systematic exploration of the moral and moral-legal problems of secession has not been attempted. The chief aim of this book is to remedy that deficiency.

This theoretical lacuna is all the more bewildering given that secession is a form of refusal to acknowledge the state's claim to political authority, and that political philosophy has taken as one of its self-defining tasks the justification of political authority and the articulation of the conditions under which the state's claim to political authority may rightly be denied.[6] Political philosophies contain theories of the right to revolution and (though often less developed) of the rights to civil disobedience and emigration, but nothing that could merit the title of a theory of the right to secede. Nor, to my knowledge, is there available a plausible account of why a theory of the right to secede is not needed.

The lack of either a normative theory of secession or an argument to show why one is not needed is especially embarrassing for *liberal* political theory. By 'liberalism', it should be recalled, I mean first and foremost the view that the state is to uphold the priority of basic individual civil and political rights of the sort listed in the U.S. Constitution's Bill of Rights—rights to freedom of expression, religion, and association, as well as political participation rights, rights of due process under the law, and equality of opportunity.[7]

The recognition of a right to secede (though not necessarily an unqualified or unconditional right) would seem to be something to which liberalism is at least *prima facie* committed. Surely a political philosophy that places a preeminent value on liberty and self-determination, highly values diversity, and holds that legitimate political authority in some sense rests on the consent of the governed must either acknowledge a right to secede or supply weighty arguments to show why a presumption in favor of such a right is rebutted.

The issue of secession, however, extends beyond the confines of liberal doctrine. It bears directly and crucially on what may be the most vigorous (and confused) debate of contemporary political philosophy: the dispute between communitarians and liberals.[8] (Communitarians such as Michael Sandel and Charles Taylor berate liberalism for its "individualism," for its alleged neglect of the importance of participation in and identification with the common good.) I shall argue that if this debate has reached an impasse, it is because both sides have failed to appreciate liberalism's resources for recognizing and securing the good of community under conditions of cultural pluralism.[9] In particular, neither side has taken seriously the possibility of secession as a way of preserving a general commitment to liberal institutions while accommodating the fact that there are some forms of community that cannot flourish within the liberal state but which it would be wrong to try to force to conform.

Quite apart from their dispute with the liberal tradition, communitarians *ought* to be thinking, and thinking hard, about secession. Any political philosophy that takes the community as fundamental must concern itself with questions concerning the boundaries of communities and the rights of groups of persons to determine their collective destiny. And this means that communitarians must face squarely the question of whether or under what conditions a group within an existing community may, with justification, separate from the larger group in order to establish its own self-governing community. Yet the chief communitarian political philosophers have failed to address this task or even to acknowledge its necessity.

Liberalism's failure to take secession seriously (or to supply reasons explaining why it is not an option) is graphically illustrated by perhaps the most influential, systematic, and comprehensive liberal view: John Rawls's theory of Justice as Fairness.[10] It is not just that Rawls offers neither a theory of secession nor an argument for why one is not needed. More strikingly, his characterization of the hypothetical social contract from which principles of justice are supposed to be derived precludes the possibility that the issue of secession will be broached at all. The imaginary, idealized parties to the contract are to assume that they are to be members of "one cooperative scheme in perpetuity."[11]

Nor would it be costless for Rawls to jettison this assumption. To do so would be to undermine, or at least seriously weaken, a type of argument that plays a central role in his justification for the principles of justice he advocates. Rawls argues that the parties to the ideal social contract must weigh the "strains of commitment": They are to ask themselves if they could sustain a sincere allegiance to the principles they choose, once those principles are actually implemented.[12] He contends that, from the standpoint of strains of commitment, his principles are superior to the chief rivals—in particular, to utilitarian principles of justice, which may require great sacrifices on the part of some individuals or groups for the sake of maximizing total or average social utility. Whatever force Rawls's strains-of-commitment arguments have is at least lessened, if not extinguished, if the parties know that they can reduce the strains of commitment by exiting from the cooperative scheme or by using the threat of exit to renegotiate the social contract on terms more favorable to themselves. Beyond the question of whether Rawls's theory can be revised to allow the question of secession to be addressed is a much more general question: Can any plausible form of ideal-contract political theory accommodate a right to secede without undermining the force of its distinctively contractarian arguments?

In defense of the general lack of any serious consideration of secession, one might reply that secession is an issue only for *nonideal* normative theory and that the first and most important task of political philosophy is to construct and support a plausible ideal theory. Ideal theory is the articulation and defense of principles of justice for a society in which these principles are *fully implemented*. (Nonideal theory, by contrast, deals with principles suitable for situations in which compliance will not be perfect.) In conditions of perfect compliance, there would be no justification for secession; hence ideal theory requires no right of secession.[13]

This response suffers from two infirmities. First, it renders inexplicable the fact that political philosophy has devoted much attention to the justification of revolution and some to civil disobedience, but almost none to secession, given that the former kinds of denial of political authority clearly fall within the scope of nonideal theory. This is most obvious in the case of revolution, inasmuch as the conditions in which revolution is usually said to be justified are precisely those in which principles of justice either are not being implemented by the state or are being actively violated by it. In other words, if it is legitimate for political philosophy to be concerned with this question of nonideal theory, why should it not be concerned with secession as well? Even if secession is an issue for nonideal theory, then, its neglect remains unexplained.

Second, the view under consideration assumes that the sole valid justification for secession is that the state is not conforming to or upholding principles of justice, that secession is justified *only* on grounds of injustice. But that assumption begs one of the most important questions a normative theory of secession must address. One cannot simply dismiss without argument the possibility that there can be circumstances under which a group living within the jurisdiction of the state may reasonably seek to achieve complete political autonomy for a quite different reason: to be able to express and sustain values other than that of justice, such as a distinctive conception of community or a particular ideal of the religious life. Suppose, for example, that a group is committed to achieving face-to-face, direct, participatory democracy of the sort that Rousseau lauded. Suppose also that it believes, with good reason, that this form of political community cannot be realized within the large state of which the group members are presently citizens. Or suppose that an ethnic group rightly believes that forming its own sovereign state is the only way to preserve its distinctive culture. The ground of a group's bid for political independence need not be that its members are being treated unjustly; and, indeed, the individual moral and constitutional rights of the group may not in any way be impaired. Yet it would be inappropriate simply to dismiss out of hand its claim to a right to secede.

Here an analogy with divorce may illuminate. Why should one assume that the only justification for divorce is that one's spouse has wronged one, violated one's rights, treated one unjustly? There may be other, quite respectable reasons for wanting to end the union: It is not satisfying the needs or aspirations for which it was undertaken, one or both parties have changed in fundamental ways, and so on. If we view political association, like marriage, not as an unalterable natural fact but as a human creation designed (at least in part!) to satisfy the needs of those who live within it, then it is far from obvious that injustice provides the only justification for dissolution.

Once we begin to consider the various arguments in favor of a right to secede, it will become clear that secession is a central issue for political philosophy. The question of whether it is to be addressed in ideal or nonideal theory will ultimately be seen as having limited significance.

II. Secession and the Main Problems of Political Philosophy

Systematic thinking about the morality of secession produces interesting results, and not just about secession. Grappling with the moral and moral-legal problems of secession forces us to reexamine most if not all of the main problems of political philosophy and to probe both the meaning and adequacy of liberalism. The nature of political obligation and authority, the meaning of citizenship, the connection between political authority and territorial sovereignty, the distinction between federal and nonfederal systems, the morality or immorality of nationalism—all of these issues and more are inescapable once we undertake to develop a normative theory of secession. Furthermore, theorizing about secession provides us with fresh and valuable perspectives on these matters and reveals the inadequacy of traditional treatments of them. More specifically, the views on secession advanced in this book will both illuminate the foundations of liberalism in surprising ways and provide a strong case for revising liberal doctrine's apparent refusal to recognize *group* rights as fundamental moral or constitutional rights. This result in turn will help to explain why liberalism, in spite of its emphasis on self-determination, diversity, and consent, has not included a right to secede but has instead remained largely silent on secession.

There is a historical explanation of the relative neglect of group rights in general, not just of the right to secede, at least in current international law.

It is something of a commonplace to note that two factors during the interwar period so discredited the notion of minority groups' rights that, since 1945, international law has largely abandoned it in favor of the idea of individual human rights. The first was Hitler's abuse of appeals to minority groups' rights. (Hitler justified his conquests of Czechoslovakia and Poland on the grounds that he was rescuing ethnic Germans residing there from persecution by non-German majorities.) The second was the failure to implement fairly and effectively the minorities treaties that grew out of the Treaty of Versailles. By contrast, the rights of minority groups had a prominent place not only in the rhetoric but also in the structure of the League of Nations. Thus it is understandable that the new international order which the United Nations attempted to forge in the aftermath of Germany's defeat would be suspicious of the very concept of minority group rights. But although this observation may explain the shift away from group rights in international law, it cannot explain the virtual absence of the notion of group rights, and especially the idea of a right to secede, in earlier liberal theory.

My hypothesis is that the issue of secession has been an embarrassment that liberals have sought to ignore because it challenges two fundamental tenets of liberalism: the *universalism* that is a chief part of liberalism's inheritance from the rationalism of the Enlightenment, and the preoccupation with *individual* rights to which liberalism has been led by its conviction that the ultimate unit in the moral universe is the individual person.[14] (It is crucial to note that this "individualism" is moral, not ontological. Liberalism in its most plausible forms need not deny that groups or collectivities exist, nor need it maintain that they partake of a lesser degree of reality than individuals, nor need it assert even that all of the properties of groups can be reduced to properties of the individuals that compose them. To repeat: Liberalism's individualism concerns what matters most morally, not what exists.)

Liberalism's universalism—its faith that what is ultimately important for purposes of moral-political theory is the capacity that we each have for leading our own lives as free, choosing beings, not our differences as Germans, Chinese, Zulus, Tamils, or Croats—leads it to be suspicious of separatist political movements and to strive, instead, for the universal implementation of a single set of principles of political order. The primary question for the liberal then becomes whether the political unit one finds oneself in satisfies those universal principles. To the liberal, concern about any other basis for choosing which political unit to belong to appears irrational or perverse if not dangerous.

Liberalism's conviction that what matters most, morally speaking, are individuals, and its hostility toward those who would devalue the individual in the name of the collective, when combined with its universalism, make it at minimum suspicious of the very concept of a group right. This suspicion has led at least some liberal thinkers to underestimate the role that group rights, including a right to secession, can play in protecting *individuals* and the values that they affirm in their lives—particularly the value they find in being members of groups.[15] This, I shall argue, is a mistake.

III. The Plan of This Book

Given the complexities of these issues, a sketch of the structure of the investigation will be helpful. The remainder of this chapter offers conceptual clarification—an analysis of the concept of secession, including a classification of the types of secession. Chapters 2 and 3 articulate and evaluate the main moral arguments for and against secession, with special emphasis both on the claims to territory that demands for secession involve and on the different grounds that may be adduced to support territorial claims. Chapter 4 sketches the main outlines of a constitutional right to secede. Although that chapter is an exercise in *ideal* constitutional design, it is nonetheless of considerable practical import. In the coming months existing countries such as Canada and the U.S.S.R. will be changing their constitutions and freshly independent ones such as Lithuania will be framing new ones. At no time has there been a greater need for clear thinking about the notion of a constitutional right to secede. To my knowledge, there is at present only one country whose constitution contains a right to secede: the Soviet Union (the Constitution of the Malay Federation included such a right for a brief period). This is likely to change.

Throughout these chapters the moral framework is illustrated by concrete, real-world examples, spanning a wide range of historical and contemporary cases of secession, from the American Civil War to Katanga's secession from the Congo, the Basques, the Baltic Republics, South Africa, and Canada. Each of these cases is discussed only to illustrate and help assess and refine the moral and constitutional analysis. No pretense is made to render comprehensive political or historical analysis. Finally, Chapter 5 summarizes and ties together the chief conclusions of the investigation.

IV. The Concept of Secession: Preliminary Clarification

It will be useful to contrast secession with other ways in which individuals or groups can challenge political authority or change their relations with the state: revolution, civil disobedience, and emigration.[16] The clarification provided here is merely preliminary. The process of trying to construct a theory of secession will further enhance our understanding of what secession is.

There is no universally accepted set of distinctions among revolution, secession, and civil disobedience. The term 'civil disobedience' in particular is accorded wider or narrower definitions by different writers.[17] The rough taxonomy employed here is not designed to answer all questions about these challenges to political authority. Its only purpose is to illuminate the topic of secession.

Unlike the revolutionary, the secessionist's primary goal is not to overthrow the existing government, nor to make fundamental constitutional, economic, or sociopolitical changes within the existing state. Instead, she wishes to restrict the jurisdiction of the state in question so as not to include her own group and the territory it occupies. The salient distinction between secession and revolution is that successful secession, being aimed only at restricting the scope of the state's power, not dissolving it, does not, like revolution, require (though it may in fact result in) the overthrow of the government. The secessionist does not deny the state's political authority as such, but only its authority over her and the other members of her group and the territory they occupy. Further, to attempt to secede is to strive for independence from the state from which one is seceding, but it need not be an attempt to achieve complete political independence. In some cases a group may endeavor to secede from one state in order to become part of another. (For example, some Transylvanians say they wish to secede from Romania and become part of Hungary.) Therefore it would be an error to define secession as separation from an existing state in order to become a sovereign state. Nonetheless, in most actual cases secessionists seek sovereign status and hence it is with secession as a mode of achieving political independence that we shall mainly be concerned.

Drawing a satisfactory distinction between secession and civil disobedience is more complex. Sometimes civil disobedience is contrasted with revolution as follows. The civil disobedient is not a revolutionary because he does not wish to overthrow the government; indeed his general attitude toward the government is that it is legitimate. Instead, through deliberately and openly violating some law or laws, he opposes certain policies or activities of the government, and he does so on grounds of political morality. For example, civil disobedients in the United States violated segregation laws on the grounds that they were both immoral and unconstitutional.

This broad definition of 'civil disobedience' is compatible with some acts of civil disobedience being directed toward the goal of secession. For instance, Gandhi's nonviolent civil disobedience aimed at Indian independence, that is, secession of India from the British Empire. It was not an effort at revolution, at overthrowing the government of Britain.

Secession is not the only way in which a group may strive to free itself from the jurisdictional authority of the state. Emigration is another. The members of a religious or ethnic group may claim a right to emigrate and thereby remove themselves from the jurisdiction of the state without challenging the state's claim to authority over all who remain within its boundaries. Thus emigration, unlike secession, challenges not the state's territorial claims but only its authority to control exit from the territory over which it claims sovereignty. Secession, by contrast, is an effort to remove oneself from the scope of the state's authority, not by moving beyond the existing boundaries of that authority but by redrawing the boundaries so that one is not included within them. To claim the right to emigrate is only to challenge the state's authority to keep one within its boundaries. To claim the right to secede is to challenge the state's own conception of what its boundaries are. To emphasize: Secession necessarily involves a claim to territory. The precise nature of this territorial claim, and the various grounds upon which it may be asserted, will be analyzed later in detail.[18]

Even if we focus only on secession as involving the taking of territory, there is currently some disagreement over the use of the term 'secession', and a problematic conceptual distinction is sometimes used to emphasize a genuine normative difference. Recently, some spokespersons for the Lithuanian government were reported to have protested the label 'secessionist', saying that because Lithuania was never legally a part of the Soviet Union it is incorrect to characterize the movement toward severing ties with the Soviet Union as secession. The normative point the Lithuanians seek to emphasize is a vital one: The fact that their country was forcibly annexed to the Soviet Union by a deal between Hitler and Stalin in 1940, followed by a sham legislative ratification, makes a great deal of difference, morally speaking. However, it is probably more perspicuous simply to make this normative claim directly, rather than embedding it in a distinction between secessionist and nonsecessionist separatist movements. For one thing, that distinction is not generally observed. Accordingly, the term 'secession' in what follows will be applied to separatist movements, regardless of whether the original union from which separation is desired was legitimate or not. But nothing of substance hangs on this distinction, and those who prefer the alternative vocabulary can easily translate my discussion into it.

At first blush it might seem that the relationships between these forms of challenge to state authority are as follows. (1) If revolution is justified, then *a fortiori* secession is justified as well, since any defects in the political order so grave as to justify a total rejection of the state's authority would surely warrant merely denying its authority over a portion of the area within its boundaries. (2) Stronger grounds are required for secession than for emigration, because the challenge to the state involved in claiming a right to emigrate is only a rejection of its authority over a group of people (or, more precisely, of the state's authority to block their exit), not a refusal to acknowledge its authority over *both* those people *and* the territory they occupy.

This second statement, I shall argue, is largely correct, although one of the chief objections to secession is also a serious objection to emigration—namely, what I shall call the argument from distributive justice, which is based on the assumption that there are limitations on the resources which a group may unilaterally decide to withdraw from the state. In the case of emigration, the resources in question are the "human capital" of the emigrants (resources that, to a large extent, may be the result of social investment) and whatever moveable property they attempt to take with them. In the case of secession, the resources also include the natural resources and fixed capital within the area whose occupants wish to secede. So, although both emigration and secession are in principle objectionable on grounds of distributive justice, the issue of distributive justice is more complex and potentially more serious in the case of secession given the loss of territory and fixed capital in addition to that of human capital and moveable goods.

The first claim—that if revolution is justified, then *a fortiori* secession is justified—is false, as I shall argue later. It is false because secession, under certain circumstances, can involve infringements of the property rights of individuals or groups, and these infringements—not just the injustices committed by the state—may be morally relevant to the question of whether secession is justified. By seceding, one group expropriates land or goods possessed by others. The moral relevance of this loss will depend upon who has legitimate title to the wealth in question. Clearly, the fact that the government has lost its legitimacy due to perpetration of injustices does not *in itself* imply that the secessionists have valid claim to the land and other goods in the seceding area. For example, opponents of the secessionist movement might argue that the people as a whole own the land, that the government is merely the people's agent—its steward or "property management firm"—and, therefore, that even extreme misconduct by the government does not *by itself* void the people's title to it, much less confer title to it upon the group that wishes to secede. Or, some persons who do not wish to secede may argue that they are private owners of some of the land or natural resources within the seceding area and that secession may be resisted because it would violate their private property rights. So even though it is true in one sense that secession is a less radical challenge to political authority than revolution, it does not follow that whenever revolution is justified, secession would be also. Such an inference is flawed because it overlooks the complexity of the territorial issue and other issues of distributive justice in secession.[19] Additional distinctions are also required. These matters are taken up in detail in Chapters 2 and 3.

A. Group Versus Individual Secession

Although the term 'secession' is usually applied only to groups, certain libertarian thinkers in recent decades have explored the idea of individual secession. They have not, however, always used that phrase, preferring in some cases to use the term 'independents' to describe those who wish to deny the authority of the state but to remain *in situ* within the borders of the state.[20] Such individuals are not revolutionaries, as they needn't have any desire either to overthrow the government or to replace it with a new political order (indeed, they may be anarchists, rejecting all forms of political order as illegitimate). Nor are they civil disobedients (if this term is taken to imply that they view the state as largely legitimate, challenging only some of its laws or policies). They are distinguishable from those who are ordinarily identified as secessionists only in these respects: They press their rejection of the jurisdictional or territorial scope of the state *as individuals*, not as members of a group, and they do not wish to constitute a new political authority distinct from that of the state. Nor do they wish to give their allegiance to a different state instead.

Individual secessionists may be thwarted group secessionists. This seems to have been true of Thoreau.[21] In the first quarter or so of the nineteenth century there was a New England secessionist movement.[22] Some New Englanders wished to secede rather than remain in a union stained by the evil of slavery. When the failure of this group secessionist movement became apparent, some individuals responded by committing acts of civil disobedience and some by covertly breaking the fugitive slave laws. Others, including probably Thoreau, felt that their only morally correct course was to attempt individual withdrawal from what they regarded as an unjust political union. It is worth noting, then, that the individual secessionist need not be a minority of one. He or she may be a member of a group that fails to achieve secession as a result of familiar obstacles to successful collective action. Even if a large number of people desire to secede as a group, they may be unable to do so because of what are called paradoxes of rationality: They may fail to overcome *free-rider* and/or *assurance* problems. In brief, a collective goal, such as secession (or national defense, or energy conservation, or pollution control, etc.), may not be achieved if a sufficient number of potential contributors to that goal decide to refrain from contributing in order to take a free ride on the contributions of others, believing that they will share in the benefits of the goal even if they themselves do not contribute. Or, collective action may falter if a sufficient number of potential contributors refrain from contributing because they lack assurance that enough others will contribute. In either case the collective good may not be achieved despite the fact that each member of the group desires it and would genuinely benefit from it and even though the means for attaining it are both known and feasible. These failures of collective action are *not* results of irrationality—for example, weakness of will—in any obvious sense. Indeed, it is the individual's *rationality*, at least so far as this is identified with means-end reasoning and the ability to determine what to do from a calculation of the costs and benefits of alternative courses of action, that seems to be the source of the failure of collective action. (Hence the label "paradoxes of rationality.") What is rational for each, namely, noncontribution, results in something that is irrational for all, the failure to achieve a good that would benefit all.[23] Individual secession, then, may be a moral response to the failure to achieve group secession.

Although I believe the question of the right to individual secession is an intriguing one, I shall not pursue it directly in this work. Instead, I shall concentrate on group secession, which is undeniably the most practically relevant form of the question, at least under current sociopolitical conditions. Some of what I say will have rather direct implications for individual secession as well. Further, if some protest that individual secession is a misnomer, believing that only groups can secede, I have no objection to that usage, and am quite happy to refer to individual independents rather than individual secessionists. Adopting this terminology, then, we can say that the main concern of this book is secession, not individual independence.

B. Central Versus Peripheral Secession

We may also contrast two quite different geographical situations in which secessionists may find themselves. In the first, which may be called central (or hole-of-the-donut) secession, the secessionists occupy and claim title to a region completely embedded within the remainder state, surrounded by territory to which the secessionists do not lay claim. (By 'remainder state' I mean simply what would remain were secession to succeed. This term is preferable to 'rump state', which suggests that the nonseceding area is the smaller portion of the presecession state—a situation that does not often obtain.) In the second, more common situation, that of peripheral secession, the territory to which the secessionists lay claim is part of but not wholly embedded within the territory of the remainder state. Central secession raises some issues that are not present in peripheral secession. In particular, central secessionists may be able to take a free ride on certain public goods such as national defense provided by the remainder state, as exclusion of the new embedded state from those benefits may be impossible or excessively costly. At the very least, such a situation raises the possibility that justified central secession might require some form of compensation by the secessionists to the surrounding state to negate what would otherwise be an unjustified gain on their part.

We might also distinguish dispersed or discontinuous group secession from continuous or consolidated group secession. In most cases the territory claimed by the secessionists will be continuous; but this need not be so. Two or more parts of the seceding area may be separated by all or part of the remainder state's territory. There are in fact historical instances of the phenomenon of geographically discontinuous states. For example, until the secession of East Pakistan under the name Bangladesh, Pakistan was divided into East and West Pakistan, separated by India.

C. National Versus Local Secession

In virtually any large-scale political unit there are subordinate units. In the United States, for example, there are the federal government and fifty state governments, and within each state there are varying numbers of counties, which in turn contain greater or smaller numbers of municipalities. This book will concentrate upon secession from states (such as Canada or the Soviet Union), but it is important to keep in mind the possibility of secession on a smaller scale, from subordinate political units. Depending upon the nature of the aims of particular secessionist groups, merely local secession may suffice. For example, if a group's only political goal is to gain and maintain control over certain functions reserved to county governments, such as zoning and local environmental policy, then forming a new county from a part of the territory of the existing one may be a more reasonable strategy than attempting to capture control of the existing county's government through ordinary electoral processes. In parts of the United States (e.g., Tennessee), some counties were formed by secession from preexisting counties.[24] The Swiss Constitution (1975) contains a provision for cantons to split into "half-cantons" but no right of cantons to secede from the Swiss Confederation.[25] Thus it allows local but not national secession.

D. Majority Versus Minority Secession

Discussions of secession usually refer to secessionists as the minority. In many, perhaps most cases, this terminology is accurate. But it need not be the case. (If, for example, the New England secessionist movement discussed earlier had grown to include the majority of persons in that region, which at the time held the majority of the population of the country, then we would have a case of the majority seeking to secede from the minority. As it turned out, the movement attracted only a small minority of New Englanders.)

Indeed, in principle the secessionist area may also be larger geographically, not just demographically. One might argue, however, that under such circumstances we should speak not of secession but of exclusion—the majority, or the group occupying the larger area, excluding the minority by redrawing the borders. Here, too, it is the distinction that matters most, not the choice of terms to mark it. A question to keep in mind is whether recognition of a minority's right to secede commits one to recognizing the majority's right to exclude.

E. Secession by the Better Off Versus Secession by the Worse Off

Morally speaking, a more interesting distinction than the immediately preceding one may be that between secession by the better off and secession by the worse off. In several actual cases of attempted secession, including Katanga's struggle to separate from the Congo,[26] Biafra's struggle to separate from Nigeria,[27] and the Basque separatist movement in Spain, the region striving for independence was materially richer and/or more economically advanced than the rest of the country.[28] Similarly, many residents of Slovenia have voiced a desire to secede from the poorer, more undeveloped regions constituting Yugoslavia.

Secession by the better off may exclude the worse off from certain important benefits that they previously received in the cooperative scheme of the unified, presecession state—benefits that they may not be able to attain either by developing their own cooperative scheme or by cooperating with third-party countries. Is such exclusion just?

If we characterize secession of the better off as exclusion, we may be tempted to assume that, by seceding, the haves are shirking their obligations of distributive justice to the have-nots. *If* distributive justice requires some redistribution of wealth from the better off to the worse off, and if this redistribution will cease if the better off citizens withdraw from the cooperative scheme that has hitherto united them with the worse off, then we will be inclined to conclude that secession by the better off is morally objectionable. If we assume that the greater wealth of those in the seceding area is due in large part to the greater natural resources of that area *and* if the natural wealth of the country as a whole belongs to the population as a whole, then we will also conclude that secession by the better off is unjust. But of course each of these two assumptions is controversial.

First, the better off may argue that they are not shirking legitimate obligations of distributive justice but are only freeing themselves from the injustice of an exploitive redistributive policy—that the fruits of their greater productivity are wrongfully being taken from them to benefit others who are not entitled to these gains. When pressed to justify their charge that existing redistributive policies are exploitive, the better-off secessionists may make either of two responses, which correspond, respectively, to two distinct theories of distributive justice. The first response is that even though justice requires *some* redistribution from the better to the worse off, the actual redistributive policies of the state *exceed* the requirements of justice, and that it is this excessive redistribution which qualifies as exploitation of the better off by the worse off. The second, more radical response is that *any* (net) redistribution is, *ipso facto*, exploitive and unjust. The latter view rests on a very controversial and austere, radical libertarian theory of distributive justice that I and many others have criticized in some detail elsewhere.[29] This theory amounts to the position that the better off do not owe any aid whatsoever to their worse-off fellow citizens (nor to anyone else, for that matter), unless they have explicitly and voluntarily promised to render such aid or unless it is required to rectify injustices perpetrated in the past. (Such a radical libertarian position is obviously incompatible with even the most minimal welfare state.)

Thus the possibility of the haves seceding from the have-nots forces us to take sides on a fundamental controversy in the theory of distributive justice: the debate between libertarian (i.e., antiredistributive) theories and welfarist (redistributive) theories, given that the former theories may regard secession by the haves as legitimate whereas the latter may judge it to be a violation of obligations to redistribute wealth within society. So, depending upon which type of theory of justice, libertarian or welfarist, we espouse, the question of whether the secessionists are the better off may make a crucial difference as to whether we judge secession to be justified.

As we have just seen, one rejoinder to the charge that secession by the better off is unjust is to argue that the presecession state has been engaging in exploitive redistribution. Another way in which the better off can defend their bid for secession is to attack the assumption that the seceding territory and its resources belong to the people of the country as a whole and hence cannot rightly be unilaterally withdrawn from the "common wealth" by the secessionists. The secessionists can rebut the charge that they are wrongfully taking the territory and its resources if they can rebut the claim of common ownership and establish, instead, that the territory and its resources belong to the secessionists, either as a collective or as individual private property owners. For example, Latvians can claim that Latvia belongs to them, not to the people of the Soviet Union, because it was unjustly annexed in 1940.

My purpose at this point in the investigation is not to resolve any of these thorny issues. It is merely to motivate the distinction between secession by the better off and secession by the worse off by indicating its relevance to the justification of secession *via* connections with fundamental issues in the theory of distributive justice. Much more will be said about these issues in Chapters 2 and 3.

F. Secession, or Merely Greater Autonomy
   ## Within the Existing State?

It is sometimes not altogether clear whether a particular political movement is best characterized as a drive for secession or merely for greater autonomy within a loose federal system. A contemporary case will illustrate. Recently the leaders of the Canadian Province of Quebec, which has a history of secessionist agitation, demanded that their region be officially recognized in the Meech Lake Accord (a proposed constitutional amendment) as a "distinct society" within Canada. Subsequently, when ratification of the accord faltered, some in Quebec threatened secession. Yet it is remarkable how unclear the difference between achieving "distinct society" status and seceding is. Canada is already a federal system, one that exemplifies a looser type of federalism than that of the United States, inasmuch as Canadian provinces have greater autonomy in important respects than do individual states in the American system. Evidently Quebec, in demanding to be recognized as a "distinct society," was requiring at the very least some further loosening of the federal bonds. However, what counts as a modification of the Canadian Federation as opposed to what counts as the dissolution of it remains a mystery.

We can imagine a continuum of degrees of closeness of political association, starting at one end with a unitary, centralized state, progressing to an extremely loose federalism, sometimes called *con*federation, and ending in an alliance (e.g., a defense treaty) among sovereign states. There may be a point or even a range of points on the continuum at which it is rather arbitrary as to whether we characterize the arrangement as an *alliance* among sovereign states or a *weak confederation*. If, as some Canadian citizens are now talking of doing, other provinces were to follow Quebec's suit in demanding greater independence, the result might be a type of political association that is not markedly different from what is expected to emerge from the integration of Western Europe scheduled for 1992 or from what may yet transpire in the Soviet Union.

The general question raised by these considerations is a conceptual one: At what point does a plea for greater independence become a demand for secession? In many, perhaps most cases, the secessionists desire not only *independence from* the existing state but also *sovereignty for* the new political unit they seek to create. Yet, as noted earlier, this need not be the case: Secessionists may wish to leave one political union in order to join another, as in the case of Romanian Transylvanians wishing to join Hungary. But let us concentrate on the more usual case whereby full independence—that is, sovereignty—is sought. Then we can answer the conceptual question in two steps.

First, we assume that the bid for secession is an effort to establish *sovereignty*. Second, we articulate a plausible list of *jointly sufficient conditions for sovereignty*. Then we can determine whether a demand for independence from the state is an attempt to secede by seeing whether what is being demanded is a new status that satisfies the jointly sufficient conditions for sovereignty. This way of posing the question avoids the confusion revealed in the following statement by Gorbachev: "We are expanding the republics' sovereign rights. And we hope that a full federation is something that . . . will resolve all the problems that have accumulated."[30] What is puzzling about Gorbachev's statement is that it refers to the future status of the Soviet Republics as that of *sovereignty* (which implies full independence), yet also assumes that they will be members of a *federation* (not merely an alliance), which usually is taken to imply something less than full independence. Perhaps a charitable reading is that he means that in a new Soviet Federation, the republics will enjoy some but not all of the rights of sovereignty.

Probably the most obvious candidate for the list of jointly sufficient conditions for sovereignty is the power to make war and peace. Only slightly more controversial might be the power to control exit and entry. One might also be tempted to add the power to coin and print money, but this is far from obvious. For example, if Western European integration in 1992 includes the use of a single currency and coinage, it does not seem to follow that every member state thereby loses its status as a sovereign nation. Even the power to control exit and entry is questionable, depending upon how it is specified. We might still speak of a European Alliance or Confederation of Nations, rather than of the Nation of Europe, if individual countries were prohibited from placing constraints on exit and entry from their territory but retained the power to determine who could become a *permanent* resident. Once we depart from the relatively clear criterion of the power to make war and peace, the situation becomes rather muddy, as indicated by the ongoing debate about whether a title such as "The United States of Europe" would be appropriate for whatever it is that results from integration in 1992.

The same point may be brought out in a different way. Some legal scholars and political activists have suggested that the law concerning relations between those native Americans living on reservations, on the one hand, and state and federal government, on the other, should be revised or interpreted so as to approximate more closely *international* law, the law of nations.[31] Doing so would amount to a shift toward recognition of native Americans or some groups of native Americans as constituting sovereign political units. But, again, there are varying degrees of autonomy; and it will remain somewhat arbitrary, or at best rather uninformative, to ignore nuanced possibilities by definitional fiat. Notice also that in most cases Indian reservations are surrounded by non-Indian territory. So if Indians on reservations achieved greater autonomy, the situation would move closer to what I have called ce tral as opposed to peripheral secession, which, as I also noted earlier, raises its own peculiar problems, especially with respect to fair contribution to public goods such as defense.

The current existence of special legal and political status for minority indigenous populations within the modern state points as well toward other possible types of combinations of autonomy and subordination—differing degrees of independence. For example, members of a minority group might be granted something akin to resident alien status or even dual citizenship. And in order to benefit from such arrangements, they need not be geographically concentrated, as is the case with Indians dwelling on a reservation.

Just as liberalism's individualism and universalism have been interpreted in ways that hinder its ability to take the issue of secession seriously, certain fundamental but rarely articulated assumptions in international law have made it difficult to consider less drastic alternatives to secession. And, paradoxically, the result has been a reluctance to acknowledge a right to secede in international law. Until relatively recently, international law was said to be the law dealing with *relations among nations*—that is, sovereign states. Since 1945, along with the greatly increased prominence of the notion of individual human rights, the conception of international law has expanded: The subjects of international law are said to include not only sovereign states but individuals as well.

With some danger of simplification, it is fair to say that, at least in the mainstream of international law since 1945, what little attention has been paid to minority rights as distinct from individual human rights has tended to treat minority groups as cultural rather than political groups, in part out of the fear that recognition of a broad "right of self-determination of peoples" would be tantamount to endorsement of a general right to secede for every ethnic group.[32] The result has been a series of lame and largely arbitrary attempts by various international bodies, including the United Nations, to endorse a "right of self-determination," on the one hand, in order to support Third World struggles against colonialism, while on the other hand restricting that right to only the colonial cases in order to avoid fueling numerous separatist movements within long-established nation-states such as Britain and Belgium. What has been largely overlooked until quite recently is the possibility of a conceptual shift that offers a way to escape the dilemma of either denying a right of self-determination or acknowledging it, but arbitrarily restricting it to decolonization.

The first step in achieving the conceptual shift—or, more accurately, the conceptual revolution—in international law is to explore the possibility that the right to secede can be domesticated by developing and gaining consensus on principled restrictions on its scope. An unlimited right to secede for any and every ethnic group or "people" would be a dangerous thing indeed; but this is not the only alternative. The appropriate response is to try to articulate substantive arguments for when secession is justified and when it is not, along with procedural and institutional constraints on the exercise of the right.

Second, international law must be transformed by the recognition that self-determination admits of degrees and, consequently, that the exercise of a right to self-determination may take many forms, with secession to form a fully independent, sovereign state being only the most extreme. To the extent that a broad range of different political statuses for groups can be accommodated in the international order, the impulse to secede may in fact be weakened. Moreover, it is becoming increasingly clear, in demanding "self-determination" or greater autonomy, that many minority groups, including some indigenous peoples, do not wish to achieve the status of full sovereignty that secession is usually thought to imply. The second step in the needed conceptual shift, then, is to recognize that there is in principle a range of political statuses that a minority group might come to have in the pursuit of greater control over its common life, short of full sovereignty, and that the traditional conceptual framework that recognizes only fully sovereign states, individuals, and minority groups that are accorded only cultural rather than political status is inadequate. Experimentation with new forms of "semi-autonomy" or "limited sovereignty" is what is needed. This book is concerned primarily with the first step—developing a theory of a limited right to secede. Nevertheless, it will also begin the exploration of alternatives to secession for achieving greater autonomy for minority groups within the modern state.[33]

The purpose of these brief remarks is only to emphasize that the concept of secession is necessarily as vague or relativistic as that of independence. Where we draw the line between moves toward greater independence that count as secession and those that do not is not so important as the recognition that there can be a variety of graded responses to those movements that sometimes issue in those most extreme forms of independence that we associate with the term 'secession'. If less radical forms of independence would sometimes prove satisfactory, it is important to know this, since they may not entail such high moral and practical costs as secession often does. One major aim of this book, then, is to consider a range of alternatives to secession and to develop a systematic way of comparing their relative advantages and disadvantages. This task is taken up in Chapter 4.

One final distinction is in order within this preliminary clarification of the concept of secession. It is a distinction not between types of secession but between secession and something that may be mistaken for it—and in a way that invites moral confusion. Suppose that at an earlier time region A and region B, which were separate sovereign states or at least were not united with one another politically, are forcibly annexed into state C. Then suppose that at some later time C is overthrown by a revolution in which the populations of both regions A and B participate, or suppose that C disintegrates from some other cause; for example, it loses a war with some fourth country D. In other words, the political union that was C no longer exists. If at this time the people of region A decide to form a sovereign state of their own and refuse to throw in their lot with those of region B, it would be incorrect to describe them as secessionists. For to secede is to withdraw from an *existing* political union (whether it is a legitimate union or not). By hypothesis, in the situation described, the previous political union C has dissolved and no new union including A and B has yet been formed.

This scenario is far from fanciful. Something very like it occurred in what had been the Belgian Congo. While the dismantling of Belgian colonial control over the Congo was occurring, a province of the colony, Katanga, declared its independence. Some of those who supported Katangan independence understandably resisted the idea that it was attempting secession, emphasizing that the political union in which it and the other parts of the Congo had been included was in reality no longer intact.

Conceptual clarity requires that we distinguish between withdrawal from an existing state, on the one hand, and the creation of a new state under conditions of anarchy, on the other. The term 'secession' is better reserved for the former, not the latter. This distinction can make a moral difference: Those who seek to form an independent state under conditions of anarchy may not be subject to some of the constraints of distributive justice that apply when an independent state is created out of a preexisting one. If no state exists, then those who seek to form their own state are not required to show that their doing so violates no valid claims to territorial sovereignty by an existing state.

With these preliminary distinctions and clarifications in mind, we may now turn to the various arguments that together constitute the moral case for secession.

Notes

1. Abraham Lincoln, *Speeches and Writings*, vol. 2, edited by Don E. Fehrenbach (New York: Literary Classics of America, 1989), pp. 357–358.

2. Frances Kendall and Leon Louw, *After Apartheid: The Solution for South Africa* (San Francisco: ICS Press, 1987).

3. Ernest Gellner, *Nations and Nationalism* (Oxford: Blackwell, 1983), Chapter 1; Michael Hechter, *Internal Colonialism: The Celtic Fringe in British National Development, 1536–1966* (Berkeley, Calif.: University of California Press, 1975), pp. 47–68.

4. For a description of the shortcomings of existing explanatory theories of secession and the beginnings of a more adequate theory, see Michael Hechter, "The Dynamics of Secession," unpublished manuscript, Department of Sociology, University of Arizona, 1990.

5. It is remarkable that the issue of secession has received no sustained and systematic consideration by the leading figures in the history of political philosophy (at least in the West). The situation is the same in contemporary political philosophy, with a few limited exceptions. Two of the most notable of these are Harry Beran's view that a consent theory of obligation implies a right to secede and Lea Brilmayer's suggestion that every sound justification for

secession includes a valid claim to territory based on a historical grievance that the territory was unjustly taken from the secessionists at some point in the past. In Chapter 2 I criticize both Beran's and Brilmayer's views. However, I have especially benefited from Brilmayer's emphasis on the point that every sound justification for secession must include a valid territorial claim. My disagreement is with her further suggestion that the only way for secessionists to establish such a claim is on the basis of a historical grievance that the territory was wrongly taken from them. In response to my arguments Brilmayer seems to have weakened this claim, now acknowledging that *in principle* secession might be justified in the absence of a valid historical grievance concerning the unjust taking of territory. However, a difference in our views persists, given that, as I shall argue in Chapter 2, there are several important actual cases of secession that were justified on other grounds. See Harry Beran, *The Consent Theory of Political Obligation* (New York: Croom Helm, 1987); and Lea Brilmayer, "Secession: A Territorialist Reinterpretation," *Yale Journal of International Law*, vol. 16, no. 1, January 1991. Professor Brilmayer kindly allowed me to read this article prior to its publication.

Very recently there have been a few brief references to the possibility of secession as a means of accommodating the deep pluralism of modern society, a pluralism of values and ways of life that many believe is encouraged by liberal institutions, but that may become a disintegrative force in liberal society. To my knowledge, however, a systematic exploration of secession—particularly one devoted to the question of whether liberal political philosophy should acknowledge a right to secede—is not presently available. The following thinkers at least raise the issue, however.

William A. Galston notes that Rawls fails to consider the possibility of secession as an option for communities that feel they cannot flourish within the liberal framework. (See Galston, "Pluralism and Social Unity," *Ethics*, vol. 99, no. 4, July 1989, p. 717.) Richard Arneson mentions the option of secession and, like Galston, endorses it: "At the limit, the federal solution approach probably ought to recognize a generalized right of political secession." (See Arneson, "Primary Goods Reconsidered," *Nous*, vol. 24, 1990, pp. 437–438.) Similarly, Bruce Ackerman, also concerned with the problem of pluralism, provides an interesting discussion of the limits of federalism and comes close to acknowledging secession as an option. (See *Social Justice and the Liberal State* [New Haven, Conn.: Yale University Press, 1980], p. 194.)

6. I distinguish between political philosophy, which is concerned primarily with the state, and social philosophy, which deals with all major social institutions, not just political ones. More specifically, the first question for (normative) political philosophy is "Can political authority be justified?"

7. Liberals can and do disagree as to whether formal equality of opportunity (the absence of discriminatory legal barriers to social offices and positions) is sufficient. But this dispute may be ignored for present purposes.

8. For a critical evaluation of this debate and an attempt to sort out its confusions, see Allen Buchanan, "Assessing the Communitarian Critique of Liberalism," *Ethics*, vol. 99, no. 4, July 1989, pp. 852–882.

9. Ibid., pp. 878–882.

10. John Rawls, *A Theory of Justice* (Cambridge, Mass.: Harvard University Press, 1971); Rawls, "Justice as Fairness: A Briefer Restatement," unpublished manuscript, Department of Philosophy, Harvard University, 1990.

11. Rawls, "Justice as Fairness: A Briefer Restatement," p. 132.

12. Ibid., pp. 123, 145, and 177–185.

13. Rawls suggested this response to the author in conversation but did not endorse it.

14. John Gray, *Liberalism* (Minneapolis: University of Minnesota Press, 1986), pp. ix–xi.

15. Allen Buchanan, "Assessing the Communitarian Critique of Liberalism," *Ethics*, vol. 99, no. 4, July 1989, especially pp. 862–865; Will Kymlicka, *Liberalism, Community, and Culture* (Oxford: Oxford University Press, 1989), Chapter 10.

16. Emigration is not a challenge, strictly speaking, to political authority (unless the state claims the authority to prevent people from leaving its jurisdiction). Rather, it is a way of putting oneself outside the scope of the political authority of the state from which one emigrates.

17. Hugo Bedau, ed., *Civil Disobedience: Theory and Practice* (New York: Western Publishing Co., 1969); Rawls, *A Theory of Justice*, Sections 55, 57, and 59; Joel Feinberg, "Civil Disobedience in the Modern World," *Humanities in Society*, vol. 2, Winter 1979, pp. 37–59.

18. Some might argue that, in principle at least, secession need not involve the taking of territory. Randy Barnett has suggested that a state, or independent political community, need not be territorially based and, hence, that if a group rejected the jurisdiction of an existing, territorially based state within which they resided and formed such a nonterritorially based political community, this would be a case of secession without the taking of territory. (Barnett, Liberty Fund Symposium on Liberalism, Federalism, and the Question of Secession, Tucson, Arizona, December 1990.) A nonterritorially based, independent political community would protect its citizens and provide services for them, perhaps by contracting for these services with territorially based states or private corporations. The Kuwaiti state in exile (after the Iraqi invasion in August 1990 and before the liberation of Kuwait) provides at least a partial model: The government of Kuwait occupied no territory of its own (other than its foreign embassies), but it had vast resources in various banks around the world. In principle, then, a nonterritorially based state could perform, or have performed for it, most if not all of the various functions that we associate with territorially based states—*if* its resources were great enough, and *if* it could count on the cooperation of territorially based states to recognize the rights of its citizens in their territories.

However, this theoretical possibility, at least under present conditions (as well as those of virtually all of world history), is not an option upon which many would be likely to stake their lives and fortunes. As was well understood by those who fought to establish Israel as a territorially based state for all Jews, in our world a people without a territory is vulnerable to the most severe violations of rights. For this reason, and because actual historical and contemporary secessionist movements do involve the attempt to take territory, I will concentrate in this book on secession as including taking control over territory.

19. These issues are taken up in greater detail in subsequent chapters.

20. Robert Nozick, *Anarchy, State, and Utopia* (New York: Basic Books, 1974), pp. 54–56.

21. Henry David Thoreau, "Civil Disobedience," in *The Variorum Civil Disobedience*, annotated by Walter Harding (New York: Twayne Publishers, 1967).

22. See James Truslow Adams, *The History of New England*, vol. 3: *New England in the Republic* (Boston: Little, Brown, 1927).

23. Brian Barry and Russell Hardin, eds., *Rational Man and Irrational Society?* (Beverly Hills: Sage Publications, 1983), especially pp. 11–50.

24. This fact was called to my attention by Haavi Morreim.

25. See the Constitution of the Swiss Federation, 1975.

26. Jules Gerard-Libois, *Katanga Secession*, translated by Rebecca Young (Madison: University of Wisconsin Press, 1966).

27. Arthur Nwanko and Samuel Ifejika, *The Making of a Nation: Biafra* (London: C. Hurst & Co., 1970).

28. Donald Horowitz, *Ethnic Groups in Conflict* (Berkeley: University of California Press, 1985), pp. 249–254.

29. Allen Buchanan, *Ethics, Efficiency, and the Market* (Totowa, N.J.: Rowman and Allanheld, 1985), pp. 74–78. G. A. Cohen, "Robert Nozick and Wilt Chamberlain: How Patterns Preserve Liberty," in J. Arthur and W. H. Shaw, eds., *Justice and Economic Distribution*, (Englewood Cliffs, N.J.: Prentice-Hall, 1978); A. E. Buchanan, "Deriving Welfare Rights from Libertarian Rights," in P. G. Brown, C. Johnson, and P. Vernier, eds., *Income Support* (Totowa: Rowman and Allanheld, 1981).

30. Mikail Gorbachev, *New York Times International*, Monday, June 4, 1990, p. A13.

31. Robert A. Williams, Jr., *The American Indian in Western Legal Thought* (Oxford: Oxford University Press, 1990); Williams, Jr., "The Algebra of Federal Indian Law: The Hard Trail of Decolonizing and Americanizing the White Man's Indian Jurisprudence," *Wisconsin Law Review*, vol. 219, 1986; Williams, Jr., "Encounters on the Frontiers of International Human Rights Law: Redefining the Terms of Indigenous Peoples' Survival in the World," forthcoming, *Duke Law Review*, 1991.

32. Lee C. Buchheit, *Secession: The Legitimacy of Self-Determination* (New Haven, Conn.: Yale University Press, 1978), pp. 1–42.

33. I hope to examine the moral foundations of the second step in the revolution in international law in another work.

2

The Morality of Secession

I. The Strategy

First, I will articulate a variety of arguments that purport to justify secession, or rather, secession under certain circumstances. For the most part these arguments rely on familiar and widely endorsed moral principles and values. However, I will endeavor to exhibit the logical structure of the arguments more clearly than is usually done, and I will subject their implicit moral and factual assumptions to careful scrutiny. Some of these prosecession arguments are flawed and some are of only limited application, but others are more compelling. The cumulative effect of these arguments is to establish a strong case for a moral right to secede.

To say that there is a moral right to secede is to say at least two things: (1) that *it is morally permissible* for those who have this right *to secede*, and (2) that others are *morally obligated not to interfere* with their seceding.[1] To have a moral right to something is to have an especially strong moral power or moral authority, the implication being that the obligation of others not to interfere with one's doing that to which one has a right is a very weighty obligation. In particular, this obligation may not be overridden merely on the grounds that doing so would maximize social welfare.[2] Thus to assert that there is a moral right to secede is to imply that preserving the liberty to secede without interference is an extremely high moral priority, that this liberty warrants special protection, and that this protection should not be compromised for the sake of competing interests, except, perhaps, in very extreme circumstances.

The proper analysis of rights is a matter of considerable controversy among moral and political philosophers. Some may endorse a richer or stronger concept of a right, according to which a genuine moral right includes features in addition to those two stated above. But for our purposes it will not be necessary to settle these disputes. My main concern is to show that under certain conditions secession is *morally justified* and that forcible resistance to it would be *morally unjustified*. Those who endorse a richer or stronger notion of a right can easily translate my subsequent references to a moral right to secede into the language of moral justification without losing anything of great importance.

After the case for a moral right to secede has been made, a similarly diverse set of moral arguments *against* secession will be presented in Chapter 3. To the extent that these arguments are cogent, they provide a *prima facie* case for resisting secession, but only a *prima facie* case. For even if they succeed in outweighing the case for secession and establish that secession, or secession under certain circumstances, is morally wrong or impermissible, it does not follow from this that the use of coercion to suppress secession is justified. This is but one instance of a more general truth: From the fact that something is morally wrong it does not follow that it is morally permissible to prohibit it by force. There can be a number of moral and practical considerations that speak decisively in favor of refraining from coercion. For example, even though lying is morally wrong, it does not follow that lying should be made a criminal offense, subject to coercive sanctions. The costs, including the moral costs of massive state intrusions into our lives, may simply be too great.

Out of the critical juxtaposition of these arguments for and against secession will emerge a substantive moral conclusion of considerable practical importance: that there is a moral right to secede, though a highly qualified one. Then, equipped with an account of the scope and limits of the moral right to secede, we can proceed to an examination of constitutional issues concerning secession.

The relationship between moral and legal rights is rather complex. A legal right, most simply, is one that is included in a legal system, in statute or common law, in a constitution, or in international law. For present purposes it suffices to say that the existence of a moral right may imply a presumption in favor of creating a corresponding legal right, but not a decisive justification for the establishment of one. Whether a moral right ought to be given legal expression will depend upon a number of considerations, and these may vary, depending upon the character of a particular legal system and the sociopolitical conditions in which it exists. Nevertheless, the chief conclusion of this part of the book will be that the moral right to secede provides a strong case for establishing a constitutional right to secede, under certain conditions. Although I shall not pursue the place of secession in international law in any direct and sustained way, the strength of the case for moral and constitutional rights to secession strongly suggests that a right to secede, under certain circumstances, ought to be recognized by international law.

II. The Case for a Moral Right to Secede

Our concern here is with reasons for seceding that are of such moral weight as to ground a right to secede. Because the aim is to ascertain the strongest case that can be made for such a right, we must consider not only arguments that have been and are being advanced to justify secession but also arguments that might be advanced but have been overlooked. As it turns out, there are no fewer than twelve distinct prosecession arguments to be examined. This number is rather surprising, since much, if not most, of the popular and scholarly debates about secessionist movements assumes that there is only one justification for seceding: the "right of self-determination."

As we shall see, however, matters are much more complex than this. For one thing, even if one assumes that there is a right of self-determination, it is a mistake to make the further assumption that a proper exercise of this right always or even frequently includes secession rather than the achievement of some other, less drastic form of political independence. The root of this mistake is the failure to see that self-determination comes in many forms. For another thing, to begin with an unexamined "right of self-determination" is to fail to dig deep enough: One needs to know why self-determination (of which sort!) is something to which a group (which group!) is entitled. For these reasons it is necessary to wend our way through a rather complex argumentative journey. In particular, the various arguments must first be sorted out one from another before we can see how they fit together. The issues are sufficiently important, and the practical implications of the moral positions are of such moment, that here, if anywhere, patience is worth the effort. A summary of the main conclusions is offered at the end of the chapter.

A. Protecting Liberty

The first justification for seceding to be explored rests upon the value of liberty. If we begin with a general presumption in favor of liberty, it seems to carry with it a presumption in favor of a right to secede. Even the most fervent advocates of liberty admit, however, that it must respect limits. The Harm Principle has been proposed to specify the proper limits of liberty. According to the Harm Principle, it is impermissible to interfere with an individual so long as her choice does not harm others.[3] But if it is impermissible to interfere with the liberty of an individual[4] so long as her choice does not harm others, then it seems impermissible also to interfere with a group of individuals' efforts to secede, if these efforts do not harm others.

Of course, not only the credibility but also the very meaning of the Harm Principle depend upon what counts as a harm.[5] One plausible suggestion, which I shall adopt here, is that a harm, in the sense relevant to the Harm Principle, is a not just a setback to an interest but a setback to an interest that constitutes the violation of a right.[6]

Not all cases in which someone's interest suffers a setback (is thwarted or frustrated) count as violations of that person's rights. For example, if I happen to have bad luck in the stock market, my financial interests suffer, but my rights have not been violated (unless I have been the victim of fraud or some other sort of dishonest dealing). In complex social interactions, especially those of a competitive nature, some harms are unavoidable and well worth suffering for the sake of the gains to all of us that such interactions bring. For this reason, the Harm Principle, which authorizes interfering with people's behavior when that behavior is harmful to others and by implication forbids interference where harm is absent, must be understood to employ a rather restricted notion of harm. The proposal to limit 'harm' to those setbacks to interest that constitute violations of rights is designed to achieve the needed restriction.

However, this necessary restriction comes at a price: To know whether secession (or any other act) may be resisted on the grounds that it *harms* others, we will need to know which interests of individuals or groups are of such moral weight that setbacks to them constitute violations of rights. In short, we will need to know what rights there are and who has them.

As we shall soon see, all arguments against recognizing a right to secede contend that secession threatens certain interests. But these arguments are incomplete and unpersuasive if they merely assume, without support, that these interests are of such moral stature that their protection justifies even the use of force to suppress secession. This assumption must be supported by argument, and in some instances the arguments turn out to be quite complex. For now, we can note simply that the general presumption in favor of liberty implies a presumption in favor of recognizing a right to secede in this sense: The burden of argument is on the opponents of secession to show that secession would cause not only harm, in some sense or other, but harm in the morally relevant sense or of the moral seriousness required to justify the use of coercion to block secession.

The case for secession based on the presumption of liberty can be elaborated and deepened, at least if a liberal point of view is granted. A liberal values the freedom of individuals and groups and seeks to safeguard it by according priority to certain basic legal rights of the sort found, say, in the U.S. Constitution's Bill of Rights or in Rawls's Principle of Greatest Equal Liberty.[7] As we have seen, these include the rights to freedom of expression, to freedom of religion, and to freedom of association; various due process rights; and the right to participate in political processes. In fact, we have simply defined liberalism, in rough and ready fashion and for present purposes, as the principle that the state must uphold the priority of these basic civil and political rights as well as equality of opportunity.[8]

Upholding these rights allows many different sorts of communities to coexist peacefully within the liberal framework. But what if there remain some forms of social life that cannot flourish there, or what if the members of some communities simply do not wish to remain within the liberal state? Should they not be allowed to free themselves of the political authority of the liberal state if they wish to do so (at least so long as their doing so harms no one else in the relevant sense)? Seen in this way, the right to secede is the logical extension of a principle of toleration thought to be central to the liberal point of view.

One may object, of course, that at most the principle of toleration or the Harm Principle provides support for a right of group *emigration*, but not for a right to secede. The natural response for the secessionist is to point out two things. First, group emigration that allows the preservation of the community, that provides a new location with conditions that would allow the community to flourish or even just to subsist, is rarely possible in modern conditions. In many instances, either the process of emigration will be too costly or no suitable place to relocate the community will be available. Second, because political institutions and their boundaries are human creations intended to serve human needs, those who find a state inhospitable to the form of social life they cherish should be allowed to form and control their own political institutions, so long as doing so does not harm others in morally impermissible ways. Again, we reach the same destination by a different route: The presumption in favor of toleration and liberty grounds a presumption in favor of secession, and the burden is on the opponent of secession to show why this presumption is rebutted. More specifically, if the costs of emigration for those who wish to secede would be very high, then it is incumbent on those who allow group emigration but deny the right to secede to show that secession threatens interests of such moral weight that the would-be secessionists must bear the high costs of emigration.

Of course, the case for secession on grounds of liberty is greatly strengthened in circumstances in which the right to emigrate is denied (as it has been for decades in the Soviet Union and in many Eastern and European countries, for example). For secession then remains the only alternative for securing independence from state control. The irony is that a regime so disrespectful of self-determination as to forbid emigration is hardly likely to allow secession if it can block it. But because my main concern is with the place of the right to secede in the political theory of liberalism, and because I take it to be relatively uncontroversial that liberal political theory recognizes a right to emigrate, the question to be pursued here is whether, granted that there is a right to emigrate, there is also a right to secede.

The most obvious, morally significant interest of others that is adversely affected by secession, and hence the most salient candidate for identifying a harm whose prevention warrants overriding the presumption in favor of liberty, is the interest of the state or of its people in preserving its territory and the resources contained within it. For recall that secessionists, unlike emigrants, challenge the authority of the state not in one but in two ways. They deny the state's jurisdiction not only over themselves but also over part of the state's present territory. *If* secession involves a wrongful taking of land and resources that belong to others, then this surely counts as a harm within the scope of the Harm Principle, and the presumption in favor of the right to secede is thereby rebutted. However, whether a taking of land is a violation of a right depends upon whether those from whom it is taken are in fact the rightful owners of it. So ultimately, whether the Harm Principle, and the respect for liberty on which it is based, speak in favor of or against secession in any particular case will depend upon who has valid title to the territory in question. Later, when we explore arguments against secession, the territorial and property rights issues will be carefully examined. At present I wish merely to note that although the argument from liberty creates at best only a qualified presumption in favor of secession, it points toward argumentative moves that are potentially more decisive and which must be taken up in due course.   More precisely, it pushes us, inevitably, toward difficult issues concerning property rights and distributive justice.

B. *Furthering Diversity*

The next argument to justify secession rests on the value of diversity. Some advocates of liberalism, including most notably Wilhelm von Humboldt and John Stuart Mill,[9] have argued that diversity either is good in itself or makes an essential contribution toward social utility. Accordingly, they have argued for a liberal state within which a great deal of diversity among individuals and groups can exist. Why they stopped at the boundaries of the state is less clear. If diversity is so important, then why restrict it arbitrarily to what can be accommodated within those boundaries? If diversity is good, then the more the better; and the secession of a group to form its own, different society increases diversity.

Yet few would hold that diversity is either intrinsically or instrumentally an *unrivaled* good. Hence the force of this argument for secession is limited. Indeed, the argument requires even further qualification. To the extent that different groups each attain *separate*, independent political existence (through secession), the result may be not diversity in any one of them but, on the contrary, homogeneity. The fact that there is diversity among *separate* political societies will not ensure that the good of diversity is being realized, because that good depends upon individuals being able to *participate in* diversity. In other words, only if the boundaries—political, intellectual, cultural, and aesthetic—of the various societies are *permeable* will individuals in one society be able to enjoy the diversity among societies. The less permeable the boundaries between the societies, the less the good of diversity will be realized if one society separates from another through secession; so the less permeable the boundaries, the weaker will be the case for secession on the grounds that it furthers diversity.[10]

In sum: The good of diversity provides a consideration in favor of secession only when there will be free interaction between the political units that secession would spawn. Appreciation for the good of diversity, therefore, does not speak in favor of a group seceding to form an insular, closed, and homogeneous society. Suppose, for example, that Kurghzis wish to secede from the Soviet Union in order to establish a closed, rigidly orthodox, Islamic fundamentalist society that tolerates very little variety in values, thought, and lifestyles. To the extent that the rulers of the new society are expected to succeed in making its borders impermeable over the long term, the case for allowing the secession to occur on grounds of the value of diversity is weakened, inasmuch as the value of diversity depends ultimately upon the ability of diverse groups to make contact with and learn from one another. To think otherwise is to make a fetish of diversity itself, while failing to see that it is a value only to the extent that it enriches the lives of those who experience it.

Apart from the mutual enrichment that contact among diverse societies may bring, there is perhaps one other source of value in diversity. Just as a wide diversity of natural species may provide insurance against ecological disasters that can occur in a monoculture, so there may be some value in keeping alive a number of distinct types of human societies, even if some are in only very limited contact with the others.[11]

This ecological argument for diversity is, however, a rather weak reed upon which to rest the case for secession, for a number of reasons. First, it is not clear why one should assume that the needed diversity can be attained only in separate sovereign states rather than within states, and hence it is not obvious that secession is necessary. Second, it can be argued that the types of disasters likely to befall humankind in the foreseeable future—such as the effects of global warming, massive environmental pollution, or nuclear war—will not respect political boundaries but, rather, will afflict virtually all human beings regardless of cultural differences among them. So, although the value of diversity does speak in favor of secession, it does not do so with a forceful voice. As we shall see, there are several much more compelling arguments for secession.

C. Preserving Liberal Purity

Secession can also be seen as a way, perhaps the only morally satisfactory way, of easing what is sometimes called the liberal paradox and of thereby preserving the purity or integrity of liberalism itself. The liberal paradox, as I shall understand it, is simply this: The tolerant framework of liberalism allows the growth of communities, political or religious (or politico-religious, as in the case of Islamic fundamentalist theocracies), that may eventually shatter the liberal framework, destroying the state-enforced system of civil and political rights. Liberalism protects freedom of religion and expression and association, but some may exercise these freedoms to achieve the goal of destroying them, either for others or for themselves. For example, advocates of single-party Marxist or Fascist dictatorships have sometimes successfully used the liberal freedoms to destroy the liberal state.

In order to prevent this destruction from occurring, the only recourse, paradoxically, may be for the liberal state to use illiberal methods. For example, the state may find it necessary to influence educational institutions so as to inculcate liberal civic virtues in children, or may even find it necessary to restrict exercises of freedom of expression whose content is dangerously illiberal—for example, pamphlets or speeches calling for the abolition of freedom of expression, for racial supremacy, or for a coercively backed state religion. In the former case, the liberal state exposes itself to the charge that its educational policy has violated a principle of neutrality essential to liberalism by using its power to impose one particular conception of the good life or of virtue upon its citizens.[12] In the latter, the liberal state will be charged with violating one of those fundamental individual rights, the right to freedom of expression, which is its constitutive role to uphold.

Allowing secession for groups whose values threaten the liberal framework, but wish only to separate from and not overthrow it, appears to be an attractive way for liberals to avoid the allegation that they had to destroy liberalism in order to save it. So, by recognizing a right to secede, liberalism provides itself with a strong response to communitarian critics who complain that the liberal state is not only hostile to some forms of community but interferes with their flourishing in ways that its own principles condemn.[13]

Furthermore, those sympathetic to the argument from liberal purity for a right to secede might go so far as to insist that groups unwilling to exist within the liberal framework and unwilling or unable to emigrate have an *obligation to secede*, not just a right to secede, and that these illiberal dissenters are justified in attempting to destroy the liberal framework from within *only* if they are denied the option of secession.

If destruction of the liberal framework from within is *revolution*, then this line of reasoning culminates in an unexpected point of intersection between the theory of revolution and that of secession: Under certain circumstances the possibility of secession undercuts the justification for revolution. So recognizing a right to secede can not only ease the liberal paradox by providing a way of protecting liberal institutions without betraying liberal principles; it can also supply illiberal groups within liberal society with an alternative to revolution while at the same time providing the liberal state with a justification for resisting revolutionary actions by those to whom it has given the option of seceding.

D. The Limited Goals of Political Association

This argument for a right to secede rests upon two assumptions: first, that the goals for which a political union is forged can be quite specific; and second, that once these goals are secured, it is permissible for a group to withdraw itself from the political union, at least if it was an autonomous or sovereign political entity at the time it entered into the union, and if it was clearly understood that the union was created for the purpose of securing these goals.

A concrete example will make both the appeal of this argument and its limitations more apparent. Suppose, as seems to have been the case, that individual American colonies, upon announcing their independence from Britain, entered a political union under the Articles of Confederation, chiefly for the express purpose of securing the independence of each from Britain. Suppose also that once the struggle for independence was won one of these units decided that because the purpose of the union had been served the union itself was obsolete, or that at the very least *it* was no longer obligated to remain within the union. Suppose, finally, that the agreement establishing the union included no provision that the union was to exist in perpetuity nor any set of procedures laying down conditions for exiting from it.[14] It is difficult to see why unilateral withdrawal would not be permissible under these circumstances. Of course, the time and manner of withdrawal might well be subject to certain moral and/or legal restrictions. In particular, the seceding unit might have certain transitional obligations to those who remained in the union. But in principle, there seems to be no sound reason to deny that there is a right to secede, under these rather specific circumstances.

This conclusion is greatly strengthened if we include the assumption, mentioned earlier, that the unit which now wishes to withdraw was at the time of entry a sovereign state. However, it is not obvious that this assumption is necessary to render the argument cogent. The status of the units that entered the American Confederation is perhaps unclear: Neither the label 'colony' nor the label 'state' is entirely appropriate. The former term ignores the fact that at the time of entry these units already had made concrete moves to sever their political subordination to Britain—in other words, that they were in the process of defending their secession from the British Empire and hence abandoning the status of colonies. And the latter term courts confusion by suggesting membership in a political union, The United States, that did not come into existence until a decade after the Confederation was created. But in fact, whether Virginia, Pennsylvania, and the rest were "states" or "sovereign states" at the time of entry into the Confederation does not seem to be morally decisive. Whether they were fully independent of all other political entities is beside the point.

What *is* relevant is whether they were bound *to each other* prior to joining the Confederation or through the Articles of Confederation themselves in such a way as to obligate them to remain in the Confederation even after its express goals had been achieved. If the situation at the time of the Articles of Confederation was as described above, there is no reason to think that such a connection existed. What this example shows is that the argument from the limited goals of political association does provide a strong case for a right to secede in circumstances such as those that appear to have obtained with respect to the American Confederation.

It should be obvious, however, that this argument is of very limited applicability; at best it justifies secession only in those cases in which (1) political union was undertaken for a specific goal, (2) the "contract" or agreement of union clearly expressed this limitation, and (3) it is clear that the goal has been secured. Further, as noted earlier, the argument is most compelling in instances in which the units that wish to exit were sovereign states in their own right at the time of entry. Within these limits the argument has strong intuitive appeal, relying as it does on our common-sense moral understanding of simple contracts or agreements for the performance of concrete actions or the attainment of limited purposes.

If we push the analogy with simple, specific, private contracts to the point of identity, we must say that the proper conclusion is not that under such conditions secession is justified but, rather, that although refusal to remain in the union is morally justified, secession, strictly speaking, is conceptually impossible. For if the performance specified in contract is achieved, then the contractual relationship dissolves; and if the political union consisted only of this contractual relationship, then once the performance is completed there is no union from which to secede.

It should be borne in mind that most real-world states, as opposed to limited agreements such as wartime alliances, are not formed by actual contract. Nor are they usually limited to the attainment of such highly specific goals. Nevertheless, as both the coming integration of Europe in 1992 and the reunification of Germany show, explicit contracts to form new political unions do occur and, of late, may be occurring with greater frequency.

E. Making Entry Easier

The preceding arguments have attempted to provide moral justifications for a right to secede. But none of those arguments addresses in any direct way the issue of whether, or in what circumstances, there is a case for including in a constitution the right to secede. The next argument is different. It is a strategic argument in favor of including a right to secede in an agreement to form a political union, rather than an argument to show that, even absent such an explicit provision, secession is morally justified. Nonetheless, it is convenient to include this argument here because it falls under the general heading of "prosecession" arguments.[15] The idea is quite simple: Especially in the case of proposals for forming political unions of an untried and experimental nature, it may be difficult to attract member units unless they are assured of an opportunity to withdraw if they wish, without excessive costs, under certain conditions. For example, some European heads of state, including former Prime Minister Margaret Thatcher of Great Britain, have expressed a reluctance to commit their countries to a new political-economic union of Europe because the nature of the proposed union itself, and hence its consequences for the well-being of particular member states, is uncertain and most likely will be clarified fully only after the initial commitment to union has been made and efforts are already under way to implement the provisions of the agreement. Such understandable reluctance might be overcome if the initial agreement itself included an explicit right to secede. Although this argument (unlike others considered thus far) does not purport to make a moral case for secession, it supplies a strong pragmatic ground for a constitutional right to secede—at least in cases where union would be to the potential advantage of all members, but where uncertainties make unconditional commitment imprudent.

Of course, even in the absence of a constitutional right to secede, continued participation in political unions, whether by individuals or groups, is usually not thought of as being literally unconditional. The traditional liberal-democratic theory of revolution, stemming especially from Locke, insists that the bonds of political obligation are broken, and the political union dissolved, when the government violates the fundamental terms of political authority, usually formulated as a list of basic individual moral rights.[16] The right to revolution is then said to be the right to overthrow a government that tramples these individual moral rights. Even when these moral rights are expressed as legal rights in the constitution, however, *the right to revolution* itself is thought of not as a constitutional right but, rather, as a purely moral right whose exercise provides an extraconstitutional check on unjust governments.

A constitutional right to secede is not, however, the only alternative to an extraconstitutional, purely moral right to revolution, as a way of capturing the idea that commitment to a political union is conditional. There are at least two other main constitutional devices, and the force of the ease-of-entry argument for secession will be sapped if it can be shown that they are superior alternatives to a constitutional right to secede.

The first is a constitutional *group veto right*, the right of a specified group—for example, a state, province, canton, or collection of such, united by a sectional interest, within a federal system—to block national legislative proposals. (Southern Senator John C. Calhoun called this the principle of "the Concurrent Majority."[17]) Recently, the Meech Lake Accord failed to achieve ratification because two provinces, Manitoba and Newfoundland, exercised their veto rights. The second alternative to a constitutional right to secede is a constitutional *right of nullification*, the right of each specified unit (for example, a province, canton, or state) to declare any item of federal legislation null and void in that group's own territory.[18]

In Chapter 4, where the constitutional issues of secession are addressed in greater detail, the comparative advantages of each of these three constitutional devices will be weighed. If either of the other two should prove superior from the standpoint of facilitating commitment to a new political union, then the force of the argument that a right to secede is desirable because it makes entry easier will clearly be diminished. But all that needs to be said at present is that a constitutional right to secede can make entry more attractive and that this is a consideration in favor of including such a right in a constitution, under circumstances in which potential members of a new union are reluctant to enter into it.

F. Escaping Discriminatory Redistribution

Liberal-democratic theory, we have already seen, recognizes an extraconstitutional, purely moral right to revolution that justifiably may be exercised when fundamental *individual* rights (the basic civil and political rights of the sort listed in the U.S. Constitution's Bill of Rights) are violated. To accommodate federal systems, we can supplement the traditional liberal individual rights with constitutionally designated *states' rights* (to delineate a division of labor between state and federal functions). This addendum yields an expanded conception of governmental injustice and a correspondingly broadened conception of the conditions for justified revolution: If the central government violates basic individual rights *or* states' rights, it may be resisted with force.

In some federal systems an additional category of constitutional rights may be included: *minority group rights*. For example, in Canada and elsewhere there are language rights for certain cultural minorities, guaranteeing an official policy of bilingualism, the inclusion of the minority language in the public education curriculum, and so on.

In Chapter 1 I observed that there are *universalist* and *individualist* strains in liberalism that tend to limit fundamental rights to a single list of individual rights for everyone. In this regard, states' rights in a federal system are not so problematic for liberalism as are minority group rights. The former can perhaps be regarded simply as a part of the constitutional structure of *administrative (or public) law*, which specifies legal relations among government entities. Traditional liberal theory, being suspicious of according moral status to anything other than the individual, is more resistant to the idea of fundamental group rights, especially if these rights are accorded only to some and not to all groups.

The Canadian philosopher Will Kymlicka has argued persuasively that liberalism should, and can with consistency, accommodate group minority rights under certain special historical circumstances. His argument proceeds in two main steps. First, he notes that some minorities in some modern liberal societies, including indigenous populations in Canada and the United States, will not be able to preserve their distinctive cultures unless they are accorded special group rights. In particular, the continued existence of their cultures may require that they be granted special rights to restrict the right of members of the majority from settling permanently in their territory or from voting in local elections, because if members of the majority were allowed to do either, they would enact or support policies that would undermine the conditions for the existence of the minority's culture. In some cases, it may also be necessary to accord the cultural minority the right to restrict the property rights of its own members by prohibiting them from selling land to nonmembers. (The same effect might be achieved by prohibiting nonmembers from purchasing land occupied by members of the group.)

The second step in Kymlicka's argument is to emphasize that preservation of a minority culture is of fundamental importance *for individuals* because belonging to a culture provides them with a "meaningful context for choice."[19] The culture supplies a needed structure for choice, which not only presents the individual with options but also endows these options with meaning in a way that enables the individual to be motivated to achieve goals and to experience fulfillment in their attainment. The power of the argument is that it provides a justification for group rights that is fundamentally *individualistic* and hence consistent with the core of liberalism. The value of a culture, and hence the justification for according special minority rights to support a culture, consists in the value of cultural membership to and for individuals.

Yet with the possible exception of minority language rights of the sort sketched above, the various provisions for minorities discussed by Kymlicka are not so much minority *rights* as legal *authorizations to cancel the immunity* from interference that is ordinarily included in the rights of all citizens in a liberal state. For example, to say that a person has a right to freedom of movement is to say that he is legally immune from attempts by others (e.g., local legislatures) to enact laws to restrict his right to live where he chooses. Similarly, if a person has a right to political participation, he has a legal immunity against attempts to deprive him of the liberty to vote in elections in the locale in which he resides. So Kymlicka's endorsement of special group rights to protect minority cultures can be reformulated as the proposal that it is permissible to authorize certain groups to limit selectively the legal immunities (or immunity-rights, as they are sometimes called) of some citizens in order to protect cultural minorities, along with the claim that doing so is consistent with liberal individualism. If Kymlicka's proposed minority rights are rights, they are the rights of a group to restrict individuals' rights (insofar as these individual rights include certain immunities)—but specifically for the sake of the individuals in the group.

Notice that if the fundamental value underlying these measures is regard for the individual—every individual, regardless of cultural differences among individuals—then they seem to be consistent with liberalism's *universalism*, properly understood. It appears, then, that in principle liberalism can be modified to recognize not only (1) individual rights (including the basic civil and political rights as well as equality of opportunity) but also (2) states' rights in federal systems (more accurately, constitutional powers for subordinate administrative units), and (3) what Kymlicka calls minority group rights (powers of groups to impose selective limitations on the immunities conferred by the usual liberal individual rights).

However, even if we construe liberal theory as including not just item (1) but (2) and (3) as well, we would not capture *all* of the conditions relevant to the legitimacy of political authority and to the justification of revolution or other forms of opposition to political authority, such as secession. Even if the central government is respecting individual civil and political rights, and "states' rights" and various minority group rights as well, it may nonetheless be perpetrating serious injustices toward certain groups. And these injustices may provide solid moral grounds for concluding that the political authority, at least insofar as it is exercised over these groups, is illegitimate and may be justifiably resisted by them. For even though it is not infringing any of the aforementioned rights, the central government may be engaging in what I shall call *discriminatory redistribution*: implementing taxation schemes or regulatory policies or economic programs that *systematically work to the disadvantage of some groups, while benefiting others, in morally arbitrary ways*. A clear example of discriminatory redistribution would be the government imposing higher taxes on one group while spending less on it, or placing special economic restrictions on one region, without any sound moral justification for this unequal treatment.

Charges of discriminatory redistribution abound in actual secessionist movements. Indeed, it would be difficult to find cases in which this charge does not play a central role in justifications for secession, although more often than not it is buried in stirring but confused rhetoric about the "right of self-determination." Here are only a few illustrations.

(1) American Southerners complained that the federal tariff laws were discriminatory in intent and effect—that they served to foster the growth of infant industries in the North by protecting them from European and especially British competition, at the expense of the South's import-dependent economy. Calhoun and others argued that the amount of money the South was contributing to the federal government, once the effects of the tariff were taken into account, far exceeded what that region was receiving from it.[20] (2) Basque secessionists have noted that the percentage of total tax revenues in Spain paid by those in their region is more than three times the percentage of state expenditures there.[21] (A popular Basque protest song expresses this point vividly, saying that the cow of state has its mouth in the Basque country but its udder elsewhere.[22]) (3) Biafra, which unsuccessfully attempted to become independent from Nigeria in 1967, while containing only 22 percent of the Nigerian population, contributed 38 percent of total revenues, and received back from the government only 14 percent of those revenues.[23] (4) At the time of its attempt to become independent of the Congo, Katanga Province contributed 50 percent of the Congo's total revenues and received only 20 percent of total government expenditures.[24]

Secessionists in the Baltics and in Soviet Central Asia protest that the government in Moscow has implemented economic policies that have benefited the rest of the country at the expense of staggering environmental damage in their regions. To support this allegation of discriminatory redistribution, they cite reports of abnormally high rates of birth defects in Estonia, Latvia, and Lithuania, apparently due to chemical pollutants from the heavy industry that Soviet economic policy has concentrated there, and contamination of water supplies in Central Asia due to massive use of pesticides at the orders of planners in Moscow whose goal was to make that area a major cotton producer in the world. Generally, a chief complaint of secessionists in so-called Third World countries is that the central government's development policies are discriminatory. For example, the ethnic group that controls the central government skews government investment toward their own people; it also engages in patronage toward them by awarding them a disproportionate share of lucrative government contracts and civil service positions (not to mention attendant opportunities for graft and other forms of corruption). In all of these cases a chief justification offered for secession is the charge of discriminatory redistribution. Although it is no doubt true that where discriminatory redistribution occurs one also usually finds violations of basic individual rights and equality of opportunity and sometimes usurpations of the power of subordinate governmental units as well, this need not be the case. And where accompanied by these other violations, discriminatory redistribution is a distinct and serious injustice.

Further, it does not appear that the injustice of discriminatory redistribution can be captured adequately by attempts to reduce it to violations of those individual civil and political rights that are here treated as definitive of the core of liberalism. The members of a group may suffer discriminatory redistribution even when its members' rights to freedom of expression or religion have not been violated, for example.

As the injustice in question involves wrongful economic loss, it might be thought that it can be accommodated by expanding the ordinary list of liberal individual rights to include an individual right to *private property*, with sufficient content to enable us to say that wherever discriminatory redistribution occurs there is a violation of such a right. Or it might be suggested that discriminatory redistribution is ruled out by a suitable interpretation of the liberal individual right of *equal protection* of the sort found in the Fourteenth Amendment to the U.S. Constitution. In either case, there would be no need for a distinct category of injustice called discriminatory redistribution and no need to include it as an additional ground for justified revolution or other modes of resistance to government authority, such as secession.

Neither alternative, however, is promising. Any theory of justice that allows for any redistribution whatsoever, including the most minimal welfare programs for the needy or disabled, or that acknowledges the need to prevent cumulative harms such as pollution or extreme concentrations of economic power that undermine individual opportunity or political equality, must concede two things: first, that the individual right to private property is a *limited* right, not a right against all interference or a right of unlimited accumulation; and, second, that the sorts of justifiable limitations on the right to private property that may be required under different circumstances are so various that it is impossible to formulate a precise legal right to private property that specifies exactly what those limits are. But if this is so, then a constitutional right to private property will not adequately capture all forms of discriminatory redistribution. Such a right will most likely either be so specific and contentful as to rule out some limitations on ownership that are morally justified or so vague and formal as to fail to serve as a gauge to determine when discriminatory redistribution has occurred and, hence, for judging those instances in which forcible opposition to the government is justified. The same dilemma seems to hold true for a *group* right to property: It seems unable to capture adequately the richness of the phenomena of discriminatory redistribution without making the right to property too broad and inflexible to accommodate reasonable limitations on that right. Some ways of supplementing the core liberal individual civil and political rights with rights of distributive justice might capture all or most forms of discriminatory redistribution. For example, suppose that liberalism's core commitment to the basic individual civil and political rights is to be supplemented with a principle stating that the social and economic inequalities are to work to the greatest advantage of the worst off, as Rawls believes. Or suppose that the core liberal civil and political rights are to be supplemented with an individual right to a "decent minimum" or "adequate level" of basic goods such as shelter, food, health-care resources, and educational opportunities, as some welfare liberals have contended. At least some forms of discriminatory redistribution may be understood as violations of these distributive rights. The point, however, is that nothing so crude as a basic individual right to private property seems capable of allowing us to discern when discriminatory redistribution has occurred and when it has not, across a wide range of cases.

For similar reasons, the multiplicity of forms of discriminatory redistribution cannot be encompassed adequately in a constitutional equal protection right. The history of disputes over the import of this right (e.g., in the United States and Canada) suggests that it is useful in direct proportion to the extent that it is given a largely procedural interpretation that makes it approximate a right of due process.[25] If this is the case, then it is hard to see how a right of equal protection, whether accorded to individuals or to groups, could capture all of the concrete forms of discriminatory redistribution.

For one thing, discriminatory redistribution can be perpetrated by a majority without any violation of legislative or judicial procedures because it is the *content* of the policy, *not the process* by which it came about or the method of its interpretation or implementation, that is unjust. Indeed, this was just the complaint of American Southerners such as Calhoun: The fact that the tariff was enacted by correct legislative processes was no consolation to those who believed it to be discriminatory. Southerners understandably feared that as the balance of power in the U.S. Congress shifted toward the North they would increasingly suffer discriminatory redistribution (as well as the destruction of their "property" in black human beings), all within the constraints of due process. It seems, then, that discriminatory redistribution is a serious injustice, and one that can justify opposition to political authority; but it also seems that discriminatory redistribution cannot be reduced to any of the rights-violations that liberalism typically takes to define the conditions for justified opposition to political authority.

Yet even if it does not involve clear violations of specific individual, group, or states' rights of the sort listed in constitutions that approximate the liberal ideal, discriminatory redistribution is a violation of a fundamental term of the "social contract" and, hence, of the conditions for legitimate political authority over those against whom it is perpetrated: namely, that government is to operate for genuine *mutual advantage*. Put negatively, the point is that government's exercise of power is legitimate only if it refrains from *exploiting* one group for the benefit of another.

In some respects the notion of nonexploitation is preferable to that of mutual advantage. Although both concepts are unavoidably vague, the latter is ambiguous as well. The same redistribution may be mutually advantageous or not, depending upon what *benchmark* is assumed as the level of benefits relative to which advantage is measured. Thus, if the level of benefits that each of two groups would receive in a situation of complete *noncooperation* is taken as the benchmark, then a system may be mutually advantageous (relative to the paucity of benefits in a situation of noncooperation), even if one group, for no good reason, is receiving the lion's share of the total benefits generated by cooperation. Clearly, then, something more than mutual advantage in this minimal sense is necessary. However, just what more is needed is unclear.

It seems preferable to employ the notion of nondiscrimination or nonexploitation, because it emphasizes the point that if the state's distributive policies are to be allowed to affect different groups differently, there must be some sound moral justification for the differences. And although the persistence of disputes about what distributive justice requires attests that what counts as a sound moral justification for differential treatment will sometimes be controversial, in many real-world cases it will be clear enough that a state's policies systematically skew benefits in ways that cannot be justified.

The condition that redistribution is not to be exploitive is fundamental as well as encompassing and general in character. Thus it is not surprising that, as we have just seen, this condition cannot be exhaustively captured by a manageably short list of specific individual or group constitutional rights. If this is the case, then any theory of political authority that restricts itself to such specific rights is inadequate.

Orthodox liberal theory, at least of the classical varieties that include no definite individual distributive rights, suffers from precisely this defect. Thus by exploring one of the most common justifications offered by real-world secession movements, the complaint of discriminatory redistribution, we are led to a fundamental theoretical insight: Liberalism's conception of the conditions that can justify forcible opposition to political authority should be expanded to include the injustice of discriminatory redistribution. More specifically, the theory should acknowledge that a group which is the victim of discriminatory redistribution has at least a strong *prima facie* case for withdrawing from the political union.

An implicit premise of the argument from discriminatory redistribution is that *failure to satisfy this fundamental condition in effect voids the state's claim to the territory in which the victims reside*, whereas the fact that they have no other recourse to avoid this fundamental injustice *gives them a valid title to it.*[26] This premise forges the needed connection between the grounds for seceding (discriminatory redistribution) and the territorial claim that a sound argument for secession must include. One good reason for accepting the premise is that it explains our intuitions about the justifiability of secession in certain central and relatively uncontroversial cases.

In other words, unless this premise is acceptable, the argument from discriminatory redistribution is not sound; and unless the argument from discriminatory redistribution is sound, it is hard to see how secession is justifiable in certain cases in which there is widespread agreement that it is justified. Consider, for example, the secession of the thirteen American colonies from the British Empire in North America (which also included Canada). Strictly speaking this was secession, not revolution. The aim of the colonists was not to overthrow the government of Britain but only to remove a part of the North American territory from the Empire. The chief justification for American independence was discriminatory redistribution: Britain's mercantilist policies systematically worked to the disadvantage of the colonies for the benefit of the mother country. Lacking representation in the British Parliament, the colonists reasonably concluded that this injustice would persist. It seems, then, that if the American "Revolution" was justified, there are cases in which the state's persistence in the injustice of discriminatory redistribution, together with the lack of alternatives to secession for remedying it, *generates* a valid claim to territory on the part of the secessionists.

The force of the argument from discriminatory redistribution does not rest solely, however, on brute moral intuitions about particular cases such as the American "Revolution." We can *explain* our responses to such cases by a simple but powerful principle: The legitimacy of the state—including its rightful jurisdiction over territory—depends upon its providing a framework for cooperation that does not systematically discriminate against any group.

G. *Enhancing Efficiency*

The next argument in favor of a right to secede is likely to appeal to no-nonsense economists, who generally scorn arguments from moral principle, giving their allegiance (if not their fervent devotion) to considerations of efficiency instead. In brief, this argument maintains that secession is justified when the division of the existing political union would promote efficiency.

History supplies numerous cases of overextended political units, far-flung empires that swelled beyond the optimum scale compatible with even minimally efficient government, given the existing conditions of technological and administrative development. In fact, it can be argued that the great commercial city-states of the Renaissance, including Florence, Venice, and Ragusa (present-day Debrovnik), eventually lost their independence and were assimilated into emerging nation-states because of precisely the opposite problem of scale: They were too small to protect their trade routes.[27] Some recent analysts have suggested that this historical trend may be reversible, arguing that advances in telecommunications, along with the relatively stable international relations of the post–World War II era, now render a new version of the city-state feasible.[28] Some are even predicting the demise of the nation-state in consequence.[29] (Note that in October 1990 the government of Odessa passed a resolution stating that this Soviet city should become a free, independent city!)

It may well be that one of the chief reasons some groups are now seriously considering secession is that they believe the prospects for peace are sufficiently good that smaller-scale political units are once again feasible. My aim here, however, is not to engage in futurist speculations. Instead, it is to take stock of the role that appeals to efficiency of scale can play in making a case for secession. And to do this, I must first clarify the relevant notion of efficiency.

By 'efficiency' here I mean *Pareto Optimality*.[30] Pareto Optimality is a characteristic of a state (i.e., an outcome) of a system of distribution or, more broadly, of a system of cooperation that has distributional effects. A state, S1, of a system is Pareto Optimal if and only if there is no feasible alternative state of that system, S2, such that at least one individual is better off in S2 than in S1 and no one is worse off in S2 than in S1. A state, S1, of a system is *Pareto Superior* to an alternative feasible state, S2, of that system if and only if at least one individual in S1 is better off in S1 than in S2 and no one is worse off in S1 than in S2. A state, S1, of a system is *Strongly Pareto Superior* to an alternative feasible state, S2, if and only if *everyone* is better off in S1 than in S2. A transition from a state S1 to a state S2 is a *Pareto Improvement* if and only if someone is better off in S2 than in S1 and no one is worse off in S2 than in S1. A transition from a state S1 to a state S2 is a *Strong Pareto Improvement* if and only if everyone is better off in S2 than in S1 and no one is worse off in S2 than in S1.

Indulging in a major but useful simplification, we can recast these concepts so as to apply, not to individuals, but to groups—the seceding group and the group that will occupy the remainder state if secession succeeds. Three scenarios can then be distinguished.

- *Scenario One*. Secession is a Strong Pareto Improvement. Both groups, secessionists as well as remainders, are better off when secession has been achieved than in the presecession state.
- *Scenario Two*. Secession is Pareto Optimal for the total group consisting of both secessionists and remainders; but only the secessionists reap an improvement from secession, whereas the remainders are neither worsened nor bettered. The transition to the

state in which secession has been accomplished is a Pareto Improvement, but not a Strong Pareto Improvement.

- *Scenario Three*. Secession is not Pareto Optimal (nor, *a fortiori*, Strongly Pareto Optimal) for the total group consisting of secessionists and remainders, nor is the transition to successful secession a Pareto Improvement for the total group. The secessionists are better off when secession is achieved, but the remainders are worse off than they were prior to secession. When the total group consisting of secessionists and remainders is considered, the state in which secession has been achieved is not Pareto Superior to the presecession state (nor, *a fortiori*, Strongly Pareto Superior to it).

Scenario One appears, at first blush, to be wholly unproblematic. Not only does no one lose, or no one lose and someone gain; everyone gains. So who could reasonably object to secession? Matters are not quite so simple, however. What has been overlooked is the possibility that the remainder group has property rights in the territory that the secessionists wish to sever from the union. If a person or a group has a property right in something (say, a piece of land), then that person has the moral power or authority to alienate it (through sale, exchange, gift, etc.) *or to continue in possession of it*, regardless of whether he would be better off alienating it. Although it is true that having a right is generally beneficial, a right authorizes the right-holder to act in ways that may not actually maximize his own welfare. (For example, if you own a piece of worthless land upon which you must pay taxes, then the fact that you would be better off if I took it from you does not make it all right for me to do so. Because you are the owner, it is your say as to whether to give it up or keep it.) So even in Scenario One, the most favorable of the three cases, considerations of efficiency do not constitute a decisive argument to justify secession. They would do so only if the remainders had no valid claim to the seceding territory or if they had a valid claim and decided to waive it. Of course, in Scenario One, considerations of efficiency can lead the one group to agree to allow the other group to secede; but if the former has a valid claim to the seceding territory, it is its agreement to waive that claim, not the fact that doing so is efficient, that justifies the secession.

The same conclusion holds, *a fortiori*, for the Second Scenario. For here the secessionists cannot appeal even to the fact that secession will benefit the remainders, but only to the fact that it will not worsen their condition. If the remainders hold valid title to the seceding territory, then the fact that secession would be a Pareto Improvement and would benefit the secessionists while not worsening the remainders does not establish that secession is justified. We might well criticize the remainders for being envious or ungenerous if they refuse to allow the secessionists to gain when this gain will cost them nothing, but we cannot conclude that the secessionists are justified in seceding without the permission of the remainders.

The same conclusions follow with a vengeance in Scenario Three. Note that this is not a case of secession on grounds of efficiency at all, if the remainder group is included in the assessment of gains versus losses, because the state in which secession has occurred is not a Pareto Improvement relative to the total group that includes secessionists and remainders. Instead, secession is a Pareto Improvement only for the secessionist group. And whether a group is morally justified in undertaking a course of action that improves its condition at the expense of another group's well-being cannot, of course, be decided by appealing to the value of efficiency. Instead, an appeal to moral principles is necessary.

The conclusion to be drawn from examining these three scenarios is that considerations of efficiency play a *subordinate* role in justifying secession. Moral considerations, valid claims to territory in particular, constrain the *justified* pursuit of efficiency.[31]

H. *The Pure Self-Determination or Nationalist Argument*

One of the most familiar and stirring justifications offered for secession appeals to *the right of self-determination for "peoples,"* interpreted such that it is equivalent to what is sometimes called the *normative principle of nationalism*. It is also one of the least plausible justifications.

The normative nationalist principle, as I understand it, states that every "people" is entitled to its own state, or, as Ernest Gellner puts it, that political and cultural (or ethnic) boundaries must, as a matter of right, coincide.[32] In other words, according to this understanding of the normative nationalist principle, the notion of self-determination is construed, in a very robust way, as requiring complete political independence—that is, full sovereignty.

The United Nations officially endorses the right of self-determination in several documents. For example, General Assembly Resolution 1514 bravely declares that "all peoples have the right to self-determination; by virtue of that right they freely determine their political status and freely pursue their economic, social and cultural development." The phrase 'freely determine their political status', lacking any qualifying language, suggests that 'self-determination' here is to be understood in the robust sense, as requiring or at least allowing complete political independence. This in turn seems to commit the UN, in its affirmation of the right of self-determination, to the view that every "people" has the right to secede if secession is necessary for achieving complete political independence.

The United Nations Charter (Article 1, paragraph 2, and Article 55), the United Nations International Covenant on Civil and Political Rights, and the

United Nations International Covenant on Economic, Social, and Cultural
Rights also proclaim a right of self-determination for all peoples.

An immediate difficulty, of course, is the meaning of "peoples."
Presumably a "people" is a distinct ethnic group, the identifying marks of
which are a common language, shared traditions, and a common culture. Each
of these criteria has its own difficulties. The question of what count as
different dialects of the same language, as opposed to two or more distinct
languages, raises complex theoretical and metatheoretical issues in linguistics.
The histories of many groups exhibit frequent discontinuities, infusions of new
cultural elements from outside, and alternating degrees of assimilation to and
separation from other groups. More disturbingly, if 'culture' is interpreted
broadly enough, then the normative nationalist principle denies the legitimacy
of any state that exhibits cultural pluralism (unless all "peoples" within it freely
waive their rights to their own states). Yet cultural pluralism is often taken to
be a distinguishing feature of the modern state, or at least of the modern
liberal state. Moreover, if the number of ethnic or cultural groups or peoples
is not fixed but may increase, the normative nationalist principle is a recipe
for limitless political fragmentation.

Nor is this all. Even aside from the instability and economic costs of
repeated fragmentation, there is a more serious objection to the normative
nationalist principle, forcefully formulated by Ernest Gellner.

> To put it in the simplest possible terms: there is a very large number of potential nations
> on earth. Our planet also contains room for a certain number of independent or
> autonomous political units. On any reasonable calculation, the former number (of
> potential nations) is probably much, *much* larger than that of possible viable states. If this
> argument or calculation is correct, not all nationalisms can be satisfied, at any rate not at
> the same time. The satisfaction of some spells the frustration of others. This argument is
> furthered and immeasurably strengthened by the fact that very many of the potential
> nations of this world live, or until recently have lived, not in compact territorial units but
> intermixed with each other in complex patterns. It follows that a territorial political unit
> can only become ethnically homogeneous, in such cases, if it either kills, or expels, or
> assimilates all non-nationals.[33]

With arch understatement, Gellner concludes that the unwillingness of people
to suffer such fates "may make the implementation of the nationalist principle
difficult." Thus to say that the normative nationalist principle must be rejected
because it is too *impractical* or *economically costly* would be grossly
misleading. It ought to be abandoned because the *moral costs* of even
attempting to implement it are prohibitive.

It is crucial to see that this criticism of the principle of self-determination
is decisive *only* against the strong version of that principle that makes it
equivalent to the normative nationalist principle, which states that each people
(or ethnic group) is to have its own fully sovereign state. For the objection
focuses on the unacceptable implications of granting a right of self-

determination to all "peoples," *on the assumption that self-determination means complete political independence, that is, full sovereignty.*

However, as a number of writers have noted, the notion of self-determination is vague or, rather, multiply ambiguous, inasmuch as there are numerous forms and a range of degrees of political independence that a "people" might attain. For example, under some conditions, a group might consider itself to have achieved its goal of self-determination if it secured the right to use its own language as an official language of the state, or if its territory was recognized as a province or state within a federation, or if the group's representatives were accorded a veto over constitutional changes or over important areas of federal legislation. 'Self-determination' need not mean full sovereignty, and hence to recognize a right of self-determination does not itself commit us to affirming that every group to which the principle of self-determination applies has a right to secede.

If the alleged principle of self-determination of peoples is either too vague to be of much use or implausible (when specified so strongly as to entail a right to complete independence and hence secession), what accounts for its popularity and longevity? My hypothesis is that the moral appeal of the principle of self-determination depends precisely upon its vagueness. It is a kind of placeholder for a range of possible principles specifying various forms and degrees of independence. These more specific principles do not express a substantive fundamental value, called self-determination. Instead, the moral force of any particular specification of self-determination depends upon the more basic values that implementing it might serve in a particular context. Once these more basic values are identified, it should be possible to dispense largely with the principle of self-determination, with its dangerous vagueness, and to concentrate on more direct arguments in favor of secession (or in favor of more limited forms of political independence).

Under certain conditions, achieving a greater degree of self-determination may be the only practical way for a group to protect itself from (1) destruction of its culture, (2) literal genocide, or (3) various injustices falling under the general heading of ethnic discrimination, including violations of civil and political rights that ought to be guaranteed to all citizens regardless of ethnicity, as well as what was referred to earlier as discriminatory redistribution. As we are concerned here with arguments to justify secession, I take up in upcoming sections of this chapter (1) the argument from cultural preservation and (2) the argument from self-defense, as justifications for that extreme form of self-determination which secession entails. Argument (3) has already been dealt with in part, under the heading of the argument from discriminatory redistribution. One point of that discussion was that whether or not the liberal doctrine of justified resistance to the state has clearly recognized it, discriminatory redistribution is a serious injustice and ought to be included among the grounds for justified resistance.

It was also noted that whether resistance to discriminatory redistribution may justifiably take the form of secession depends, in the end, upon whether the need to eliminate the injustice of discriminatory redistribution is sufficient to establish a valid claim to territory on the part of the secessionists (and to override whatever claims to territory others may have to the seceding area).

Similarly, whether injustice in the form of violations of the civil and political rights of members of ethnic groups justifies not only revolution, as liberal doctrine concedes, but also secession, along with the taking of territory that the latter entails, will depend upon two things: first, whether there is any other practical and morally acceptable way of avoiding these injustices that does not involve the taking of territory; and, second, if there is not, whether the practical necessity of seizing territory in order to avoid injustice generates a valid moral title to that territory. These complex issues deserve special attention and will be taken up later. For the present, however, this conclusion can be proffered tentatively: The argument from self-determination may be understood either as appealing to self-determination for all peoples or ethnic groups as a fundamental value or as something instrumentally valuable for securing other, more basic values, such as cultural preservation, survival, or justice. If the former, then the principle of self-determination must be rejected, at least insofar as the principle is interpreted so strongly as to entail a right to secede. If the latter, then the argument from self-determination can be dropped in favor of an examination of those arguments to which it reduces.

Before we proceed to those arguments, it is worth noting an important connection between the nationalist argument for secession and the argument from discriminatory redistribution. As observed earlier, not just the worse off but the better off, too, may claim to be victims of discriminatory redistribution and seek to escape the continuation of this injustice by seceding. It is on precisely this ground that many Slovenes, for example, advocate severing their region from the poorer and less developed areas of Yugoslavia.

Yet the same people may well accept policies within their own region that distribute wealth from the rich to the poor. What this suggests is that whether a group views itself as a victim of discriminatory redistribution will depend in part upon how it conceives of the boundaries of its own identity—whether it regards those to whom some of its resources are being transferred by government redistribution policies as *its own people* or as an alien group. Thus whether the reunification of Germany will succeed may depend in large part upon whether West Germans see the massive transfers of wealth from themselves to East Germans as redistribution to another people or as redistribution among one people, a matter of the wealthier members of a family helping their less fortunate relatives. The greater the identification of the benefactors with the recipients, the less likely the benefactors are to see themselves as suffering the injustice of discriminatory redistribution.

So, on the one hand, the presence or absence of a sense of distinct ethnic identity can determine whether or not discriminatory redistribution even becomes an issue, and hence whether it comes to fuel a secessionist movement. On the other hand, a policy of discriminatory redistribution can contribute to the emergence of a group's sense that it is distinct and to its desire to form an independent state: The members of a group may come to construct a common identity in part out of the recognition that they are all victims of the same enemy. The process by which a group becomes a force striving for a state of its own is usually a complex one in which a political and literary elite forges a strong sense of identity by convincing people that the economic disadvantages they suffer are the result of ethnic discrimination, and continued discrimination may impede assimilation, preventing a disadvantaged group from losing its ethnic distinctness. And when the members of a group perceive that they are barred from economic advancement available to others, the goods that membership in their distinct ethnic culture provides to them may become all the more important. This circumstance in turn may lead them to seek political autonomy in order to preserve their distinctive culture.

In some cases, however, a secessionist movement may be motivated by the desire to preserve a distinctive culture even when the members of the group in question are no longer the victim of discriminatory redistribution or other forms of discrimination. This may in fact be the case with Quebec. Some, perhaps the majority of Quebecois advocating secession do so on grounds of cultural preservation, not discriminatory redistribution or another injustice, although most would probably maintain that they have suffered serious discrimination until very recently. For this reason the issue of cultural preservation is worth considering, in its own right, as an independent argument for secession, even though in many cases the perceived need to preserve a culture will be closely tied to the grievance of discriminatory redistribution.

I. *Preserving Cultures*

Some have contended that by itself the need to preserve a culture can justify secession. Again Quebec can serve as a case in point. The Meech Lake Accord, as was already noted, contains a special provision recognizing French Canada as a "distinct society," and one reason given for including it was that doing so was thought to be necessary for the preservation of French Canadian culture. To frame the argument in this manner, however, may be too impersonal, too abstract. Its true force lies in the idea that the members of a culture who believe that their culture is threatened with disintegration feel that their very identities are imperiled, that in losing their culture they will in some sense lose themselves, or a significant part of the selves they value most.

To evaluate this justification for secession, two undertakings are required. First, we must explore the value of cultural preservation and try to chart its scope and limits. Second, we must ascertain whether there are other, less drastic measures than secession that can help provide sufficient protection for a culture. What counts as sufficient protection will depend upon how valuable the preservation of a culture is, and that in turn will depend upon what constitutes the value of a culture.

On the view endorsed here, the chief value of culture is more accurately characterized as the value of *cultural membership*. In other words, a culture is valuable first and foremost because of its contribution to the lives of the individuals whose culture it is. A culture's value will be enhanced, of course, if it also enriches the lives of others who are not members of it but who benefit from indirect contact with it.

The key point is that whatever value a culture has is its value *for individuals*. It is extremely important to emphasize, however, that this does not assume a conception of value that is "individualistic" in any unacceptable sense of that much abused term. To say that culture is good (and only good) by virtue of the contribution it makes to the lives of individuals is not to assume that the good of those individuals is egoistic or purely self-regarding, nor that cultural membership is only an instrumental or extrinsic good for them. None of this is implied, although critics of liberalism's "individualism" often suggest that it is.

There are two ways in which cultural membership can contribute to the good of an individual. In only one of them does cultural membership not qualify as an intrinsic good. And in neither does the good of cultural membership depend upon any assumption that the individual is egoistic or that her good is exclusively self-regarding. First, as we have already seen, Kymlicka has correctly noted that membership in a cultural community can be vital for the individual because it provides her with a meaningful context for choice.

This important point warrants more elaboration than Kymlicka gives it. The culture not only makes *salient* a manageably limited range of alternative goals, rescuing the individual from the paralysis of infinite possibilities; it also does so in such a way as to endow certain options with *meanings* that allow the individual to *identify with* and be *motivated by* them. Finally, the culture serves to *connect* what otherwise would be fragmented goals in a coherent, mutually supporting way, offering ideals of wholeness and continuity, not only across the stages of a human life but over generations as well. Without the context for meaningful choice supplied by a culture, the individual may feel either that nothing is worth doing because everything is possible or that life is a series of discrete episodes of choice, each of which is diminished in value because of its utter unconnectedness with the others. The landscape of choice may seem so flattened and featureless that movement seems pointless, and the sense that one's life is a journey in which milestones can be reached may evaporate. With some simplification, we can say that the first source of the value of culture is that it provides an appropriate *structure* for the individual's pursuit of the good life. To repeat: Nothing in this account of the first source of the value of culture assumes that the content of the individual's goals is egoistic or purely self-regarding.

What Kymlicka neglects to observe—and what renders his view vulnerable to charges of excessive individualism—is that cultural membership is valuable also because, at least for most individuals, *participation in community* is *itself* an important ingredient in the *content* of the good life, not just a part of its structure. Participation in community, for many people, at least, is a fundamental intrinsic good, not merely a structural condition for the successful pursuit of other goods or a means of acquiring them. In many cases the community that is most important in the individual's life will be a cultural (as opposed to a political, professional, or aesthetic) community. Nothing in liberalism or its understanding of human good precludes it from acknowledging this basic truth.[34]

Proponents of the argument under scrutiny must go farther than the statement that cultural membership, and hence the preservation of culture, is a good. They must show that there is a *right* to cultural preservation and that this right justifies secession. However, this alleged right, if it exists, cannot be a right to cultural *stasis*—a right to preserve a culture just as it is at present. The basis of the alleged right is the good that cultural membership achieves for individuals, and this good does not require an unchanging culture.

For the same reason, an appreciation of the value of cultural membership cannot by itself even support a right to the continued existence of any particular culture. What is important is that an individual be able to belong to a culture, some culture or other, not that he be able to belong, indefinitely, to any particular culture.

Of course, in practice this distinction will frequently be of little consequence because an individual whose culture disintegrates will sometimes not be able to become a fully participating member of another culture. This may be the case with some members of indigenous populations, including some North American Indians. The impact of white culture and technology in some instances may have rendered the traditional culture unviable, or at the least has so damaged it that membership no longer provides great benefits to the individual but instead imposes many serious liabilities. Yet for a number of reasons, including a shameful record of injustice and neglect, those whose cultures have been most severely damaged also have been barred from genuine assimilation into the culture the whites brought.[35] However, this is not always so. In some cases individuals can leave the sinking ship of one culture and board another, more seaworthy cultural vessel.

Tragically, the members of a dying culture may not always be willing to abandon it and give their allegiance to a new way of life, even when one is available to them.[36] The following type of case, which may be all too common, creates a dreadful moral dilemma. Consider the indigenous culture mortally wounded by the onslaught of "civilization," because the material base for its fundamental ways of life has been destroyed. (Such was the case with the destruction of the bison herds upon which the Plains Indian cultures were built.) Without this material base, which cannot be restored, the culture may not be able to supply in sufficient degree the goods that make cultural membership valuable and whose preservation provides grounds for secession or other forms of political autonomy, or even for according the group special rights. Indeed, any attempt to prolong the life of the moribund culture will not only fail but will also make the members of the group worse off by impeding their assimilation into the "civilized" culture. Yet the members of the group remain steadfast in their desire to try to preserve the culture. They are like people who refuse to be rescued from their sinking lifeboat because it is *their* craft and because any other vessel seems alien and untrustworthy to them. Instead, they demand that we provide them with timbers and pumps (special group rights, greater autonomy, and/or other resources) to shore up what we have every reason to believe is a doomed vessel. The dilemma is this: Should we respect their preferences and render aid that we reasonably believe will only be detrimental to them, or should we act so as to promote their well-being even though this means rejecting their choices?

Notice that there is a dilemma here even for the strongly antipaternalistic. Even if one is willing to allow competent choosers to bring ruin upon themselves, it is quite another matter to provide them with resources to pursue a path that will prevent their children, and successive generations as well, from achieving the goods of membership in a viable culture. This problem deserves far more attention than can be given here. Despite the complications it introduces, the chief point I wish to make is that there is a limitation on the right to preserve a culture: Because the value of cultural membership is not limited to membership in one particular culture, and because individuals whose culture is damaged will in some cases be able to affiliate successfully with another culture (at least if they are given the resources to do so), there is, strictly speaking, no right to the perpetual existence of any one particular culture.

There is another reason why the right to cultural preservation cannot be understood as the right to whatever is necessary, including secession, for each and every culture to survive indefinitely. As was seen in our assessment of the pure self-determination or nationalist argument for secession, there simply may not be sufficient usable space and other resources for every culture to have its own autonomous territory. And the cultural preservation argument, as an argument for secession, assumes that the culture requires its own autonomous territory if it is to survive.

Yet another important limitation on the alleged right to cultural preservation is that some cultures may be so pernicious as to warrant no protection at all, much less the protection afforded by granting them their own territory. Indeed, some cultures are so heinous that they may be and should be destroyed. It would be little short of bizarre to say that the Nazis had a right to preserve their culture, even if one quickly added that this right was overridden by the fact that the culture in question was a genocidal barbarism erected on a tissue of grotesque lies and racist mythology. (Nazism, which included distinctive conceptions of the family, of the individual's relationship to society, and of virtue, and which also possessed its own peculiar aesthetic and art forms, does seem to qualify as a culture.) Such a culture has no right to preserve itself. So if there is a right to cultural preservation, it may be ascribed only to cultures that are not beyond the moral pale.

Finally, it is important to understand that the argument from cultural preservation assumes that the need to protect a culture is of such moral weight as to *generate* the valid territorial claim that justified secession requires. This argument, then, does not *begin* with a preexisting claim to territory. Instead, its *conclusion* includes such a claim.

In this regard the argument from cultural preservation for secession is to be contrasted with the argument from rectificatory justice to be considered below. The latter argument justifies secession as the reappropriation of territory that was unjustly taken (as in the case of the U.S.S.R.'s annexation of Lithuania, Latvia, and Estonia) and hence relies on a *preexisting* territorial claim. If the need to preserve a culture is to count as an independent justification for secession, then, it must be shown that at least under certain conditions this need generates a valid claim to territory in the absence of a historical entitlement to territory (as in the argument from rectificatory justice). In other words, if the argument is to succeed, it must at minimum establish that autonomous control over territory is *practically necessary*—that it is the only effective way to preserve the culture.

Keeping in mind these limitations on the right to preserve a culture, we must next ask whether there are other, less costly ways in which the existence of a culture may be protected. And as our special concern is with the place of secession in liberal theory, we must try to determine what resources a liberal order in particular has for protecting imperiled cultures while still accommodating them within its borders. Because the argument from cultural preservation assumes that under certain circumstances control over land is necessary for cultural survival, the questions to pose are these: (1) How might a group achieve forms of control over land other than the full control of territorial sovereignty that secession entails? (2) Would such alternative forms of control suffice to provide endangered cultures with whatever protection they are entitled to?

There are at least two major mechanisms for control over land (short of secession) available within a liberal framework. The first already exists within all liberal societies: *the laws of property and contract*. These laws enable members of groups, including cultural groups, to pool individual property into collective, jointly owned property. Throughout the history of liberal societies certain groups have done just this, and they have done so in part out of a recognition that collective control over real property was necessary for the survival of their distinctive shared goals and ways of life. Examples are plentiful, but only two will be mentioned here: religious orders (which establish monasteries and convents) and groups such as the Nature Conservancy (which purchase land in order to prevent it from being developed in ways that threaten wildlife habitat). In brief, the individual rights of property and contract fundamental to liberal societies can be used to create group rights that can afford communities a significant degree of control over land and natural resources. Of course, the property rights that groups can acquire in this way fall short of the territorial sovereignty that successful secession brings; but in some cases at least, the former, more limited type of control may suffice. Whether it does will depend upon the nature of the cultural group and the relationship between the survival of its distinctive features and the degree of control its members are able to exercise over land.

Some (like Kymlicka) believe that the resources of ordinary contract and property law are not always sufficient to provide endangered cultures with adequate control over land and resources. Accordingly, they propose a second form of control not already found in all liberal regimes: *special group rights*. These rights might be of several different sorts. But in each case they would be designed to provide special protections for vulnerable minority cultures. For example, as we have already noted, Indians may be granted the right to establish longer residency requirements for non-Indians in areas occupied by Indians in order to prevent the formation of voting majorities that would enact laws that erode Indian culture. Or tribes might be given the right to require that their children be taught their native language in public school and might be guaranteed public funds for doing so. Neither of these approaches, however, deals directly with the issue of control over territory and its influence on the preservation of culture.

In contrast, minority cultures may be protected by according them *special group property rights*. This can be done by granting minority group governmental units (e.g., tribal governments for Indians) the authority to enact special property laws that place restrictions on the ability of individuals or groups within the minority community to alienate land. As we have seen, this in effect is the right to restrict the ordinary individual right to private property, by limiting the individual member's liberty to buy and sell property.

Put more positively, granting such a right to a minority group or its governmental unit amounts to empowering it *to create new collective property rights directly*, rather than by members of the group forging them through cooperative exercises of their ordinary individual property and contractual rights. If the special right accorded to the minority governmental unit allows the creation of these new collective property rights (or restrictions on preexisting individual property rights) through majority voting procedures or any method other than unanimity, then protecting the territory and hence the culture by this method may prove easier than relying on ordinary contractual and property rights, because the latter require the voluntary agreement of *all* concerned. Avoiding the requirement of unanimity can be a distinct advantage of special group property rights over individual property rights. (But the cost of securing this advantage, of course, is that the individual is deprived of her power to veto decisions concerning the use of land through the exercise of her individual property rights.)

Yet another way to protect a minority culture would be to empower the minority to impose obstacles to entry into its territory by nonmembers and to impose exit costs on members who wish to leave. For example, instead of forbidding the sale of Indian lands to non-Indians, tribal governments might simply enact a surcharge on real estate transactions involving non-Indians as well as a special tax on non-Indians who rent land or dwellings on Indian territory. And in order to discourage Indians from leaving areas in which they are concentrated and, hence, from contributing to a situation in which they lack the population mass to sustain their culture, tribal governments could impose exit taxes and/or tax the profits on sales of property by members when they leave the territory.

What all of these methods have in common is that they are attempts to sustain conditions thought to be necessary for the preservation of a minority culture. Each involves granting the group in question, acting through its government, the right to restrict the rights otherwise held by individuals. Some methods grant groups varying degrees of control over territory, short of territorial sovereignty. To the extent that these special rights to restrict rights are exercised by majority rule within the group they can be seen as instances of the group *binding itself*—that is, limiting the freedom of its members for the sake of preserving the collective good of sustaining the culture. Self-binding can be a valuable means for preserving values.

So far we have noted only how special rights to limit the entry and exit of *people* into the cultural minority's territory, and how special rights to create limits on the alienation of land from the group's territory, can help protect a culture. But some cultural minorities complain that it is the intrusion of alien lifestyles and alien culture themselves that threaten the survival of their cultures.

However, if the reason a cultural minority seeks secession is to control its own borders in order to limit alien cultural influences, then in principle this goal might be achieved by less drastic measures than secession. For example, a tribal government or the government of a territorially concentrated religious community such as the Amish or Mennonites might be granted the authority to enact laws that create barriers to the entry of cultural influences that threaten to undermine the community's values. Some communitarian authors, including Michael Sandel, have proposed precisely this measure. Sandel suggests that a community ought to be empowered to protect itself against a type of activity that "offends its way of life,"[37] such as the dissemination of "pornography" within its area. In other words, just as there are ways of protecting the territorial base of a culture other than by establishing complete territorial sovereignty through secession, so there are other ways of protecting a community's culture from destructive alien cultural influences.

These differing possibilities raise an important and perplexing question for liberal political theory—one that to my knowledge has never before been posed, much less answered. From the standpoint of liberal values of freedom and tolerance, is it preferable to empower local communities *within* the state to restrict individual rights (e.g., to private property, or to freedom of expression) or to allow (or require!) communities that seek to do so to secede, to separate from the state?

The initial response is likely to be: Obviously it is more consonant with liberal values to allow the group in question to secede than to compromise individual freedom and toleration within the liberal state! Yet from a liberal standpoint, the second alternative has one clear advantage: *If* the liberal state retains ultimate control over entry to and exit from illiberal enclave communities within its borders, then individuals will have some freedom of choice to participate in these communities or not. Conversely, if illiberal communities are allowed or encouraged to secede, the liberal state's recognition of their sovereignty implies a presumption that those communities will control access to and exit from their territory. Even if liberalism champions the right to emigrate, the recognition of sovereignty that goes along with acceptance of secession at least implies a greater degree of *de facto* control over entry and exit than is possible if the group stays within the liberal state.

So, at least from a liberal point of view, there is a presumption in favor of *non*secessionist methods for preserving minority cultures—even if some of these methods involve limitations on liberal individual rights. And as we have just seen, there are a number of measures, from special property laws, to minority language rights, to constitutional rights of nullification and group veto, that can help to preserve minority cultures, without the radical step of secession. For this reason the cultural preservation argument for secession is of limited force. The burden is upon its proponents to show the inadequacy of strategies for cultural preservation that employ combinations of individual rights and various special minority group rights. Only if these alternatives are inadequate, or if the state refuses to utilize them, can the need to preserve cultural identity justify secession. Whether or not a right to secede, rather than some combination of individual and other group rights, will best protect minorities admits of no general answer. It will depend upon the particular circumstances.

Another, more fundamental limitation of the argument from cultural preservation should be acknowledged. So far I have argued only that there are alternatives to secession for preserving cultures and that liberalism favors some nonsecession alternatives, other things being equal. Later, when antisecessionist arguments are explored in detail, we will examine a serious challenge to the idea that a group has a right to secede when the goal of secession is to establish an illiberal state *that limits the opportunities of its citizens to exit from it.* There I will elaborate an argument that I merely sketch at this point: At least from a liberal point of view, the obligation to protect future generations from a regime that violates their rights while allowing them no escape from it can rebut what would otherwise be a sound justification for secession. The force of this argument stems from a distinction between allowing competent individuals to destroy their own freedom and allowing them irrevocably to deprive others of their freedom without their consent.

It was emphasized earlier that if the argument now under consideration ›is to be an independent justification for secession, it must show that, at least under certain conditions, a group's need to preserve its culture can *entitle it to territory*; that is, this need can *generate* a valid claim to territory where none previously existed. There are two cases to distinguish. The state from which the cultural preservationists are attempting to secede may have valid title to the seceding territory, or it may not. In the former case it is implausible to say that the need to preserve a culture, even when other means fail, justifies overturning the state's territorial claim and transferring title, as it were, to the secessionists. Any such principle would be unacceptable for at least two reasons. First, it treats valid territorial claims too lightly, according them too little substance. Second, because the notion of a culture and hence of a cultural group is so expansive and vague, the principle is a recipe for intolerably excessive international instability and thus is subject to the same objection that was raised against the "people's right of self-determination," or normative nationalist principle, encountered earlier. Therefore, the principle that the need to preserve a culture can overturn a state's valid claim to territory ought to be rejected.

So if the argument from cultural preservation is to have any prospect of success, as an independent argument for a *right* to secede, its application must be restricted to the second type of case, that in which the state from which secession is attempted does *not* have a valid claim to the seceding territory.

Of course, more than this is needed if the argument is to be fully convincing: The area in question must not be subject to a valid territorial claim by any third party either. For it is obviously not enough for the secessionists to establish that the state has no valid claim to the territory. To make a strong case that their need to preserve their culture entitles them to the territory, they must also show that no other group or state has a valid claim to it.

We can now pull together the various conditions that would have to be satisfied if the argument from cultural preservation is to succeed in justifying secession as a matter of right. (1) The culture in question must in fact be imperiled. (2) Less disruptive ways of preserving the culture (e.g., special minority group rights within the existing state) must be unavailable or inadequate. (3) The culture in question must meet minimal standards of justice (unlike Nazi culture or the culture of the Khmer Rouge). (4) The seceding cultural group must not be seeking independence in order to establish an illiberal state, that is, one which fails to uphold basic individual civil and political rights, *and* from which free exit is denied. (5) Neither the state nor any third party can have a valid claim to the seceding territory.

The principle on which the fifth condition rests is this: The need to preserve a culture, though it is a morally significant interest, is not as weighty as either a grievance of injustice against the state or the need to protect a group against literal extinction, and it cannot *overturn* (override or extinguish) a valid territorial claim and generate a new one for the group in question. At most, it can generate a new valid claim to territory for the group whose culture is imperiled if the territory in question is *not* the subject of a valid territorial claim by anyone else. The principle that underlies condition (5) seems plausible because it recognizes that groups have a morally significant interest in preserving their cultures without giving excessive priority to that interest.

Are all of these conditions met in the case of Quebec? Conditions (3) and (4) no doubt are. Conditions (1), (2), and (5) are much more problematic. Quebec already enjoys important group rights, including language rights, and a limited veto right over constitutional amendments. Further, like every other province, Quebec has the right to reenact within its own jurisdiction legislation that has been shown to be in violation of the Federal Charter of Rights and Freedoms. (This limited right of nullification is provided by the so-called "notwithstanding" clause of the current Canadian Constitution.) Each of these powers can be employed by Quebec to help preserve its cultural identity.

It is difficult to know what further special arrangements, short of secession, might have been provided to afford further protection for French-Canadian culture had the Meech Lake Accord not broken down, thereby aborting any exploration of how the "distinct society" clause might be spelled out in practice. One possibility, at least in principle, would be to go beyond the "notwithstanding" clause and provide a general right of nullification, a right of the province to void any and all federal legislation in its jurisdiction. However, the fact that the First Ministers of the Provinces of Manitoba and

Newfoundland used their group veto rights over constitutional amendments
to kill the Meech Lake Accord, apparently because of objections to the
"distinct society" clause, suggests that further special group rights are not likely
to be incorporated into the Canadian Constitution in the foreseeable future.
Nonetheless, it cannot be denied that both the basic looseness of the Canadian
Federation and the existing special arrangements (especially language rights,
the limited provincial right of nullification under the "notwithstanding" clause,
and the limited provincial veto over constitutional amendments) do provide
substantial protections for French culture.

Whether or not they are sufficient to protect the culture is an empirical
(i.e., factual) question. Yet, to my knowledge, the political debate in Canada
on the issue of Quebec's secession is somewhat lacking in sustained discussion
of data indicating whether current arrangements are in fact adequately
protecting French-Canadian culture or whether it is imperiled.

It is true that the vagueness of the notion of "culture" creates formidable
problems for designing sound empirical research tools to answer this vital
question. Nonetheless, there are some "hard" data that bear on the issue. For
example, is the use of French among those who can speak that language still
on the decline in Quebec? Is the number of non-Francophones in Quebec
increasing? Is the number of educational and artistic activities dealing with
distinctive French or French-Canadian themes decreasing? Are fewer citizens
of Quebec identifying themselves in surveys as French-Canadians (rather than
as Canadians)? *If* it should turn out that the answer to all of these and similar
questions is "no," what evidence is there that current arrangements to preserve
that culture are inadequate and, hence, that secession is necessary?

If there turns out to be solid data to support affirmative answer to some
of the preceding questions, we could then perhaps conclude that French
culture in Quebec is declining—or at least that it is contracting, so to speak.
But whether a reduction in the proportion of persons in the province using
French means that the culture is *imperiled*, as opposed to declining or
contracting relative to its previous extent, depends upon what the critical mass
of language-users is that constitutes the minimum for the continued viability
of the culture. And reasonably accurate estimates as to what the critical mass
is may be hard to come by.

Nonetheless, it is reasonable to assume both that the prevalence of
French language in the province is crucial to the survival of the culture and
that a continued reduction in the use of French is a matter of serious concern.
But how, exactly, would full sovereignty for Quebec solve the problem of the
decline of the use of the French language there?

Quebecois who advocate secession frequently argue that a chief reason
for the decline of the proportion of Francophones in the province is the fact
that immigrants to Quebec are much more likely to be or to become
Anglophone than Francophone. First, the majority of immigrants to any part

of Canada are more likely to speak English than French if they speak either language. Second, because English is the dominant language in Canada as a whole, immigrants maximize their mobility and hence their economic opportunity by learning English rather than French. Third, for those immigrants to Canada who hope to use it as a stepping-stone for eventual emigration to the United States there is also a strong incentive to learn English rather than French. Fourth, English is still to a significant extent the language of commerce, and hence of economic advancement, in Quebec. Yet so long as Quebec is part of Canada, so the argument goes, it is unlikely that these conditions will change. For one thing, freedom to emigrate from one province to another is likely to exist in relatively unrestricted form so long as the provinces form one country, simply because this freedom is, in the minds of many, an essential element of what it is to be a Canadian citizen.

It is important to note that those who appeal to the facts about emigration in arguing for sovereignty for Quebec —and hence for its secession from Canada —must assume that if Quebec were an independent state, then either (1) the remainder of Canada would not allow free immigration into it from Quebec and emigration from Quebec into the United States would be sufficiently limited by the United States, or (2) Quebec would restrict immigration to Canada and the United States.

It is true that a sovereign Quebec could restrict emigration of its citizens to the United States or Canada if it wished—though this would be a serious infringement of individual liberty. But an independent Quebec would have no control over whether the rest of Canada (and the United States) continued a policy of allowing persons from Quebec to emigrate to the United States if Quebec permitted them to try to do so. In the end, then, the strength of this particular version of the argument from cultural preservation, as an argument for secession, depends upon some rather conjectural predictions about what emigration policies are likely to exist after Quebec becomes independent. My point here is not to speculate on the answers to the relevant empirical questions; rather, I wish only to emphasize that they are crucial to the moral justification for secession on grounds of cultural preservation and to urge that more attention be focused upon them.

Whether or not an investigation of the language-use data (and a recognition of the speculative character of the argument from emigration patterns) convince one that the satisfaction of conditions (1) and (2) is in doubt, a case can be made that condition (5) is satisfied for at least part of the territory within Quebec's borders. It is true that Quebec was incorporated into English Canada by conquest. Hence the validity of the Canadian Federation's claim of territorial sovereignty is a rather weak basis upon which to rest a case for resisting secession. However, the claim of French-speaking Canadians to all of Quebec is also quite problematic because part of that area was similarly gained by conquest from Indians, some of whose descendants are living and can be identified. Further, the original French territory was in fact only a narrow strip of land along the St. Lawrence River. More than one-half of the total area of present-day Quebec was ceded to the province by the British after the British conquest. And there can be little doubt that this donation of territory was made by the British with the understanding that Quebec was to remain united with the rest of English Canada, or at least that if disunion should occur the French would not be free to take the ceded land with them.[38] So at most, the Canadian Federation's lack of clear title to Quebec would support secession on grounds of cultural preservation only for those parts of Quebec that are not subject to whatever valid territorial claims existing Indians groups may have and were not part of the territory ceded to Quebec by the English. One might well conclude that the territorial claims are sufficiently muddy on either side that the issue must be settled on other grounds.

Once these complexities are appreciated, one cannot but be struck by the extreme oversimplification with which the issues of Quebec secession are often debated. It is not surprising, then, that our examination of the argument from cultural preservation does not yield a conclusive answer to the question of whether secession by Quebec, solely on the grounds that secession is necessary to preserve French culture, would be justified. Nonetheless, the analysis offered here has made considerable progress by locating two neglected issues that must be addressed if that question is to be answered: Can other measures short of secession provide adequate protection for the culture? (In particular, are there constitutional options or further special group rights that would do the job?) And would secession merely perpetuate historical injustices to Indians? Quite independent of the particular case of Quebec, the analysis has also advanced a set of five conditions that must be satisfied if secession on grounds of cultural preservation is to be justified. As these conditions together impose very significant constraints, the conclusion to be drawn is that the argument from cultural preservation, like a number of the other prosecession arguments already canvassed, is of rather limited utility. Only rarely will the need to preserve a culture justify secession.

J. Self-Defense

Although the distinction between a group's right to preserve its culture and its right to defend the very existence of its members against lethal aggression is sometimes blurred by rhetoric about "cultural genocide," there is a great difference. Even when the right to preserve a culture does not offer a compelling justification for secession, the right of self-defense can do so, under certain circumstances.

'Defense' here implies an effort to protect against a lethal threat, a deadly attack by an aggressor. Not every effort at self-preservation is a case of self-defense because what endangers may not be an attack by an aggressor. (It might be, for example, a natural disaster.) Hence the concept of a right of self-*defense* is distinct from and narrower than that of a right of self-*preservation*.

The common law, common-sense morality, and the great majority of ethical systems, both secular and religious, acknowledge a right of self-defense as including a right to use force against an aggressor who threatens lethal force. For good reason this is not thought to be an unlimited right: Among the obvious restrictions on it are (1) that only that degree of force necessary to avert the threat be used, and (2) that the attack against which one defends oneself not be provoked by one's own actions. If such restrictions are acknowledged, the assertion that there is a right of self-defense is highly plausible. Much more problematic is the assertion that the right of self-defense includes a right to use force *against an innocent third party* in order to defend oneself against deadly attacks from a second-party aggressor. Each of these limitations, including the last, is pertinent to the alleged right of groups to defend themselves.

The argument under consideration has two variants. The first, in which a group wishes to secede from a state in order to protect its members from extermination by that state itself, is the most obviously compelling. Under such conditions the group may either attempt to overthrow the government, that is, to engage in revolution; or if strategy requires it, the group may secede in order to organize a defensive territory, forcibly appropriating the needed territory from the aggressor, creating the political and military machinery required for its survival, and seeking recognition and aid from other sovereign states or international bodies. Whatever moral title to the seceding territory the aggressor state previously held is *invalidated* by the gross injustice of its genocidal efforts. Or, at the very least, we can say that whatever legitimate claims to the seceding territory it has are *outweighed* by the claims of its innocent victims. We think of the aggressor's right, in the former case, as dissolving in the acid of his own iniquities, and, in the latter, as being pushed down in the scales of the balance by the greater mass of the victim's right of self-defense. Whether we say that the evil state's right to territory is invalidated (and disappears entirely) or merely is outweighed, it is clear enough that in these circumstances its claim to territory should not be an insurmountable bar to the victim group's seceding, if this is the only practical way to avoid its wrongful destruction.

The second variant of the argument makes the more controversial claim that to defend itself against an aggressor a group may secede from a state that is not itself the aggressor and that it may do so even if, as will often be the case, the use of force is involved. This amounts to the assertion that a group's need to defend itself against literal genocide can *generate* a claim to territory of sufficient moral weight to override the claims of those who until now have held valid title to it and who, unlike the aggressor state in the first version of the argument, have perpetrated no injustice to invalidate or override their title.

Perhaps the closest analog to this would be the common-law *defense of necessity*, according to which property rights may be infringed if doing so is necessary to avert some great evil. For example, I may trespass on your land to prevent a serious crime. But the chief difference, of course, is that in the case of secession from one state to avoid a threat to survival from another, there is not so much an infringement of a property right as the denial of one property right and its replacement by another. A concrete though hypothetical example will be useful.

Suppose the year is 1939. Germany has inaugurated a policy of genocide against the Jews. Jewish pleas to the democracies for protection have fallen on deaf ears (in part because the Jews are not regarded as a nation—nationhood carrying a strong presumption of territory, which they do not possess). Leaders of Jewish populations in Poland, Czechoslovakia, Germany, and the Soviet Union agree that the only hope for the survival of their people is to create a Jewish state, a sovereign territory to serve as a last refuge for European Jewry. Suppose further that the logical choice for its location—the only choice with the prospect of any success in saving large numbers of Jews—is a portion of Poland. Polish Jews, who are not being protected from the Nazis by Poland, therefore occupy a portion of Poland and invite other Jews to join them there in a Jewish sanctuary state. They do not expel non-Jewish Poles who already reside in that area but, instead, treat them as equal citizens. (Note that from 1941 until 1945 something rather like this occurred on a smaller scale. Jewish partisans, who proved to be ferocious and heroic guerrillas, occupied and defended an area in the forests near Brody, Poland, and in effect created their own ministate, for purposes of defending themselves and others from annihilation by the Germans.) Unless one holds that existing property rights, including the right of Poland to keep all its territory intact, supersede all other considerations, including the right of an innocent people, utterly lacking in effective allies, to preserve its very existence from the depredations of mass murderers, one must conclude that the Jews would have been justified in appropriating the territory necessary for their survival.

The force of the self-defense argument derives in part from the assumption that the Polish Jews who create the sanctuary state *are not being protected by their own state, Poland*. The idea is that the state's authority over territory is granted to it so that it may provide protection for its citizens—all its citizens—and that its retaining that authority is conditional upon its providing that protection. In the circumstances described, the Polish state is not providing protection to its Jewish citizens, and this fact voids its territorial authority.[39]

If this line of reasoning is cogent, then we have another illustration of a point made earlier during the discussion of the argument from discriminatory redistribution. In some cases, even where secessionists have no historical title to the territory they desire, and hence no basis for justifying secession as the reclaiming of what was wrongfully taken, weighty moral considerations favoring secession, in this instance the right of self-defense, may be sufficient to generate a new title to territory, thus transforming existing property rights and thereby justifying the taking of territory that secession necessarily involves.

It would be a mistake to assume that this type of case is fanciful simply because it is hypothetical. One of the strongest arguments for recognizing a Kurdish state or an Armenian state may be that only this status, with the territorial sovereignty it includes, will ensure the survival of these peoples in the face of genocidal threats. So there can be and indeed are situations in which the right of self-defense grounds a right to secede.

K. Rectifying Past Injustices

This is perhaps the simplest and most intuitively appealing argument for secession and one that has obvious application to many actual secessionist movements, including those currently in progress in the Soviet Union. It contends that a region has a right to secede if it was unjustly incorporated into the larger unit from which its members wish to separate. The act of unjust incorporation may have occurred in either of two ways: The seceding area may have been directly annexed by the currently existing state, or it may have been unjustly acquired by some earlier state that is the ancestor of the currently existing state. The Baltic Soviet Republics, as we have already seen, exemplify the first scenario. The secessionist movement in Bangladesh is an instance of the second. Bangladesh, along with other regions in the Indian subcontinent, was incorporated into the British Empire by conquest. When colonial rule ended, Pakistan, consisting of East and West Pakistan, was created. East Pakistan, taking the name Bangladesh, later seceded from Pakistan and, with the help of India's military, won its independence by force.[40] This second scenario raises its own special issues. Here it will be more fruitful to focus on the simpler first scenario, because it provides the most direct and compelling illustration of the argument from rectificatory justice.

That argument's power stems from the assumption that in these cases secession is simply the reappropriation, by the legitimate owner, of stolen property. The right to secede, under these circumstances, is just the right to reclaim what is one's own. This simple interpretation is most plausible, of course, in situations in which the people attempting to secede are literally the same people who held legitimate title to the territory at the time of the unjust annexation, or at least are the indisputable descendants of those people (their legitimate heirs, so to speak). But matters are considerably less simple if the seceding group is not closely or clearly related to the group whose territory was unjustly taken, or if the original group that was dispossessed did not have clear, unambiguous title to it. But at least in the paradigm case—one in which the secessionists are the group that was wronged or at least are the indisputable legitimate successors to it—the argument from rectificatory justice is a convincing argument for a moral right to secede. (The difficulty, which we will explore later in some depth, is that the history of existing states is so replete with immoral, coercive, and fraudulent takings that it may be hard for most states to establish the legitimacy of their current or past borders.)

Under some circumstances, however, the considerations of rectificatory justice which establish that there is a right to secede are not sufficient to show that those who have the right ought to exercise it or that they ought to exercise it now. Here, as with other rights, there can be compelling moral reasons for not doing what one has a right to do, or for postponing the exercise of one's right in order to avoid inconvenience or even catastrophe for oneself or others. To repeat: Sometimes one ought not to do what one has a right to do.

The appeal of the argument from rectificatory justice is so strong that one might be tempted to assume that it provides the *only* conclusive argument in favor of secession. And some writers have in fact argued that a sound justification for secession must always be founded on a claim of rectificatory justice—on the assertion of a right to recover territory that was unjustly appropriated by another at some earlier point.[41] Let us call this *the historical grievance version of the territoriality thesis*. The territoriality thesis states that every sound justification for secession must include a valid claim to territory. In other words, it must be the case that the secessionists have a right to the territory in question. The historical grievance version asserts that the valid claim to territory that every sound justification for secession includes must be grounded in a historical grievance concerning the violation of a preexisting right to territory.

As the survey of prosecessionist arguments thus far suggests, this view on the justification of secession is too restrictive. It is one of the main theses of this book that there are some cases in which secession is justified even in the absence of a historical grievance about the unjust loss of territory. Although the historical grievance version of the territoriality thesis is wrong, it contains a grain of truth. The grain of truth is that a sound justification for secession must include a justification for taking the seceding territory, and that the simplest, most obviously compelling justification for taking the seceding territory is that doing so is merely reappropriation by the owners of what was wrongly taken from them. The error is the assumption that the secessionists' taking of territory can be justified only by establishing that it is a reappropriation of property that was previously wrongfully taken by others. The point is that there are other ways in which secessionists can establish valid title to the territory. We have just seen one instance of this: the hypothetical example of a Jewish sanctuary state in Poland in 1939.

But regardless of whether that particular example convinces, it is worth observing that there have been a number of major secessionist movements that have not based their claims on historical grievances about unjust seizure of territory. Furthermore, and much more important, at least some of these are cases of secession that are widely thought to be justified. For example, the American Revolution was a successful attempt by a part of the British Empire in North America, which included Canada as well, to secede from that empire. (As noted earlier, it was not strictly speaking a revolution, since no attempt was made to overthrow the British government but only to free the American colonies from its control.) Yet this secession was not based on any appeal to a historical grievance concerning the wrongful taking of territory. Similarly, the American Southern secession of 1861 was not based on any alleged historical grievance about unjustly acquired Southern territory.

It is of course controversial, if not utterly inflammatory (except in South Carolina and a few other places), to suggest that Southern secession, like the American secession from the British Empire in North America, was justified. As we have already seen, the tendency to assume that Southern secession was clearly unjustified stems from the contaminating effect of the slavery issue. Yet our analysis of the argument from discriminatory redistribution indicates that *if* Southern secession had *not* been undertaken at least in great part to preserve the evil of slavery, a plausible justification for it might have been made on grounds of discriminatory redistribution. Indeed, as was suggested earlier, the best justification for the American secession from the British Empire was also the argument from discriminatory redistribution: Britain's taxation and trade policies were designed to enrich England at the expense of the colonies, and the colonies' lack of representation in the British Parliament virtually guaranteed that this injustice would continue. But if this is the case, then we have a second instance in which the justification for secession does not depend upon a valid historical grievance concerning wrongful taking of property, and the historical grievance version of the territoriality thesis is again shown to be false. The fact that discriminatory redistribution can justify secession shows that the historical grievance thesis is wrong.

There is a further similarity between the case of the American colonies and that of the Southern states. Unlike the colonists, Southerners did enjoy legislative representation. However, because the North's population was growing so much faster than the South's, the North was rapidly gaining power in the House of Representatives; and because more new states were likely to be free than slave states, the South expected to lose power in the Senate as well. Hence Southerners had reason to believe that the discriminatory redistribution they believed they were already suffering would not be rectified but, instead, would only increase because the rules of the legislative game were stacked against them. (They also believed, not unreasonably, that as their political power in Washington eroded, the North would eventually destroy slavery and would probably do so without violating the letter of the Constitution.) In both the case of the colonists and that of the South, secession may have been the only alternative, given that the rules of the political game—in particular, the rules governing representation—systematically worked to the group's disadvantage and that there was no expectation that they would change.

It may in fact be the case that existing *international law* tends to accord legitimacy only to those secessionist movements that can establish a historical grievance regarding unjust loss of territory (regardless of whether international law explicitly endorses the historical grievance thesis or not). But it begs the moral question to assume that existing international law is above criticism. If there are sound justifications for secession that do not make the right to secede derivative upon a right to rectify past unjust takings of territory, then there will be a case for modifying international law regarding secession. But here I wish to emphasize that whether or not the argument from rectificatory justice is the sole justification for secession, it is, at least in its most direct application, a plausible one. The next argument for a right to secede, the argument from consent, though initially plausible, makes the opposite error of those who assume that only a historical grievance concerning territory can justify secession: It overlooks the importance of establishing a valid claim to territory altogether.

L. Consent

Works of political philosophy contain a number of different arguments from consent, and they are seldom clearly distinguished from each other. One of the few political philosophers who has even briefly discussed secession, Harry Beran, first argues that consent is a necessary condition for political obligation and then infers from this thesis about consent that there is a right to secede.[42] His idea is quite simple: Unless the right to secede is acknowledged, groups will sometimes remain subject to the state's power without consenting to it. So if one agrees that consent is a necessary condition for legitimate political authority, then one must recognize a right to secede. Merely allowing people the option of emigration as a way of withholding consent is insufficient because in many cases either emigration will be prohibitively costly or there will be no opportunity to relocate in a state that is any more satisfactory.

This view can be attacked in two ways: By criticizing the thesis that consent is necessary for political obligation, or by denying that if consent is necessary for political obligation, then there is a right to secede when consent is lacking. I shall do both: First I will argue that consent is not a necessary condition for political obligation, and then I will show that even if it were, much more would be needed to show that there is a right to secede.

The thesis about the connection between consent and obligation is not the highly implausible claim that a citizen must consent to each and every law or policy, that he or she may accept or reject every law or policy at his or her discretion. This latter view is a denial of the existence of political authority, not an account of a necessary condition for its existence.

The more persuasive thesis about consent is that persons are under a general obligation to obey the laws of the state only if they consent to be governed by it, that they tacitly consent by accepting the benefits which the state confers on them, *and* that *not renouncing* these benefits counts as *accepting them*. Chief among these benefits are the personal security and freedom that life under the rule of law provides. Consent is said to be tacit in that no written or oral statement by the individual or group is thought to be necessary.

As a number of critics of this view have observed, the difficulty is not with the idea of tacit (or implicit) consent *per se* but with the assumption that what counts as tacit consent is merely refraining from renouncing benefits.[43] On Locke's version of the consent view, merely continuing to reside within the borders of the state while enjoying its benefits constitutes tacit consent. Because some of the most important benefits (such as security from attack from without) are *public goods*, available to all within the borders of the country if they are available to any, the only way to "renounce" them (without changing the borders of the country) may be to cease residing there.[44]

The problem is that although cases of tacit consent do exist, this does not seem to be one of them. We are justified in saying that someone tacitly consented to something only where certain rather special conditions of a rule-governed, conventional sort obtain. For example, a person who already possesses appropriate authority, such as the chairperson of a meeting, announces that a certain course of action will be taken unless there is an objection, there is adequate opportunity for objections to be raised, members of the group can object without untoward costs, there is an understanding as to what counts as objecting, and so on. Merely continuing to reside in a country, and thereby enjoying the benefits provided by the state, is a far cry from satisfying anything like these sorts of rather specific conditions.[45]

Furthermore, as the legal scholar Lea Brilmayer has pointed out, if the foregoing example of tacit consent is apt, there is an even more fundamental difficulty. If silence or continued participation in the aforementioned meeting is to count as consent to the course of action in question, the person proposing or initiating the action must *already possess authority* over the group. But if this is so, then whatever else the notion of tacit consent can explain, it cannot explain that person's authority. Similarly, it is hard to see how tacit consent could explain political obligation, that is, the obligation to obey political authority, if the conditions for tacit consent include the assumption that political authority already exists.[46]

These and other dissatisfactions with the consent thesis have led some theorists to conclude that the real issue is *fairness*, not consent. They contend that political obligation rests on a moral *duty of fair play*. The state, through the contributions of other citizens, provides me with important benefits. My continuing to enjoy these benefits without obeying the laws that make them possible would be unfair to my fellow citizens. But if I do renounce these benefits, then my obligation ceases.

Most criticisms of the fair play approach have concentrated on showing that it fails as an account of what is *sufficient* for being politically obligated. The libertarian philosopher Robert Nozick, for example, has argued that merely continuing to receive benefits is not sufficient for being obligated to the benefactor. His point is that, as a general account of how we come to be obligated, this is much too strong: If it were correct, others could obligate us simply by imposing benefits on us.[47] Or, more accurately, we would be morally bound to obey those who imposed the benefits or to contribute to the continued production of those benefits or to take whatever steps are necessary, no matter how costly to us, to ensure that we no longer partook of those benefits. Nozick rightly concludes that this is an unacceptable account of the genesis of obligations.

Our concern, however, is with the thesis that accepting or refraining from renouncing the benefits the state provides is a *necessary* condition for being politically obligated. Even if this thesis is granted, we are a long way from having a justification for secession, for two reasons: First, there are other ways of renouncing the benefits of political association than by seceding; and, second, even if political obligation is severed by refusal of benefits, more is required to justify secession than the severance of political obligation. A valid claim to territory must also be established: It must be shown that the secessionists have a right to the territory.

The most obvious alternative to secession as a way of renouncing the state's benefits is emigration. However, as has frequently been noted, for many people emigration will at best entail severe costs. Even if a favorable alternative country exists and will receive such people, the costs of relocating may be high. But in many cases the situation is much worse than that: The only option may be emigration to an equally or more uncongenial state. Worst of all, there are some individuals—for example, some recent refugees from

Vietnam, the "boat people"—who can find no country willing to admit them. So whatever plausibility the fair play approach has as an argument in favor of secession depends upon the assumption that emigration is not a morally acceptable alternative for renouncing the benefits of cooperation. For if both ways of renouncing benefits were freely available, then there would be no case for secession, since secession not only involves renouncing the benefits of continued membership in the political association but also entails the taking of land.

This brings us to the second gap between the fair play principle and the right to secede. The fair play argument for secession would do only part of the job of justifying secession even if it were wholly unobjectionable. It would not by itself touch the territorial issue because it does nothing either to establish the secessionists' claim to territory or to refute the antisecessionists' charge that secession is a wrongful taking of the state's land. Similarly, even if various objections to the consent argument could be successfully met, the most that argument would establish is that those who do not consent are not obligated. It would not show that they may appropriate territory, and hence it would not show that secession is justified. The consent and fair play arguments can at most demonstrate the conditions under which the state no longer has authority over people; they cannot show when the state no longer has control over territory. So arguments from consent and fair play, contrary to initial impressions, cannot even *in principle* justify secession.

For the same reason, even if it could be shown that either tacit consent or receipt of benefits is *sufficient* for political obligation, the fundamental issue of territorial sovereignty would remain untouched, as would that of the state's authority if the latter is taken to include authority over land as well as people. Tacit consent or receipt of benefits would be *sufficient* for political authority—where political authority includes territorial sovereignty—only if territorial sovereignty were already assumed.[48]

This simple but important point can be illustrated as follows. Suppose that a group of people illegally and unjustly came to occupy a piece of land claimed by another group. Suppose that the members of the first group tacitly consent to be governed by the political apparatus established by this group. Or suppose that the first group provides benefits to its members, which they accept, making no effort to renounce or avoid them. Whatever obligations are thereby generated among members of the first group, the question of which group has legitimate title to that piece of land remains unresolved. So regardless of what position we take on either the tacit consent view or the fair play view, each of which can be construed as stating either necessary or sufficient conditions for political obligation, these views provide no arguments for (or against) secession, contrary to what some writers, including Beran, have assumed.

M. Summary: The Case for a Right to Secede

Before the moral case for a right to secede can be conclusively evaluated, it is necessary to see what the other side of the ledger holds. Accordingly, the moral arguments against secession are taken up in Chapter 3. At present, however, this much can be said: Although some prosecession arguments fail, including the argument from consent and the pure self-determination argument, and others, such as the self-defense argument, the argument from cultural preservation, and the argument from the limited goals of political association, are of very limited application, a variety of considerations taken together make a strong case for a moral right to secede under certain circumstances. Among the strongest arguments and most widely applicable arguments for a right to secede are the argument from rectificatory justice and the argument from discriminatory redistribution. Under extreme conditions, secession may also be justified on grounds of self-defense and, perhaps more controversially, in some cases where it is necessary for the preservation of a culture.

III. Individual and Group Rights?

Some assume that there is something incongruous, if not outright inconsistent, about a political philosophy that would supplement the basic individual civil and political rights associated with liberalism with a right to secede, a group right. In short, they are skeptical of the conceptual and normative coherence of a system containing both individual and group rights.

Before we can answer this skeptical challenge, we must clarify what a group right is and how it differs from an individual right. My aim here is not to provide a comprehensive analysis of group rights. Instead, it is to show that with respect to one important sense of 'group right', one that applies to the right to secede, to rights of nullification and of group veto, to collective property rights, and to minority language rights, there is nothing inconsistent or incoherent about a system that includes these as well as the traditional liberal individual rights.

For our purposes, the chief difference between an individual right and a group right is this: Individual rights are ascribed to an individual, who in principle can exercise the right independently, in her own name, on her own authority. (The qualifier 'in principle' is important here because in practice it may not be possible for the individual to exercise her right unless the right is effectively guaranteed by appropriate institutional arrangements—courts, an enforcement mechanism, etc.) Group rights are ascribed to collections of individuals and can only be exercised collectively or at least on behalf of the collective, usually through some mechanism of political representation whereby a designated individual or subset of the group purports to act for the group as a whole. In addition, the good secured by the right is most often a collective good in the sense that if it is secured it will be available to all or most members of the group. Moreover, if we think of rights as serving certain interests, we may also say that the interests served by group rights are individuals' interests, *qua* members of the group, in the collective goods of the group—that is, their interests in participating in the common activities and in pursuing the shared goals of the group.[49]

The right to secede, as we have been understanding it, is a group right. In some cases the group is already politically organized and recognized, as a state, or canton, or province, or, in the case of Lithuania, a "Republic." In other cases, the group to which the right to secede is ascribed—for example, the Kurds—may not be politically organized or recognized as a legitimate political subunit. Secession, as we have been exploring it (i.e., as opposed to "individual independence"), is a kind of collective action, whereby a group (whether officially recognized as a legitimate political subunit or not) attempts to become independent from the state that presently claims jurisdiction over it and, in doing so, seeks to remove part of the territory from the existing state. Thus a right to secede is a right, ascribed to a group, to engage in collective action whose purpose is independence from the existing state, where the coming to be independent includes the taking of territory. In most, if not all, cases the collective action that constitutes the exercise of the right to secede will involve some internal political organization, including some mechanism of representation, of the group. For example, the Lithuanian legislature, speaking on behalf of the Lithuanian people, attempts to exercise what it and they take to be the group's right to secede; or the leaders of the Kurds, purporting to represent their people, attempt to secede from Iraq.

The rights of nullification and of group veto also satisfy our two criteria for group rights: At least as conceived by those who advocate them, they are rights ascribed to (politically recognized) groups, not to individuals (e.g., states or provinces in a federation), and they are to be exercised collectively, through mechanisms of political representation.

In this chapter we have also examined collective property rights as a device for protecting minority cultures. By ascribing certain rights to control the buying and selling of land on reservations to Indian tribes rather than to individual Indians, the U.S. and Canadian governments have equipped Indians with the legal tools that, with varying degrees of success, can be used to protect Indian cultures. Again, the right in question satisfies both criteria for a group, as distinct from an individual right: It is ascribed to a group (a tribe or a collection of tribes), and it can be exercised only through some form of collective action, usually a process of representative democracy of some sort. For example, federal legislation may empower a tribe, acting through its elected officials, to restrict the sale of land currently owned by Indians to non-

Indians; or it may impose special taxes on sales of land of certain sorts, in order to provide a disincentive for breaking up parcels of land.

The notion of minority language rights is ambiguous, and not everything placed under this broad heading may count as a group right. For example, if by a minority language right one simply means the right of every member of a minority ethnic group to be free to speak his or her language without interference, then it would be more accurate perhaps to call this a negative individual right. However, when ethnic minorities such as French Canadians or Croats press for language rights, this is not all they have in mind. In addition to the negative right of noninterference they typically desire a positive right to public resources for language education, as well as recognition of their language as one of the official languages of the larger state or, in some cases, as the official language of their own region.

Further, the ethnic minority may include in its demand for language rights the legal authorization to limit or forbid the speaking, teaching, or writing of the majority language in certain contexts. For example, cities in Quebec have enacted laws making it illegal to display signs in English that are visible from the street. Although the minimal negative right to speak one's language may not qualify as a group right, the more robust language rights that ethnic minorities usually demand do satisfy both the criteria: They are ascribed to groups, not individuals, and they are exercised or implemented through collective processes, usually involving internal political organizations of a representative sort.

Those still reluctant to acknowledge the existence of group rights might argue that each of the group rights mentioned can be "reduced" to a collection of individual rights. For example, the right of nullification, though officially ascribed to a people or their political subunit, can be reduced to a collection of individual rights to participate in a decision to secede.

The proposed reduction, however, seems seriously incomplete: It is impossible to spell out the content of the decision in which the individual has a right to participate without referring again to the group. This is so because what is being decided in the process in which the individual participates is whether the group (not the individual) should sever its ties with the state, remove the territory from the state's jurisdiction, and then establish its own state (or join another state, as the Romanian Transylvanians seek to do). If an individual right is one that (at least under favorable institutional arrangements of adjudication and enforcement) can be exercised independently by an individual, then the right to secede (like the rights of nullification and group veto) is not an individual right. Its exercise requires collective action, even though we can speak of the individual rights that members of the group have to participate in that collective action. The same holds true for collective property rights and robust minority language rights. All of these are group rights in the sense specified above: They are ascribed to groups and must be exercised collectively, through political mechanisms, on behalf of the group. So the question is whether liberalism can accommodate any or all of these group rights.

To those who assume that a mixed-rights theory is untenable, it should first be pointed out that classical liberal democratic theory contains at least one fundamental group right: the right of the people to form a political association, to empower the state to protect their fundamental rights. Locke, for example, held that the people may exercise this right when forming an original political society or when the existing political authority has lost its legitimacy through violations of basic individual rights. Furthermore, Democratic Federalism, which is preeminently a liberal political doctrine, also includes group rights—the rights of constitutionally recognized, politically organized groups. For in *democratic* federal systems the rights ascribed by the constitution to subunits (e.g., cantons or provinces) are to be understood, ultimately, as collective rights of the citizens of those subunits. Finally, many existing constitutions in what are generally recognized as liberal states include both individual and group rights, without any obvious evidence of incoherence or inconsistency. So it is simply a mistake to say that liberalism, either in theory or in practice, wholly excludes group rights.

Perhaps those who balk at the idea of a mixed system of rights assume (1) that the only justification for individual rights must be "individualistic" and (2) that "individualism" cannot recognize group rights. Both assumptions are false.

First, as I have argued at length elsewhere, the most important individual rights can be justified on "nonindividualistic," collectivist, or communitarian grounds.[30] For example, the rights to freedom of expression, of religion, and of assembly and association, though ascribed to individuals, provide valuable protections *for groups* and their shared values. Historically, these basic liberal civil and political individual rights have been a strong bulwark against attempts to destroy or dominate various *communities* with the state. They allow individuals to partake of the good of community by protecting existing communities from interference from without and by giving individuals the freedom to unite with like-minded others to create new communities. Further, there are at least four weighty practical advantages to ascribing these rights *to individuals* rather than to groups.

First, individual rights to freedom of religion, thought, expression, and association facilitate rational, nonviolent change in existing communities as well as the rational, nonviolent formation of new communities. Individual rights do this by allowing individuals who are dissatisfied with current forms of community to advocate and to try to develop alternatives even when the majority of their fellow members (or the official leaders of the community) do not share their views. If rights to freedom of expression, association, thought, and religion accrued to communities, not to individuals, then they would protect *existing* communities from intrusions by other communities or state agencies. But they would provide no protection for the formation of new communities or the modification or reform of existing ones, insofar as either of these latter types of change originates in the beliefs of an individual or a minority.

Second, the state's recognition of individual rights to freedom of religion, thought, expression, and association allows prompt appeals for the protection of a community's interests. For if these rights are ascribed to individuals, then all that is needed to trigger official protective action is a violation of the rights of *one* member of that community. In contrast, a group right, a right ascribed to the community rather than to individuals, would presumably have to be invoked through an official process involving a collective decision procedure of some kind. The costs of exercising a group right may therefore be considerably higher and the process of doing so more ponderous.

Third, to the extent that the exercise of a group right entails a political structure within the group (i.e., a structure consisting of leaders or representatives, or other official bodies), group rights encourage hierarchy and create the possibility of opposition between the interests of those who control the exercise of the right and the interests of other members of the group. Thus, those who control the exercise of the right may find it in their interest not to exercise the right in ways that would be beneficial to some or all other members of the group. Moreover, those who control the group's rights may use this special power for ends quite unrelated to the considerations that make the rights valuable. Individual rights, in contrast, do not require this sort of hierarchy and do not encourage the abuses it can bring. Tying together the second and third points, we can note that if a group right is to be exercised through a democratic process, there may be significant delays and other decision costs; but if it is exercised through some nondemocratic, hierarchical process, there are dangers of abuse of power by those who control its exercise.

A fourth, related point is that individual rights are inherently antipaternalistic in a way that group rights are not. In the case of a group right, some individual or subset of the group has the ultimate say as to whether to exercise the right. Even if others decide on the basis of a sincere commitment to doing what is best for that individual or subgroup, they are the ones who are in control. For all four of these reasons, then, there are distinct advantages to individual rights, at least so far as the basic civil and political rights are concerned—even if we focus exclusively on the value of having these rights for protecting and promoting the goods of community. In other words, there is a strong communitarian case for these individual rights. So the first assumption of those who believe a mixed system of rights is incoherent is seen to be false: It *is* possible to give a justification for at least some of the more central individual rights that is nonindividualistic, in the sense that the justification does *not* assume that individuals are egoistic (i.e., that their interests are exclusively or even primarily self-regarding). On the contrary, we have just seen that these individual rights can be justified by showing how valuable they are to those for whom shared ends are extremely important, who value the goods of community intrinsically, and who identify strongly with the community. So the first assumption of those who believe that mixed-rights theories are incoherent, and that the justification for individual rights must be individualistic in the sense of being egoistic and unable to accommodate the goods of community, is shown to be false.

The second assumption of those who reject mixed-rights theories is equally erroneous: It *is* possible to provide an "individualistic" justification for group rights. In fact, this chapter has done exactly that. Recall the argument from the need to preserve a culture. There it was noted that one very strong argument for according certain special group rights to minorities in certain circumstances is that their having these rights may be necessary if the group is to be able to preserve its distinctive culture, the way of life with which its members identify and which gives meaning to their pursuits and projects. Among these special minority group rights are language rights and special collective property rights, as noted earlier. The right to secede is only one of a number of possible group rights that can serve the function of protecting minority cultures.

Yet in the same discussion it was also shown that the value of a culture—and hence the justification for according these group rights in order to protect that value—can be explained in "individualistic" terms in this sense: The value of a culture is the value of cultural membership, the value *for the individuals* who are members.

This is *not* to say that a member of a cultural group or community values the culture chiefly or even in part as something that is instrumentally good for himself, nor that his interest in the goods of cultural membership is egoistic. On the contrary, the assumption employed in the argument for group rights as necessary for preserving cultures was that participation in a culture is, at least for most individuals, something that is intrinsically good, and that part of what it is to be a member of a community and to partake of communal goods is to adopt the perspective of "our" interests rather than "my" interests. So in this sense, although the arguments for group rights presented earlier are individualistic, insofar as they ultimately justify those rights by reference to the value that group membership has for individuals, they are *non*individualistic if 'individualism' is interpreted narrowly to imply egoism, exclusively self-regarding interests, and the absence of shared intrinsic ends.

It is true that some of its opponents assert that liberalism is individualistic in the objectionable sense, that it assumes egoistic motivation and denies shared ends; but this is a caricature of all but the most extreme and least plausible versions of liberalism. As was noted in Chapter 1, liberal individualism is a moral, not an ontological, doctrine.

Liberals hold only that the individual is what matters ultimately, morally speaking. They are not committed to an ontology that denies the existence of groups, nor even to one which asserts that all purported properties of groups can be reduced to properties of individuals. These ontological disputes are irrelevant to liberalism.

Liberal theory can cheerfully acknowledge a number of theses that facile critics of liberalism have assumed are inconsistent with it: that participation in groups is an intrinsic good; that in order to describe the interest that individuals have in participating in groups it is necessary to make reference to institutions and social practices, not just to features of individuals; and that the institutional or social concepts used to describe the interests that individuals have in belonging to groups and pursuing shared ends are not reducible to preinstitutional or presocial concepts. My point is not that no one who has called himself a liberal has ever rejected any of the foregoing theses but, rather, that the more plausible versions of liberalism have never denied them or needed to.

Finally, the analysis of what it is to assert that there is a right advanced earlier in this chapter makes it clear that there can be both individual and group rights. To simplify somewhat, according to that analysis, the concept of a right includes two elements that are especially pertinent here: the assertion that it is permissible for the right-holder(s) to engage in certain activities or to exercise control over certain objects or territory, and so on; and the assertion that others have a weighty obligation not to interfere with the right-holder(s) in that regard, or, in the case of positive or welfare rights, a weighty obligation to provide the right-holder(s) with the item in question.

The analysis also emphasized that rights-statements are conclusory and hence must be supported by morally relevant reasons. In some cases, the balance of morally relevant reasons will justify ascription of a right to individuals as individuals (as I have argued is the case with basic civil and political rights such as the rights to freedom of expression, religion, and association); in others, to a group or to individuals as members of a group, and on condition that the right is to be exercised collectively, on behalf of the group (as in the case of minority language rights or group property rights). It is important to understand just where the burden of argument lies in the dispute between advocates of liberal political theory and those whom I have characterized as caricaturing it: Those who ascribe extreme and implausible motivational and ontological theses to liberalism must show that the best versions of liberalism depend upon such views, and this they have not done.

We have no reason, then, to assume that there is any inconsistency or incoherence in a system of rights that contains both individual and group rights. Whether any particular mixed system is harmonious or not will depend upon the nature of the rights it includes, how they fit together, and whether their various justifications are compatible. Until systems of rights are articulated more clearly than is usually done, not much can be said in the abstract one way or another. This book begins the task of examining the possibility of a mixed system that encompasses the familiar liberal individual rights and some group rights, including a right to secede.

Notes

1. Allen Buchanan, "What's So Special About Rights?" *Social Philosophy & Policy*, vol. 2, issue 1, Autumn 1984, pp. 61–83; Joel Feinberg, "In Defense of Moral Rights," The Romanell Lectures, 1990 (three unpublished lectures).

2. Ronald Dworkin, *Taking Rights Seriously* (Cambridge, Mass.: Harvard University Press, 1977), pp. 184–205.

3. For the best critical formulation of the Harm Principle and the larger moral view that supports it, see Joel Feinberg, *Harm to Others*. Vol. 1, *The Moral Limits of the Criminal Law* (New York: Oxford University Press, 1984).

4. This statement assumes that the individual is competent or that the behavior in question is substantially voluntary. For alternative accounts of this threshold condition, see Joel Feinberg, *Harm to Self*, vol. 3, *The Moral Limits of the Criminal Law* (New York: Oxford University Press, 1986), pp. 98–172; and Allen Buchanan and Dan W. Brock, *Deciding for Others: The Ethics of Surrogate Decisionmaking* (Cambridge: Cambridge University Press, 1989), pp. 17–86.

5. Feinberg, *Harm to Others*, pp. 31–36.

6. Ibid., pp. 31–104.

7. John Rawls, *A Theory of Justice* (Cambridge, Mass.: Harvard University Press, 1971), p. 250, states the Principle of Greatest Equal Liberty as follows: "Each person is to have an equal right to the most extensive total system of equal basic liberties compatible with a similar system of liberty for all." On p. 61 of the same work he enumerates the basic liberties: "The basic liberties of the citizen are, roughly speaking, political liberty (the right to vote and to be eligible for public office) together with freedom of speech and assembly; liberty of conscience and freedom of thought; freedom of the person along with the right to hold (personal property); and freedom from arbitrary arrest and seizures as defined by the concept of the rule of law." For Rawls the right to hold personal property does *not* include the right to private property in the means of production.

8. As was noted in Chapter 1, there is controversy among liberals as to how equality of opportunity is to be understood, but there is agreement that it is to include at least the absence of discriminatory legal barriers to social offices and positions. Here it is worth observing that the basic liberal rights, including the right to equality of opportunity, are usually thought of as *individual* rights. The issue of secession forces us to question liberalism's tendency to focus exclusively on individual rights, inasmuch as the right to secede is a group or collective right.

9. John Stuart Mill, *On Liberty* (New York: Bobbs-Merrill, 1959). Mill indicates his indebtedness to von Humboldt's *The Limits of State Action* by taking a quote from it as the motto for *On Liberty*: "The grand, leading principle, towards which every argument unfolded in these pages directly converges, is the absolute and essential importance of human development in its richest diversity."

10. I thank George Rainbolt for making this point clear to me.

11. For this point I am indebted to Dale Jamieson.

12. For contrasting accounts of liberal neutrality, see Joseph Raz, *The Morality of Freedom* (Oxford: Oxford University Press, 1986), pp. 110–133, and Will Kymlicka, *Liberalism, Culture and Community* (Oxford: Oxford University Press, 1989), pp. 76–83, 95–97.

13. William Galston makes a similar point, in "Pluralism and Social Unity," *Ethics*, vol. 99, no. 4, July 1989, p. 717.

Depending upon what theory to justify the state's use of coercive power the liberal espouses, the problem of coping with groups that threaten to shatter the liberal framework from within will be more or less severe. In his later essays Rawls employs what I shall call a Traditionist justification for principles of justice. He also endorses what he calls the Principle of Democratic Legitimacy, according to which the state's use of coercion to implement principles of justice must satisfy this condition if it is to be morally justified: It must be possible to justify the coercion *to* those to whom it is applied. See Rawls, "Justice as Fairness: A Briefer Restatement," unpublished manuscript, Harvard University, Department of Philosophy, pp. 135, 138, 142. It is the combination of these two views, one concerning the justification of coercion, the other concerning the justification of principles of justice, that greatly exacerbates the liberal's problem of how to deal with illiberal communities in a liberal state. According to Rawls's Traditionist view, principles of justice are justified by appeal to arguments that begin with the assumption that those to whom the justification is addressed already espouse certain normative ideals of the person. A normative ideal of the person, very roughly, is a conception of what is morally valuable about and appropriate for persons and hence implies prescriptions for how persons ought to live and interact with one another. The justifications for principles of justice build upon our preexisting allegiance to these ideals.

The term 'Traditionist' is appropriate because, according to Rawls, the ideals are embedded in a particular tradition or, as he sometimes says, a particular political culture. The ideals upon which his arguments for his favored principles of justice allegedly rest are those of equality and freedom. Thus in attempting to justify what he takes to be the correct liberal principles of justice, Rawls claims to construct his hypothetical contract situation, which he calls the original position, and from which principles of justice are to be chosen, in such a way as to express the ideals of freedom and equality. These ideals are said to be present as normative beliefs in the citizens of modern liberal societies and to be partly exemplified in their political institutions.

The Traditionist justification has a profound limitation: The arguments that build upon the ideals of freedom and equality will justify the principles of justice only to those who espouse those ideals. Rawls fails to take seriously the possibility that there are groups existing within the liberal society who are alienated from its traditions and political culture, who do not espouse its ideals of freedom and equality.

If we are restricted to a Traditionist justification, then, we cannot justify liberal principles of justice to such persons; nor, for the same reason, can we justify coercing them in the name of those principles. But recall that the Principle of Democratic Legitimacy, which Rawls also endorses, implies that forcing such persons to conform to the rules of the liberal framework would be an illegitimate use of state power because it is not possible to justify coercing them *to them*. Allowing secession is a way, perhaps the only way, for Rawls to preserve both his Traditionist justification and the Principle of Democratic Legitimacy.

Notice that merely allowing emigration does not seem to solve the problem. Suppose those alienated from the political culture choose not to emigrate. If we coerce them to comply with the principles of justice so long as they remain in our liberal society, this coercion will not be justified according to the Principle of Democratic Legitimacy. For that principle states that we may coerce others only if we can justify *to them* that use of coercion, and the justification, if it is of the Traditionist sort, cannot reach them because it builds on ideals that, by hypothesis, *they* do not espouse. At best it seems that, if they refuse to emigrate, we are justified in requiring them to choose between secession and subjection to our liberal principles, on the grounds that (1) if they choose not to secede they thereby voluntarily submit themselves to the liberal state's authority and (2) where political authority is accepted voluntarily the Principle of Democratic

Legitimacy does not apply or is trivially satisfied. (In other words, if a person has voluntarily accepted political authority, then we may say either that the state's use of coercion against him is thereby justified to him or that his voluntary acceptance makes justification of that authority otiose.) So it appears that the possibility of emigration does not relieve the tension between Traditionist justifications for principles of justice and the Principle of Democratic Legitimacy, and that, at least for those who wish to hold both consistently, secession may be the only remedy for the paradox of liberalism. Yet as we have seen, Rawls, who employs a Traditionist justification and subscribes to the Principle of Democratic Legitimacy, dismisses secession out of hand.

14. The title of the Articles characterizes them as Articles of "Perpetual Union."

15. James M. Buchanan suggested to the author that what I call the ease-of-entry argument is the strongest practical argument for a right to secede.

16. John Locke, *Second Treatise of Government*, edited by Richard H. Cox (Arlington Heights, Ill.: Harlan Davidson, Inc., 1982), pp. 134–148.

17. John C. Calhoun, *A Disquisition on Government* (New York: Liberal Arts Press, 1953), pp. 19–31.

18. The Canadian Constitution contains something similar to a right of nullification in its "notwithstanding clause": "33. (1) Parliament or the legislature of a province may expressly declare in an Act of Parliament or of the legislature, as the case may be, that the Act or a provision thereof shall operate notwithstanding a provision included in section 2 or sections 7 to 15 of this Charter." See Canadian Constitution, Part I, section 33 (1), *Canadian Charter of Rights and Freedoms*, as amended, December 22, 1987.

19. Will Kymlicka, *Liberalism, Community, and Culture* (Oxford: Oxford University Press, 1989), Chapter 10.

20. Peter Aranson, "Calhoun's Constitutional Economics," forthcoming in *Constitutional Economics*, 1991.

21. Donald Horowitz, *Ethnic Groups in Conflict* (Berkeley: University of California Press, 1985), pp. 249–254.

22. Ibid., p. 250.

23. Arthur Nwanko and Samuel Ifejika, *The Making of a Nation: Biafra* (London: C. Hurst and Co., 1970), p. 229.

24. Jules Gerard-Libois, *Katanga Secession*, translated by Rebecca Young (Madison: University of Wisconsin Press, 1966), pp. 187–220.

25. John E. Nowak, Ronald D. Rotunda, and J. Nelson Young, *Constitutional Law*, 3d ed. (St. Paul, Minn.: West Publishing Co., 1986), Section 14.1.

26. We shall see later that the situation is a bit more complex than this simple statement of the needed premise suggests. The complication is that since the people, not the state, are strictly speaking the owners of the territory, there may be cases in which injustice by the state does not void the people's title to the territory. This problem will be taken up later when the notion of territorial sovereignty is analyzed in detail.

27. Fernand Braudel, *The Mediterranean and the Mediterranean World in the Age of Philip II*, vol. I, translated by Sian Reynolds (New York: Harper and Row, 1966), pp. 338–341.

28. Jane Jacobs, *Cities and the Wealth of Nations: Principles of Economic Life* (New York: Random House, 1984).

29. A major difficulty involved in achieving any such massive reduction in the scale of political units is this: Any state that undertook such a reduction would expose itself to domination unless it had assurance that other states would undertake similar reductions or unless it could count on a large state being its protector.

30. Economists sometimes employ the Kaldor-Hicks concept of efficiency instead of the Pareto notion. S2 is Kaldor-Hicks efficient relative to S1 if and only if in going from S1 to S2 those who gain from this transition *could compensate* those who would lose so that no one would be worse off than she was in S1 and at least one person would be better off than she was in S1.

The main points for which I argue in this section concerning efficiency arguments for secession can be stated in terms of Kaldor-Hicks Efficiency as well as the Paretian notion of efficiency.

31. For an examination of the relationship between justice arguments and efficiency arguments concerning the use of markets, see Allen Buchanan, *Ethics, Efficiency, and the Market* (Totowa, N. J.: Rowman and Allanheld, 1985).

32. Ernest Gellner, *Nations and Nationalism* (Oxford: Blackwell, 1983), p. 2.

33. Ibid., p. 2.

34. Allen Buchanan, "Assessing the Communitarian Critique of Liberalism," vol. 99, no. 4, July 1989, pp. 867–871.

35. This is not to suggest, however, that assimilation was never attempted. See David H. Getches and Charles F. Wilkinson, *Federal Indian Law*, 2d ed. (St. Paul, Minn.: West Publishing Co., 1986), pp. 111–122; and F. Cohen, *Handbook of Federal Indian Law* (Charlottesville, Vir.: Michie Co., 1982 ed.), pp. 127–143.

36. I am indebted to Dale Jamieson for clarifying this point to me.

37. Michael Sandel, Introduction, *Liberalism and Its Critics*, edited by Michael Sandel (New York: New York University Press, 1984), p. 6.

38. Quebec Act, 1774.

39. This is not to imply that the titles of private Polish citizens to the land in question are thereby voided. However, the founders of the Jewish sanctuary state could argue that all that is required is that private landowners be compensated for their losses and that their land be returned if the danger passes.

40. E. S. Mason, R. Dorfman, and S. A. Marglin, *Conflict in East Pakistan: Background and Prospects*, cited in Subrata Roy Chowdhury, *The Genesis of Bangladesh* (New York: Asia Publishing House, 1972), p. 11, n. 18.

41. This was the view of Lea A. Brilmayer, who has since acknowledged that "one can imagine" secession might be justified on other grounds. See Brilmayer, "Secession and Self-Determination: A Territorialist Reinterpretation," *Yale Journal of International Law*, vol. 16, issue 1, January 1991. However, one needn't rely on imagination—history suffices: The case of the secession of the American Colonies from the British Empire illustrates the point that secession on grounds of discriminatory redistribution is justifiable.

42. Harry Beran, *The Consent Theory of Political Obligation* (New York: Croom Helm, 1987), pp. 37–42.

43. For an especially lucid and well-argued criticism of consent theory on this point, see John Simmons, *Political Obligation* (Princeton, N.J.: Princeton University Press, 1979), pp. 75–100.

44. A public good is a desired state of affairs that requires the contribution, which involves a cost, of all or some members of a group. The public good produced is available to all members of the group, the exclusion of noncontributors being impossible or impractical.

45. Simmons, *Political Obligations*, pp. 75–100.

46. Lea Brilmayer, "Consent, Contract, and Territory," *Minnesota Law Review*, vol. 74, no. 1, October 1989, pp. 6–10.

47. Robert Nozick, *Anarchy, State, and Utopia*, pp. 90–95.

48. Brilmayer, "Secession and Self-Determination: A Territorialist Reinterpretation," pp. 186–187.

49. Some have suggested that an additional feature is distinctive of group rights: The interest of no single individual in the group in the collective good secured by the right is sufficient by itself to justify the obligation on others which the right includes. Joseph Raz, *The Morality of Freedom* (Oxford: Oxford University Press, 1986), p. 208.

The sort of group right in which I am chiefly interested in this work is one which (in principle) can *be exercised*. The right to secede, the right to nullify, and group veto rights are all *exercisable* rights. A group exercises the right to secede by seceding (or it may choose not to exercise it); a group may (or may not) exercise the right to nullify by nullifying a piece of legislation, and so on. Whether the group actually will succeed in obtaining the end of the exercise of a given exercisable right will depend, of course, upon a number of factors, including whether or not others allow them to do so. For that reason we may say that these rights are exercisable in principle.

Some rights, including some group rights, are not exercisable, even in principle. For example, if, as I have suggested, groups have a right not to be subjected to discriminatory redistribution, then this is best described as a *negative claim-right*, not an exercisable right. (The group may assert that it has this right, and thereby make a claim on the state, namely, that it not subject the group to discrimination; but this is not the same as exercising the right in the way in which a group's right to secede or an individual's right to vote can be exercised).

My view of the relationship between the right to secede, as an exercisable group right, and the nonexercisable group right against nondiscrimination, is as follows. If the state persists in violating the group's right against discriminatory redistribution, and if there is no effective, morally acceptable alternative to secession for ending this discrimination, then the group has a right to secede. To say that it has this right, and that it is an exercisable right, is to say that the group has the moral power or authority to do something, namely to secede, and that it may choose to actualize this power or exercise this authority or not. And to say that the group has the moral authority to secede is not merely to say that it is at liberty to do so (that is, that the group's seceding would not be wrong, that the group has no duty not to secede), but also that the state has a duty not to interfere with its seceding if it chooses to do so.

50. See Buchanan, "Assessing the Communitarian Critique of Liberalism," pp. 858–862.

3

The Moral Case Against Secession

Appeals to moral principle are not the exclusive prerogative of those who advocate secession. The other side can mount arguments purporting to show not only that secession is morally unjustified but also that it is morally permissible to resist secession with deadly force. The antisecessionist positions to be considered are presented first and foremost as arguments for the conclusion that there is no moral right to secede and that opposing secession with force is justified, with the additional implication that there is no sound moral case for a constitutional right to secede. However, in the end they are best construed as arguments to show only that the moral right to secede is *limited*, or that if a right to secede is to be included in a constitution, then it should be framed as a limited right and formulated in certain ways and not others. Articulating and critiquing these arguments will advance us further toward a specification of the scope and limits of a moral right to secede and put us in a position to address the question of constitutional design from a firm moral grounding.

I. Protecting Legitimate Expectations

This justification for forcible opposition to secession boldly assaults the secessionists' strongest citadel, denying that secession is justifiable even in cases where the secessionists have a valid grievance that the land they occupy was illegitimately annexed to the state. There are two versions of the argument. Both contend that the alleged right to secede is defeated by an appeal to the legitimate expectations that would be thwarted if secession were allowed to occur.

To illustrate the first version, a concrete example will be useful. Suppose, contrary to fact, that the Soviet Constitution did not include a right to secede. Suppose also that Lithuanians claim that they have a moral right to secede nonetheless, because their country was forcibly and unjustly annexed by the Soviet Union in 1940. At this point the antisecessionist objects that we cannot be held hostage to history. The present reality is that for more than fifty years Lithuania has been part of the Soviet Union. During that time expectations —reasonable expectations—have been generated. Many people, including non-Lithuanian Soviet citizens who had no part in the original injustice, have constructed their lives in accordance with these expectations. Allowing secession would thwart the expectations and thereby disrupt the life-plans of many innocent people. This first variant of the argument may be called the simple argument from expectations.

Proponents of the simple argument admit that the secessionists whose territory was unjustly annexed have a right to secede, but they assert that this right is *overridden* by the moral weight of the legitimate expectations of others who were not party to the injustice. The critical issue, however, is this: What counts as a *legitimate* expectation, and when does a legitimate expectation have sufficient moral weight to override a valid claim of right?

Once again, an analogy to a simpler case proves instructive. Surely the fact that *I* did not myself steal the ill-gotten goods upon whose enjoyment I have come to rely does not by itself show that the person from whom they were stolen has no right to them or that whatever right he has is overridden. Why should the matter be any different in the case of thefts perpetrated by groups or states? The flaw in the simple argument is that it fails to develop a notion of legitimate expectations robust enough to defeat the assertion of a right to secede based on considerations of rectificatory justice.

The simple argument can, however, be strengthened somewhat by the addition of what may be called the *pragmatic premise*. It asserts, in effect, that historical grievances fade with time—that the right of rectification itself can evaporate, or at least that the priority on satisfying this right can abate as the original injustice recedes into the past.

The idea here is *not* that the passing of time itself wreaks these moral changes, but rather that, given the fact that the pages of world history are so crowded with unjust takings, stretching back so far into the past, we must, if somewhat arbitrarily, close the books at some point. In short, *there must be a moral statute of limitations*. To fail to acknowledge a moral statute of limitations would produce unacceptable disruption of the international order, with endless recriminations about ancient wrongs vying for priority.

The difficulties raised by this twist on the argument are exceedingly daunting. Clearly, any comprehensive moral account of secession would have to take a stand on the pragmatic premise. Perhaps the only reasonable alternative would be for the international community, presumably through institutions of international law such as the International Court of Justice, to adopt a *convention* of granting a strong presumption of legitimacy to existing states' claims to territory, subject to the proviso that these claims can be defeated by strong evidence of unjust takings occurring within but not earlier than, say, three or four generations.

It is worth noting, however, that some recent claims to land that are much older than this have been honored, at least when they were clearly documented. Recently approximately 300,000 acres of land in Maine were returned to the Penobscot and Passamaquoddy tribes—land taken in violation of a treaty signed over one hundred fifty years ago.[1] It is true, of course, that this was a property settlement within a nation and hence was not a threat to territorial sovereignty in the way that secessionists' claims to territory are. However, because the awards of land were made to the tribes, not to individuals, and because American law recognizes a degree of independence for Indians, this case is not simply one involving a title dispute among private citizens of a nation. It lies somewhere between ordinary title disputes among private citizens and boundary disputes in international law. Consequently, it cannot simply be dismissed as irrelevant to the issue at hand—namely, the question of whether it is justifiable to set a statute of limitations on claims to territorial sovereignty. What the Indian case suggests is that where documentation is clear, quite old claims ought to be honored and that legal systems will sometimes recognize this need.

However, this conclusion should be tempered by the recognition that in general a change of ownership among individuals or groups within a state will be much less disruptive than the redrawing of national boundaries. So even if the decision in the Indian case is appropriate, one cannot conclude straightaway that it would be wrong to adopt an international convention specifying a temporal limitation on claims to territorial sovereignty as grounds for secession. The real issues are the length of the temporal limitation, the nature of exceptions to it, and the evidentiary standards for establishing that the temporal limitation has been exceeded or that an exception obtains.

Even if it is granted that the passage of time (or, more precisely, the multiplicity of competing historical claims and the need to limit major disruptions for large numbers of people) can legitimize expectations to the point of expunging or overriding a preexisting territorial right, the interval would presumably have to be substantial. It would certainly have to be more than one lifetime. To view the matter otherwise would be to fail to appreciate the fact that persons—persons now living—have been wronged, that their rights, not just those of the faceless dead of earlier generations, have been violated, and that redress can still be made to those persons. So even if we enhance the simple expectations argument by admitting the problematic pragmatic premise, the resulting argument is of sharply limited application. For instance, it is incapable of providing a sound case against Lithuanian secession. That wound is too fresh, the identity of the aggressors and the victims too unmistakable.

Dissatisfaction with the simple argument, even when buttressed by the pragmatic premise, can motivate a second version of the argument from expectations. At least one legal scholar writing on secession as a matter of international law has suggested that under certain conditions—namely, when a valid claim of *adverse jurisdiction* can be made—the expectations in question are legitimate and can defeat the assertion that the historically wronged group has a right to secede and can serve to justify forcible resistance to secession.[2] This variant of the argument purports to remedy the defect of the first by specifying an adequate notion of legitimate expectations; and it does so without the crude subordination of right to stability that the pragmatic premise represents. The chief idea is that where adverse jurisdiction has occurred, expectations are legitimate, in a suitably strong sense, because a *change of ownership* has taken place. The occupiers have come to have a right to the land they inhabit, whereas the right of the previous owners has been extinguished.

In the common law, 'adverse possession' refers to a means by which a person or a group may come to have a legal property right in something, usually land, that was the property of another, without his voluntarily alienating his right to it by sale, exchange, gift, or bequest. What I have called adverse jurisdiction is simply the notion of adverse possession applied to territorial sovereignty. A claim of adverse possession is valid if and only if these conditions are satisfied.

1. Possession or occupation (by the nonowner) is open—that is to say, easily knowable by anyone in the vicinity.
2. The owner has the opportunity freely to protest the other's possession or occupation of the property, or otherwise to seek to validate his own title to it, but does not do so.
3. The possession or occupation by the nonowner is continuous for some period of time (usually specified by statute).
4. The possession or occupation is exclusive. (A plurality of distinct claimants to title by adverse possession defeats the claim of any one of them.[3])

Assuming that each of these requirements has an analog in the case of adverse jurisdiction, it should be clear that the argument from adverse jurisdiction will rarely apply in real-world cases of secession because requirement 2 will hardly ever be satisfied. Either there will be protest against the unjust occupation or protest will be absent because the occupying power has repressed it or made it too costly (as has been the case until very recently in Lithuania and other Soviet Republics where secessionist movements are grounded in historical injustices). In many cases, condition 4 will not be satisfied either.

Suppose we accept the idea of adverse possession and transfer it from its home in the common law to the case of the state. If the conditions for adverse jurisdiction were satisfied, then the would-be secessionists would lose the right to secede by losing a valid territorial claim or property right to the area they wish to sever from the state. Put another way, the adverse jurisdiction argument attempts to specify the conditions under which the expectations of antisecessionists have sufficient weight to rule out a right to secede insofar as the latter right presupposes that the secessionists have a valid claim to the seceding territory. Thus understood, the adverse jurisdiction argument, unlike the earlier simple argument from expectations, does not first recognize that there is a right to secede (based on a right to recover stolen territory) and then contend that under conditions of adverse possession that right can be overridden by a new and weightier property right. Instead, the argument's conclusion is that when the conditions of adverse jurisdiction are satisfied, *there is no right to secede*, because the property right on which the right to secede depended no longer exists. If there is no property right, there is no property right to be vindicated, and if there is no property right to be vindicated, then secession cannot be justified as an exercise of rectificatory justice.

To summarize: The difficulty with the adverse jurisdiction argument is that even if it is sound, its range of application is very narrow (primarily because condition 2, and possibly 4 as well, will rarely be satisfied). The reverse is true of the simple expectations argument. It will apply to almost every case of secession in which the original annexation was unjust, because secession will almost always thwart some expectations of innocent third parties; but it will in every case fail to justify resisting secession because its notion of legitimate expectations is too thin. It appears, then, that neither version of the argument from expectations does much to undermine the justification of secession on grounds of rectificatory justice. The second (adverse possession) version may show that in principle no right to secede may exist in spite of unjust annexation, owing to the fact that the seceding area has lost its right to the territory through adverse possession. But this theoretical possibility is a remote one because the conditions for adverse possession will generally not be satisfied in precisely those cases in which annexation was unjust.

The first (simple) variant of the argument does not succeed, even in principle, in showing that secession may be rightly resisted. Proper sensitivity to expectations might provide a reason for those who possess the right to secede not to exercise it, or to postpone their exercise of it, or to adopt a gradualist approach to seceding, or to supply some form of compensation to innocent parties whose expectations will be thwarted by secession. But none of this is to say that the moral weight of the expectations in question shows that there is no right to secede, nor that this right may be overridden.

II. Self-Defense (as a Justification for Resisting Secession)

Historically, some opponents of secession, including perhaps Lincoln, have at least appeared to appeal to the larger political unit's right to preserve itself.[4] If uncharitably construed, this contention shamelessly begs the question, amounting to a flat denial of the right of secessionists to redraw the political boundaries on the ground that if this is done the state *as it was* will no longer exist. But at issue here, of course, is precisely the question as to whether it is permissible to redraw the political boundaries so that the larger unit no longer exists but is replaced by two or more smaller, independent units.

There are, however, two other, somewhat more promising interpretations of the self-defense argument. On the first, secession may be forcibly resisted if it is incompatible with the continued independent *existence* of the remainder state. On the second, secession may be forcibly resisted if it would undermine the *economic viability* of the remainder state, even if the continued independent existence of the remainder state is not at risk.

Consider the second variant. Unless fleshed out, the notion of economic viability is too nebulous to support the weight of the argument. If the economic viability of the remainder state requires that those who remain in it continue to enjoy *presecession* levels of economic well-being, then the economic viability version of the self-defense argument against secession is quite unconvincing for the simple reason that there is no right to the economic *status quo* as such, either for individuals or for groups.

Unfortunately, this dubious principle of entitlement to the *status quo* is frequently applied in *domestic secession*—that is, divorce. In the United States courts often adjudicate settlements in accordance with the principle that divorce is not to worsen the spouse's economic condition, even if ensuring this outcome means a significant lowering of the other spouse's level of material well-being. This principle assumes that the fact of marriage itself generates a right to the economic *status quo* of the marriage.

Of course, it is not difficult to think of cases in which a fair divorce settlement would require one spouse to provide support to the other even at the cost of lowering his or her own standard of living. For example, in many cases the wife supports the husband's graduate or other professional training, or at least forgoes opportunities for enhancing her own income-earning capacity in order to further his career or education. Under such circumstances, a just settlement may require that she be compensated, even if this worsens the condition of the husband to a point far below the level of economic well-being he enjoyed during the marriage. Similarly, if there was a prenuptial agreement guaranteeing one spouse that he or she would not fall below a certain income level should the marriage be dissolved, this too would suffice to justify a transfer of resources from the other spouse, even if the result was a significant lowering of the latter's prospects relative to the marital *status quo.* But to assume—in the absence of either of the two foregoing special circumstances—that the mere fact of marriage creates a right to the economic *status quo* is quite implausible. The principle of entitlement to the economic *status quo*, in both its political and domestic applications, has little to recommend it.

'Economic viability' might be interpreted in either of two other ways, however. On the first interpretation, economic viability in the remainder state would be achieved if secession did not depress the material well-being of those in the remainder state below some *adequate level* or *decent minimum*. On the second, economic viability is taken literally: Secession is said to be prohibited if it would result in such economic loss to the remainder state that the latter could not continue to exist at all, or at least not as an independent state. This latter interpretation reduces the argument from economic viability to the first version of the self-defense arguments noted at the beginning of this section, according to which secession may be forcibly resisted if it threatens the existence of the remainder state as an independent, sovereign state.

The first version of the economic viability argument evidently rests upon the assumption that there is something like a right to an adequate level or decent minimum of economic goods or material well-being. This, of course, is in itself a controversial assumption about what distributive justice requires. Moreover, the inherent vagueness of the notion of a decent minimum or adequate level may prompt one to question whether anything so indeterminate could be the object of an entitlement, an obligation of right, as opposed to an encouragement to exercise the virtue of charity. Nevertheless, even if we waive these difficulties and grant that there is a right to a decent minimum or adequate level of economic goods or material well-being, it does not follow that the presecession state has the right to use force against the secessionists to see that this right is upheld. That conclusion would not follow even if it could be shown that *someone or other*, or the better-off societies collectively, has an enforceable obligation to ensure that the adequate level or decent minimum is preserved. It also would be necessary to show that *the secessionists* have such an enforceable obligation. I am aware of no sound argument for such a conclusion.

On this first interpretation, the self-defense argument against secession is really not about self-defense at all, nor even about economic viability as such. It is about obligations of distributive justice. The case at issue has already been touched upon in Chapter 1, in the context of secession by the haves from the have-nots. The question is whether obligations of distributive justice can preclude secession—or, more precisely, whether there is an obligation to share wealth with others in the existing state that supplies a decisive reason against seceding from that state. This difficult question is taken up in a subsequent section of this chapter when we investigate the wrongful taking (or distributive justice) argument. For the present we are concerned only with self-defense arguments against secession properly described.

On the second interpretation, economic viability is understood in a more Spartan fashion and one more consonant with the notion of a right of self-defense: Secession may be forcibly resisted if successful secession would so cripple the economy that the remainder state would not be able to continue to exist at all, at least not as an independent, sovereign state.

Even if we grant this appeal to self-defense in principle, its range of application in real-world cases of secession is extremely constrained. For if those in the remainder state are able to reconstitute their economy by developing new foreign trade with the seceded state or with others (even though this may mean a reduced level of economic well-being), then it will rarely be the case that secession would literally render the remainder state's economy nonviable.

One should not, however, be too quick to concede that the Spartan version of the argument from economic viability is sound even *in principle*. Suppose that if Quebec were to secede from Canada what remained of Canada would not be viable (either economically or militarily or both) as a sovereign state. Suppose further, however, that the remainder state, Canada *sans* Quebec, could solve its problems by voluntarily joining itself to the United States. Finally, suppose also that Canadians would not lose any important civil or political rights, or otherwise suffer injustice, by becoming citizens of the United States. (Note that this last assumption is at best very questionable: By becoming American citizens Canadians would lose some important legal entitlements to social services, including health care, which many regard as a matter of justice.) *If* all of these conditions obtained, would it be plausible to say that the mere fact that Canada without Quebec would not be viable as a sovereign state entails that Quebec should not be allowed to secede? Surely not. (Whether *other* considerations against secession might be decisive is another question, of course.)

Undaunted, the proponent of the self-defense argument against secession may pull in her perimeter to strengthen her case. She will concede that it is not justifiable for a state forcibly to resist secession in order to preserve its independence when the alternative to independence is annexation by a reasonably just state. Instead, her argument will be that a state may resist secession, with force if necessary, if successful secession would make it vulnerable either to the physical destruction of its populace and its wealth or to assimilation by a seriously unjust state. Let us label this the ultrasurvivalist version of the self-defense argument against secession.

The first thing to note is that this is more a scorched-earth policy than an orderly strategic retreat for the antisecessionist. For clearly this version of the argument has an even narrower range of application than the earlier, less extreme versions. In many cases, secession will only lower the level of economic well-being of the remainder state or require it to annex or ally itself to another state in order to remain economically viable; and in at least some of the latter cases, this can be accomplished without a threat to the survival or the civil and political rights of the citizens.

The ultrasurvivalist argument requires even further qualification, however. For if states (or their citizens) have a right of self-defense against actions that would produce mass destruction of life or loss of basic rights, it is surely a limited one, just as an individual's right of self-defense is limited.

In other words, the right of an individual to defend himself is not a right to do *whatever* is necessary for his survival. Both morality and the common law recognize a number of distinct limitations on the individual's right of self-defense.[5] One such limitation seems especially pertinent. One cannot validly claim to be exercising one's right of self-defense if one is a *culpable aggressor*. For example, if you break into a man's home, attack him, and he defends himself, you cannot kill him and then reasonably protest in indignation that you were only exercising your right of self-defense! Similarly, if the state violates the rights of a group within its jurisdiction and the members of that group seek to secede, the state or those who support it cannot justify crushing the secession movement by claiming that they are only exercising the right of self-defense, even if it happens to be true that if secession succeeded the remainder state would not survive.

There is another putative limitation on the right of self-defense that, as we have already seen in Chapter 2, is even more controversial: the prohibition against using force against *innocent third parties* to defend oneself against threats to one's survival by a second party who is a culpable aggressor. Suppose that a group G, occupying a certain territory within state A, desires to secede but not on the grounds that it or its members have been treated unjustly. Suppose that the other citizens and leaders of the state reasonably conclude that it is virtually certain that if G is allowed to secede, an evil neighboring state, B, will attack and subjugate state A. Is A justified, by a right of self-defense, in coercing G to remain within A so as to avoid A's conquest by B? Surely there is at the very least a weighty presumption that an individual may *not* use coercion against an innocent individual in order to protect himself against a culpable aggressor. And there is no obvious reason to conclude that matters stand any differently if we assume that a state (or group) has a right of self-defense. So there is at the very least a strong presumption that a state may not use force to block an otherwise justified secession in order to secure its own survival against a lethal threat from an aggressor. The question is whether there are exceptional circumstances in which this presumption is rebutted.

In the case of the self-defense argument *for* secession considered earlier, we saw that there can be extreme conditions that overcome this presumption—the hypothetical case of the Jewish sanctuary state in Poland made that point. It is important to see as well, however, that there is a crucial difference between the treatment of innocent parties in the case at hand and the plight of the Jews in 1939. In the latter cases, the state has failed to live up to a fundamental condition of its authority over the territory: It has not provided to all of its citizens equal protection from threats to life. Further, our example assumed that the Jews who appropriated the land for self-defense did not expel its current occupants but, rather, allowed them to be included as fellow citizens. Given these morally relevant differences, it is not inconsistent to hold that there are some extreme cases in which the right of self-defense can justify secession, but also that in general the same right does not justify resisting secession with force.

There are some special cases of self-defense, however, that provide a stronger case for forcibly resisting secession. Suppose that G entered into the union to form state A in order to achieve a common defense, or suppose that G has accepted and benefited from efforts for common defense to which the other citizens of A have contributed. If G unilaterally withdraws its contribution to the common defense by seceding, at a time when there is a genuine danger to the remainder state, then perhaps A would be justified in forcibly resisting G's efforts to secede. The international analog here would be a situation in which two sovereign states had made an alliance for their common defense and then one abandoned the alliance, exposing the other to danger. In such a case the other party might well be justified in trying to sustain the alliance through the use of force, if no other means were available and effective.

Notice, however, that if we apply this reasoning to secession and not just to defensive alliances between sovereign states, it would at most justify coercive resistance to secession *only* where there is a high probability that secession will be followed by an attack by a third party that is likely to be successful and severely damaging, if not lethal to the citizens of the remainder state. Nothing less could justify coercion against innocent third parties (in the absence of an explicit agreement to continue to associate, as in the case of a treaty or an alliance).

Moreover, whatever force the argument might have in the case of secession would be undercut if the seceding group were willing to enter into an alliance for the common defense with the remainder state or to postpone its secession until after the substantial danger of invasion by a third party passes. What seems clear enough is that a state cannot correctly claim a right of self-defense in order to justify resistance to secession merely by invoking *speculative* dangers or merely by pointing out that its capacity for self-defense will be *lessened* if secession occurs. Appeal to the right of self-defense, then, cannot show that there is no right of secession. Even in the case where the ground for secession is not unjust treatment of those who wish to secede, the right of self-defense at best provides a justification for blocking secession only under rather severely circumscribed conditions.

Some who have seemed to appeal to a right to self-defense, and in particular, Lincoln, may in fact have had in mind something quite different. Lincoln believed that the United States' right to defend itself from dismemberment was a special case, that this right was derived from a *higher obligation to humanity*, not only to present but future generations as well. Rightly or wrongly, Lincoln was convinced that *the fate of democracy in the world* depended on the success of the American experiment, that if the Union dissolved, political freedom and all its fruits might "perish from the earth."[6] It was probably for this reason, and not because he espoused any of the above-mentioned, uncompelling, self-defense arguments, that he was willing to wash the country in blood to preserve the Union.

Properly understood, this is not so much an argument from self-defense *per se* as an argument for self-defense *in order to avert a moral catastrophe*. And to the extent that it is *more justifiable* to coerce innocent third parties to avert great harm to many *other* innocent persons than merely to save *oneself*, the moral catastrophe argument is a stronger argument than any *self*-defense argument.

Whether or not the situation in which Lincoln found himself was one that, as he believed, required forcible resistance to secession in order to avert a moral catastrophe, there certainly can be such cases. Suppose, for example, that preserving the political union of a powerful democratic state were necessary if that state were to be able to lead a successful defensive war of the democracies against a ruthless totalitarian foe hell-bent on enslaving the world (as the Nazis tried to do). Under such extreme conditions forcible resistance to secession might well be justified, especially if the state resisting secession could truthfully say that the secessionists had no legitimate grievance that they were being treated unjustly by the state, but only wished to secede for less morally weighty reasons not having to do with justice. (For example, they wish to form a small-scale, direct, participatory democracy or to cultivate a closed fundamentalist theocracy that will tolerate no heterodoxy within its confines.)

Without pretending to have supported a fully decisive answer to the question of whether armed opposition to secession would be justified under such dire circumstances as those described in the Nazi example, I think it correct to conclude that the argument from self-defense in its most forceful forms (including the moral catastrophe version) once again provides a justification for forcibly resisting secession only under stringently confined circumstances. In many cases secession neither threatens the literal survival of the remainder state nor is likely to result in moral catastrophe to large numbers of innocent third parties. So, like all of the antisecessionist arguments vetted thus far, the argument from self-defense is incapable of showing that there is no right to secede. The next argument for resisting secession attempts to take the high moral ground by appealing to the value of democracy.

III. Protecting Majority Rule

The general idea to be plumbed here is that recognizing a right to secede undermines constitutional democracy: If a minority has the option of seceding whenever the majority makes decisions it opposes, then the principle of majority rule is thwarted. Here, too, there are several distinct arguments to be assessed.

According to the simplest and least persuasive of these, the minority is unconditionally bound by majority decisions. So a minority group may not legitimately secede if a majority decision goes against it. Similarly, if a bid for secession is defeated by majority vote, then efforts to secede are illegitimate and may therefore be resisted with force. The gross defect in this argument, of course, is that it relies on the simplistic assumption that whatever a majority decides binds all members of the polity, regardless of the content of the decision. Yet surely if the majority adopts policies that violate individuals' rights, its decisions are *not* binding and it cannot justify the use of coercion against those who would oppose it, whether by attempting secession or otherwise, simply by asserting that its decisions *are* binding.

Once it is conceded that the scope of majority rule must be limited by constraints on substantive outcomes (in particular, by respect for an appropriate list of individual rights), a somewhat more plausible anti-secessionist argument comes into view. To distinguish it from the simple majority rule argument, let us call it the *constrained majority rule argument.* It proclaims that the state may oppose secession with force, if need be, so long as the state upholds individual rights for all and so long as the majority, expressing its will through fair, constitutionally authorized voting procedures, rejects secession.

There are two serious objections to this version of the argument from democracy. First, it begs the question by assuming that majority rule is constrained only by *individual* rights, given that precisely what is at issue is whether *groups* have rights and in particular whether some groups, at least, have a right to secede. And we have already seen in Chapter 2 that there is a strong case for such a right. Further, as was also observed, even if we assume initially that the only rights are individual rights and the only injustices are violations of individual rights, we cannot take it for granted that the only legitimate ground for secession is that the state has acted *unjustly*. For we have seen, drawing on an analogy with divorce, that we cannot dismiss the possibility that a union, whether political or personal, may be unilaterally dissolved (subject to whatever requirements of distributive justice may apply, that is, conditional upon a fair property settlement), even if the party who wishes to do so has not been treated unjustly. (For example, a group might wish to secede in order to realize its own distinctive vision of democracy, even if it is suffering no injustice.) We also saw that under certain specified conditions, the need to preserve a culture can justify secession, even in the absence of injustices.

The argument that secession may be blocked in order to protect majority rule can be construed in yet another way, however. Call it the *participatory commitment version* of the argument. It contends that if a group voluntarily participates in majority rule procedures without protesting their legitimacy (e.g., by boycotting elections or committing acts of civil disobedience), and if the outcome of those procedures falls within the bounds specified by individual rights or other constitutional constraints, then it is illegitimate for that group to reject the outcome of majority rule by attempting to secede.

Once again American history provides a possible illustration. Some Unionists apparently believed that because the South had voluntarily participated in the national elections of 1860 (at least it had not abstained from them in protest), the South was thereby obligated to accept the outcome (at least so long as the outcome violated no constitutional constraints). The core idea of the procedural constraint version of the argument from democracy is a familiar one: Voluntary participation in a decision-procedure counts as an undertaking to abide by its results, at least so long as the latter fall within appropriate limits, mutually agreed upon in advance. Thus some Unionists complained that it was unfair for the South to play the electoral game as long as it suited its purposes (expecting the North to abide by the results when it did), but to withdraw unilaterally from the game when the outcome went contrary to its wishes.

Several comments are in order here. First, even if this argument is sound, its utility is quite limited. It provides a case against secession only when the secessionists do not withdraw from the majority process in protest. But even in instances in which they do not withdraw, there are problems. The question of when participation in majority rule procedures is *voluntary* and when it is not is a complex issue in itself. However, regardless of how that thorny question is resolved, it appears that a minority's obligation to accept the outcome of majoritarian procedures is diluted, if not dissolved, if nonparticipation is either known in advance to be an ineffectual means of protest or entails excessive costs to the minority (for example, retaliation by the majority). Finally, even if a currently existing minority can be considered bound to the (constitutionally constrained) outcome of a majoritarian procedure in which it voluntarily participated at a certain time, it is hard to see how *its* behavior or the obligation that behavior engenders can bind *future* minorities at later times.

None of the arguments from majority rule considered thus far supplies a convincing justification for denying the right to secede. Yet the notion that secession threatens majority rule still has an intuitive plausibility that has thus far eluded us.

IV. Minimization of Strategic Bargaining

There is, in fact, a related though distinct argument that does a better job of capturing the truth behind the allegation that recognizing a right to secede undermines democracy. In conditions in which the majority views secession by a group G as a prohibitive cost, G's threat to secede can in effect serve as a veto. G can use the *threat* of secession to ensure that the majority's will does not prevail, even when the majority's decision would respect constitutional limits. To prevent such strategic behavior, it is necessary to refuse to acknowledge a right to secede. And for the same reason, it is also permissible to deprive the threat of secession of credibility by forcibly opposing secession.

Though not without merit, this argument discards the baby with the bath water. Given that there is a strong case for a right to secede (as we saw in Chapter 2), a more appropriate response is to devise constitutional mechanisms to give some weight *both* to the interest in secession and to the interest in preserving majority rule. The most obvious way to do this would be to allow secession under certain circumstances, yet to minimize the danger of strategic bargaining with the threat of secession by erecting inconvenient but surmountable constitutional barriers to secession. For example, the constitution might recognize a right to secede but require a strong majority (say, three-quarters) of those in the area in question to endorse secession by a referendum vote.

This first type of hurdle is the analog of an obstacle to constitutional amendment that the U.S. Constitution itself establishes. The latter stipulates that a proposed amendment must receive a two-thirds majority in Congress and be ratified by three-quarters of the states.

The purpose of allowing amendment while erecting these two strong (i.e., nonsimple) majority requirements is to strike an appropriate balance between two legitimate interests: the interest in providing flexibility for change and the interest in securing stability. Similarly, the point of erecting inconvenient but surmountable obstacles to secession is not to make secession impossible but to avoid making it too easy. An alternative would be to impose an exit cost—a secession tax, if you will.

The possibility of devising such constitutional mechanisms, which will be examined in considerable detail in Chapter 4 when we take up the problem of framing a constitutional right to secede, blunts the edge of the strategic bargaining argument against secession. That argument shows only that the exercise of a right to secede should be constrained by procedural hurdles and/or substantive exit costs, not that there is no such right. In contrast, the next argument to be explored, if successful, shows that secession may be and indeed ought to be denied altogether, at least in certain cases.

V. Soft Paternalism[7]

A group might wish to secede, not because its members' civil and political rights have been violated, nor because it has suffered discriminatory redistribution, nor because it is reclaiming territory unjustly taken from it, but because its form of life cannot flourish in a society that *does* respect the individual civil and political rights that constitute a liberal society. For example, some communities may not be able to preserve and transmit to successive generations their distinctive values under conditions of freedom of expression. Some groups in the United States claim that this is so. For example, some religious fundamentalists protest that a lack of censorship in public school curricula and in popular entertainment undermines their efforts to inculcate (what they take to be) Christian values in their children.

Those who adhere to liberal values may be willing to let competent individuals freely discard their own rights, and yet they may consistently resist secession to form an illiberal state because the secessionists will be depriving not only themselves but also their children and future generations of these rights. According to this argument, then, resistance to secession is justified not for the sake of the secessionists themselves but for the good of others whose liberties and opportunities will be adversely affected by secession and who had no say in the decision to secede.

This is a very strong argument for resisting secession, but only, of course, against secession to form an illiberal society in which people will not be given an opportunity to make an informed and free choice between a liberal and an illiberal form of life. It has no force if there is freedom to exit the illiberal society. So although the soft paternalism argument fails to show that in general there is no right to secede, it does establish a significant limitation on that right by supporting the conclusion that those who would secede to form an illiberal society from which there is no exit have no right to do so.

In establishing this conclusion the soft paternalism argument also exhibits the limitations of secession as a way of easing the liberal paradox. The liberal paradox, we saw earlier, is this: The tolerant framework of liberal society allows the growth of communities that may eventually shatter it; and in order to prevent this from happening, the liberal state may be forced to employ illiberal methods.

Allowing secession for groups whose values threaten the liberal framework but who are willing to separate from it, rather than insisting on overthrowing it, is a way for liberals to avoid the allegation that they had to betray liberalism in order to preserve it. We have just seen, however, that any form of liberalism that acknowledges the validity of soft paternalist intervention must limit the right to secede to cases where the seceding society will be liberal or, if illiberal, will allow exit for those who wish to live under liberal conditions. Unfortunately, those communities that raise the problem of the liberal paradox in its most acute form are likely to restrict exit if they can.

VI. The Threat of Anarchy

The next justification for secession, unlike the soft paternalist argument, purports to be perfectly general in its application, rejecting the right to secession altogether. It contends that if secession is permitted there will be no end to it. The result will be chaos. If large groups are allowed to secede, why not small groups; and if small groups, why not individuals? The *reductio ad absurdum* of the right to secede is the prospect of the limiting case of anarchy: not Everyman's home his castle; rather, Everyman's yard his country. Even if the process of fragmentation does not reach this far, recognition of a right to secede is very likely to produce more fragmentation than is tolerable. From Lincoln to Gorbachev, those who oppose secession have raised the alarm of "anarchy!"

This argument proceeds by sleight of hand. It assumes, quite without warrant, that a right to secede must be an *unlimited* right—a right of virtually anyone to secede for virtually any reason. But one doesn't have to allow everything just because one allows something. We have already seen that the right to secede cannot be an unlimited right. Even the combined weight of all the prosecession arguments surveyed in Chapter 2 supports only a limited right to secede. The chief limitations are of two sorts: those imposed by the fact that some reasons for secession are morally decisive and some are not (and that the morally decisive reasons apply only to some cases of secession), and those imposed by appropriate procedural and substantive conditions on the constitutional embodiment of the moral right to secede. (In Chapter 4 various procedural and substantive conditions on a constitutional right to secede are explored in greater detail.)

Even where there is no constitutional right to secede, a proper understanding of the limits of the moral right to secede provides a principled way of avoiding the equation of secession with anarchy. To take but one prominent example: The prediction of anarchy gains credibility because there is a tendency to assume the validity of the *normative nationalist principle*, the principle that all "peoples" or ethnic groups have a *right of self-determination*. It is true, as we saw in our critique of prosecessionist argument from self-determination, that widespread efforts to act on *this* principle would entail unacceptable disruptions, dislocations of peoples, and almost certainly horrendous loss of human life. But we also saw that this principle, and hence its use as a justification for secession, must be resolutely rejected.

Of course, the proponent of the antisecessionist argument from anarchy may reformulate his objection to take all of this into account. He may reply that even if it is true that fragmentation would be contained within acceptable bounds *if* secessionists observed the proper moral and constitutional limits of a right to secede, they will not do so—and the result will be intolerable.

This new version of the argument, though not quite so crude as the first, is still less than convincing. Paradoxically, it simultaneously overestimates and underestimates the force of morality in the world of action.

Secession is not a new idea, and whenever it has been attempted its proponents have tried to justify it from a moral point of view. Moreover, as we saw in Chapter 1, a number of prominent documents of international law, including UN Resolutions, have apparently endorsed an unqualified principle of self-determination, thus supplying an extremely broad moral slogan to justify almost limitless secession. Yet actual attempts at secession have been relatively infrequent, compared to the high number of groups that might aspire to political independence. As was observed earlier, virtually every existing large state in Europe began as an empire and contains two or more distinct ethnic groups. Nevertheless, in spite of the fact that both the potential number of secessionist movements is extremely high and the moral slogans for justifying them are readily available, there have been relatively few serious secessionist movements.[8] Furthermore, most secessionist movements fail and do so at great cost to the secessionists.[9] So, on the one hand, the shrill cry that recognizing a right to secession is a recipe for anarchy seems to accord moral ideas an exaggerated power in the world of action.

On the other hand, if the proponent of the anarchist objection admits, as he should, that the right to secession is a limited right, his contention must be that in practice people's moral motivation will not be strong enough to enable them to observe in their actions what they themselves take to be the moral limits of the right. But this amounts to the claim that moral ideas are virtually impotent. Yet the proponent of the anarchist objection supplies no reason why we should accept his assumption that moral ideas about the justification of secession have this peculiar combination of power and impotence. One might just as well say that we should not acknowledge the moral ideal of personal autonomy because if we do, people will run amok, committing all sorts of atrocities in its name.

The saner approach is to admit that this moral ideal, like all others, can be abused, and then to set about the task of determining the scope and limits of the ideal in its implications for how one ought to act *and* ensuring that the ideal is embodied in institutions in such a way that its proper scope and limits will be duly observed. This is precisely what I am attempting to do in the case of the right to secession. Moreover, there is a certain touching naivete in the antisecessionist argument under consideration: The horse is already well out of the barn. The question is not whether to recognize a right to secede but, rather, how to domesticate it. For many political actors in today's world the issue is not so much "Shall we recognize a right to secede?" as "Assuming that a right to secede is becoming a key item in practical political discourse, how can we utilize clear moral thinking and wise institutional design to enable us to live with it?" For all of these reasons, the argument that any particular instance of secession may be opposed because tolerating secession will lead to unacceptable fragmentation ought to be rejected.

VII. Preventing Wrongful Taking

This source of opposition to secession has already been alluded to on more than one occasion. Two quite distinct versions of the argument can be isolated. What they have in common is that both purport to justify resistance to secession on the ground that secession involves *wrongful taking*. They differ, however, as to the nature of the wrongful taking. The first version may be called the *lost investment argument*; the second, the *stolen territory argument*.

A historical illustration of the lost investment argument makes its appeal evident. In the two decades preceding Southern secession, the federal government of the United States spent several million dollars improving Southern waterways (especially the Mississippi River), building and maintaining coastal fortifications (some of which were designed by Robert E. Lee, later commander in chief of the secessionist forces), and undertaking various other public works. When the Southern states seceded they made no serious effort to achieve the political equivalent of a negotiated property settlement in a divorce. They simply appropriated these federal investments (beginning with Fort Sumter). In doing so they supplied the North with a reason to resist secession, one grounded in considerations of distributive justice or, more specifically, in the morality of property rights.

The most obvious limitation of the lost investment argument is that the reason for resisting secession it supplies can be removed if the secessionists pay *fair compensation* to the remainder state for its lost investments (and/or for secessionists' expropriation of the private property of individuals who do not wish to secede). But the question of what counts as fair compensation is an enormously complex issue. At this point I will sketch only one relevant factor that reveals an interesting connection between the compensation question and secession on grounds of discriminatory redistribution. The nature and relevance of this factor can again be illuminated not only by the case of Southern secession but by contemporary cases as well.

One justification that Southern secessionists might have given for *not* compensating the federal government for the expropriation of its investments was that this was only the South's due—partial payment for what it had lost through discriminatory redistribution. In fact, Peter Aranson cites data showing that the total revenue extracted by the federal government from the South (mainly as a result of the redistributive effects of the tariff) far exceeded the value of federal investment in the South.[10] Similarly, if the Basques secede from Spain and in doing so expropriate state facilities without offering compensation, they might endeavor to justify their actions by pointing out that the revenue the government of Spain derives from the Basque area is approximately three times greater than what it infuses into that region.

My point is not that these crude calculations are accurate (nor that by themselves they are conclusive evidence of discriminatory redistribution). Nor am I assuming that victims of discriminatory redistribution are justified in confiscating state property whenever they choose, in order to offset their unjust losses, without even attempting to achieve a fair, negotiated property settlement. Instead, I only wish to emphasize two points. First, the lost investment version of the wrongful taking argument is not really an argument against secession as such. It is an argument for resisting secession when and so long as secessionists refuse to cooperate in a just property settlement that includes whatever compensation is appropriate for state and/or private investment in the seceding region. Second, whatever compensation secessionists owe for the investments of others in the seceding region must be offset by a fair estimate of whatever effects of discriminatory redistribution they have suffered.

A case can also be made for requiring the state to compensate the seceding group for the costs of governmental inefficiencies or constraints on economic development, in instances in which the seceding region was unjustly annexed. Thus the Lithuanian government had a good point when it replied as follows to Gorbachev's demand for compensation for Soviet investment in that country: Wait until you see the bill for fifty years of socialist economic mismanagement!

A further complication, which can only be flagged here, is the question as to whether or to what extent social investment in the productive powers of the secessionists themselves is to be included in investments for which compensation is owed. There are close parallels here with the standard argument that states advance to justify prohibiting emigration. The Soviet Union and its satellite countries for decades defended their denials of requests for permission to emigrate by saying that emigrants would take with them "human capital" (an odd phrase in the mouths of Marxists!) that the state has invested in them through public education and training.

I would not attempt a definitive solution of this issue. However, it is crucial to emphasize that citizens in such regimes typically have little say over the nature of the investments the state chooses to make in them, are frequently not free to refuse them, and have extremely limited options for making their own investments in their own productive powers since private property is largely forbidden and private education is unattainable. Taken together, these considerations do much to undercut any argument that the state's investment in people's productive powers is a moral bar to emigration or secession.

Regardless of how the "human capital" issue is settled, considerations of distributive justice impose significant limitations on the right to secede. However, the possibility of fair compensation to the remainder state (or to private citizens within it who will lose property as a result of secession) means that problems of distributive justice pose no more of an insurmountable barrier to secession than the need for a fair property settlement does for divorce.

The lost investment argument, then, supplies no decisive justification for resisting secession. It shows only that, at most, the state would be justified in resisting secession if this were the only way to preserve its investment *and* (as is not the case with the U.S.S.R.'s investment in Lithuania) it has a valid property right in that investment. Further, if it can extract adequate compensation for the investment without thwarting secession, then *ceteris paribus* the state has no justification for opposing secession.

This latter point is extremely important: It reveals a crucial difference between the lost investment argument and the stolen territory argument. In our discussion of the former, the assumption has been that the only property at issue is the state's investment in the territory. The secessionists' claim to territory itself is not in dispute in this argument. In the stolen territory argument, by contrast, the justification for resisting secession lies precisely with the charge that secession involves the wrongful taking of territory—the state's territory.

The second, stolen territory version of the argument, then, alleges a more fundamental loss of property: a part of the territory of the state itself. Notice that *if* this charge could be made good, an offer of *compensation* by the secessionists may not be an acceptable response. For if a fundamental property right has been violated, as this argument contends, then compensation is not enough. Analogously, if you take my home from me, you do not erase my grievance by writing me a check for its market value. A fundamental property right is a right to continued possession, not merely a right to be compensated if the object is taken from one.[11] Hence if a case of secession involves the wrongful taking of state territory, then compensation for the loss removes the justification for resisting secession *only* if there are weighty reasons in this case for making an exception to the ordinary distinction between a fundamental right to property and a mere right to compensation. We have already seen, in the discussion of the prosecessionist argument from self-defense (illustrated by the hypothetical example of a Jewish sanctuary state in Poland in 1939), one strong candidate for a case in which the ground for secession has such overwhelming moral weight that it extinguishes an existing property right to territory and generates a new property right. This, however, is an extreme case. In less extreme cases, if those who oppose secession can show that secession would infringe the state's right to its territory, they will have a substantial reason for resisting secession, even if the secessionists offer compensation for the territorial loss. The general principle at work here is simple to formulate but difficult to apply concretely: Compensation for the wrongful taking of territory is acceptable only if the moral interest in secession is sufficiently weighty to override the state's property right in the seceding territory. (Of course, the state may choose to accept compensation if it wishes, even in cases where it is not morally required to treat compensation as being sufficient.)

In some actual cases of secession, however, the matter is not nearly so complex, and less controversial principles yield a more determinate resolution. As was already noted, the Soviet claim that Lithuania may be forcibly prevented from seceding until it pays compensation for the U.S.S.R.'s investments in that country is all but ludicrous, quite apart from the fact that Lithuania's losses from discriminatory redistribution would at least partly cancel the investment debt. The Soviet claim rings hollow for the simple reason that Lithuania was unjustly and forcibly annexed into the Soviet Union. Because it had no legitimate title to the territory in the first place, whatever investments the U.S.S.R. made there were made at its own risk. In other words, the U.S.S.R. has no valid claim to the investment because of the circumstances under which the investment was made. (Analogously, if you force your way onto my land, take over my house, and then proceed to make improvements in it, I owe you no compensation for your investment when I finally succeed in expelling you.)

The deeper difficulty with evaluating the application of the stolen property version of the argument lies in another quarter altogether: What exactly are we to make of the claim that a certain parcel of land is *state territory*? In other words, when does the state have a valid claim to the territory in question, and what is the nature of that claim if it is valid? Whether—or, rather, under what conditions—the stolen property argument provides a sound justification for forcible opposition to secession cannot be determined until these questions are answered.

Answering them requires us to confront more squarely an intimidating problem that has already surfaced at several points in our investigation: *the territorial issue*. We first encountered it when we saw that every attempt to justify secession must include a territorial claim—a justification not only for severing the secessionists' obligations to the state, for concluding that those *persons* are no longer subject to the state's authority, but also for taking a part of what the state considers to be *its territory*. Subsequently, we saw that there can be several distinct grounds on which secessionists may base their claim to the territory in question.

In the preceding discussion the terms 'state's territory' and 'state's property' have sometimes been used interchangeably in contexts in which nothing hinged on the distinction. But in fact there is a distinction, one that becomes important once we delve more deeply into the territoriality issue. At least under modern conditions, the relationship between the state and its territory is *not* the same as that between a person and the land which is her private property. It may be true that in earlier periods of history a ruler or ruling family was thought to own the territory of the state, to possess it as a piece of private property. But modern states, whether socialistic or capitalistic, are not conceived of in this way. This is perhaps clearest in states where private citizens own land; they, not the state, are the property holders. But even where there is virtually no private property in land, the official rationale, at least, is that the state holds and administers the land and the resources it contains, and defends the borders *for the people*, that is, the citizens collectively. Thus the relationship between the state and "its" territory is that between an agent and the principal that authorizes the agent to perform certain functions on the principal's behalf.

Further, insofar as the state also acts on behalf of future generations of the people in preserving the legitimate territory for them, it functions as a trustee, with future generations of citizens as beneficiaries of the trust. To the extent that principal/agent and trusteeship relationships are usually thought of as distinct, it is perhaps most accurate to say that the relationship between the state and the territory partakes of both. 'Territorial sovereignty', therefore, signifies not a property right ascribed directly to the state but, rather, a complex relationship among the state (the agent), the territory, and the people (the principal), with the state acting on the people's behalf to preserve the territory not only for the present but for future generations as well. Territorial sovereignty is best understood as a set of *jurisdictional* powers over territory, conferred upon the state, not as a special kind of property right.

Even in countries such as France or Britain or the United States, where much land is privately owned, there is something called public land (or state land). However, even this is not properly characterized as the property of the state or of government officials. Instead, the state or the government is the *trustee* of the land, on behalf of the people. A trustee who is granted authority to exercise certain forms of control over land is not the owner of the land but, rather, the agent of those who are, and the trustee acts for the benefits of others. In the case of public or state land, whether in a socialist country in which there is little or no private property in land, or in a capitalist country in which much if not most land is privately held, the *trustors*, those on whose behalf the state or government acts as a trustee, are future generations of citizens.

So when a state resists secession on the grounds that it involves a wrongful taking of part of its territory, the basis of its action should be understood as the charge that specific, existing private property rights of various citizens would be violated if secession occurred, and that the taking of whatever public lands are also included in the seceding territory would also deprive the people, understood as an intergenerational community, of that which is theirs and which the state is also supposed to protect.

The distinction between a property right properly speaking and territorial sovereignty also enables us to make sense of a possible situation that would otherwise seem a contradiction in terms. In a state where all land (and natural resources) within the state's borders is privately owned, it would still make sense to talk about the state's territory in the territorial sovereignty sense, even though there would be no state land in the sense of public land—that is, no land directly held by the state in trust. To speak of the state's territory in such a case is not to say that the state owns all the land within the borders. Rather, it is to say that the state is authorized to exercise certain limited forms of control over all the citizens' private property (e.g., the power of eminent domain), and to control the borders surrounding it, so as to discharge the protective functions that are the basis of its authority.

Consideration of this extreme case of total private property helps us to isolate what territorial sovereignty is by avoiding the tendency to confuse it with public land or state property. Territorial sovereignty, as I understand it, is simply the authority to control borders (to regulate entry and exit, and to protect against invasion) and to administer within these borders laws designed to protect property rights and other rights of citizens, including future citizens who will come to exist.

Because territorial sovereignty, at least in modern states, is a form of agency that includes an element of trusteeship, it does not in itself include unlimited, wholly discretionary authority to *change* the borders of the state, any more than I would be authorized to sell a piece of your land that you merely instructed me to manage and conserve for you and your heirs.

The state as agent/trustee may have authority to alienate a part of the territory; but when it does, its reasons for doing so must be compatible with the idea of its being a trustee for the people, conceived of as an intergenerational community. The presumption is that the legitimate territory of the state is to be kept intact. This presumption can be defeated only by weighty reasons, closely connected with the welfare of the people as a whole, and not just the people of the present generation.

If the state is not itself the owner of the territory but, rather, the agent of and trustee for the people, then the authority of the state's actions regarding territory, the moral warrant for its behavior, clearly depends upon the legitimacy of the people's title to the territory. This simple fact has portentous—some will say very disturbing—consequences for the morality of secession. The sobering truth is that even the most cursory "title search" would in most cases reveal that at least some parts of most of the areas over which territorial sovereignty is now claimed were unjustly acquired by conquest, genocide, or fraud.

Marx once remarked that capital comes into the world dripping blood and dirt from every pore. The same can be said of the birth of most states. An appreciation of this fact might lead one to conclude that the justification for secession is easier than one might have first thought. If in so many cases the state's claim to territorial sovereignty is so shaky, then the justification for dismembering the state will be that much easier. There is much truth to this, but matters are not quite so unambiguous. No such simple inference from the dearth of valid titles to territorial sovereignty is warranted for two reasons: First, from the fact that the *state* lacks valid title to the territory it does not follow that the *secessionists* do have valid title; second, precisely because of the dearth of clear titles, there are significant practical and moral considerations that favor adopting a convention that accords substantial weight to existing boundaries, a moral statute of limitations of the sort discussed earlier.

Keeping the foregoing distinctions in mind, I can now offer a tentative answer to the question: Under what conditions are secessionists justified in claiming a right to the territory they wish to sever from the state? Assuming that they wish to establish an independent state of their own, as will usually be the case, the question can also be formulated thus: When does a secessionist group have a justified claim to territorial sovereignty over a piece of land over which the state claims territorial sovereignty? This way of formulating the question makes it clear that the territorial component of a justified secession includes two components, not one: establishing that the state does not have sovereignty over the territory, and establishing that the secessionists do or should have sovereignty over it.

Given the seamy origins of most states, the first step will generally be easier than the second. There are two chief ways in which secessionists might execute the first step: They can argue that the state wrongly acquired the territory, appealing to historical fact to establish an unjust taking (as in the case of the Baltic Republics); or they can try to show that the state lacks clear title even if it did not unjustly take the territory from them.

Consider each alternative. If history reveals not only that the territory was unjustly taken but that it was taken from the secessionists, then, as we saw in the argument from rectificatory justice in Chapter 2, the secessionists have established that the state lacks legitimate title and that they do have a valid title. In other words, this way of executing the first step automatically achieves the second step as well. (The chief complication of this approach is what was referred to earlier as the moral statute-of-limitations problem: Are all historical grievances, no matter how ancient, to have the same moral standing, or should some partly arbitrary convention be adopted to confine the list to "recent" injustices; and if so, how recent?)

Suppose, however, that the state did not unjustly take the territory from the secessionist group. Its title to the territory may be faulty for other reasons. Perhaps the origins of its *de facto* sovereignty over that land are shrouded in the mists of history, or perhaps it acquired all or some of that portion of its current territory through unjust or nefarious means, not from the secessionist group but from some other group or groups. Under such conditions, a strong case could be made for saying that the state does not have a valid claim of territorial sovereignty over the seceding area; but the same might be true of the secessionist group. At least in terms of *historical* entitlement, they, too, may lack clear title.

This may be an accurate description of the situation in Quebec. The claim that English Canada, which forcibly annexed Quebec in an imperial war of naked conquest, lacks valid title to Quebec is much more plausible than the contention that the Quebecois have valid title to all of it. For one thing, the French acquired at least some of the territory in unjust ways from the various Indian tribes (some now extinct, or virtually so, and others readily identifiable) who originally occupied the land. For another, some portions of present-day Quebec were ceded to the province by the English after unification.

Other instances in which neither potential unionists nor potential secessionists can make convincing claims of territorial sovereignty to the seceding area on the basis of historical entitlements are not hard to find. For example, in some parts of South Africa, Bantu-speaking peoples (in particular, Zulus) from the North arrived in sparsely inhabited areas at about the same time that Europeans (Trekboers from the South) did. Both were land-hungry, militaristic, cattle-based societies, and both displaced, subjugated, or killed indigenous populations in their paths. Thus the situation in much of South Africa was not the typical one in which a European colonial power arrived late on the scene and subjugated a large, established native population.[12] One might well conclude, therefore, that history reveals no clear title to territorial sovereignty, at least for some portions of the area that falls within South Africa's borders. Where this is the case, the justification for secession or the lack of it *cannot be decided on grounds of historical entitlement to territory.* Other factors must decide the moral issue. Nevertheless, showing that a "no clear title either way" situation exists removes one obstacle to justifying secession, by refuting the state's claim that secession may be resisted because it would be an unjust taking of the state's legitimate territory.

We have already encountered more than one way in which the case for secession might be made on grounds other than historical entitlement (i.e., by using arguments other than that of rectificatory justice). Suppose that the secessionist group seeks to protect itself against genocide or discriminatory redistribution or wishes to secede to preserve its distinctive culture, or to realize an ideal of small-scale participatory democracy with a strong sense of political community. *If* it were the case that neither the state, the secessionists, nor any aggrieved third party held valid title to the seceding territory, then the primary moral case for secession would thereby be made. Of course, full justification for secession, or a particular path toward secession, would require the satisfaction of other conditions as well. (For example, appropriate compensation for lost investments would have to be made, and reasonable efforts would have to be undertaken to minimize adverse impacts on third parties. And if the secessionists intended to form a society that denied basic individual rights, a condition of recognizing their territorial sovereignty would be to insist on a limitation on it—namely, that citizens of the new, illiberal state must be free to exit it if they wish.)

There is yet another way in which the case can be made that the state does not have valid title. The secessionists can try to show that even though there was no unjust taking in the past, and even though the state has until now had valid title to the territory, *it has now lost it*—it no longer has territorial sovereignty over the seceding area. There are at least two ways in which this loss might occur. First, the state might be persisting in certain forms of injustice against the people of the seceding area—serious discriminatory redistribution or violations of their civil or political rights or equality of opportunity. If secession is the only way to remedy this condition of injustice, then the state's unjust behavior, and by implication the trustors' failure to make their trustee cease perpetrating these injustices, voids the claim of territorial sovereignty, at least to the area in which the victims of the injustices reside.

This conclusion assumes that the secessionists are the chief or sole victims of state-perpetrated injustice. If the government is engaged in wholesale violations of its citizens' rights in the other regions as well, the matter is perhaps murkier. Under such conditions it is clear enough, however, that the citizens in general have a right to revolution, a right to overthrow the unjust government. But whether, upon successful completion of the overthrow of the unjust government, a particular region has the right to form an independent state is another matter. The right to do so is questionable because participation of the citizens in other regions in the overthrow of the government indicates that in perpetrating injustices the government was acting *without the people's authorization*—it was not acting within the terms of its trusteeship. Consequently, the unjust actions of the *government* under these conditions may void not the *trustors'* (i.e., the people's) claim to the territory but only the government's claim to territorial sovereignty. Hence, if secession, not merely revolution, is to be justified in these circumstances, the secessionists must also show that the people have lost their right to the seceding territory. The point is that state-perpetrated injustice does not by itself achieve the voiding of the territorial claim that is the first, necessary condition for justified secession. However, selective, discriminatory injustice toward the people of one region, at least when the rest of the people make no serious effort to prevent the state (their agent) from perpetrating it, can serve to void the claim to territorial sovereignty, thus clearing the first hurdle in the path toward a sound justification of secession.

The second way in which a state that had hitherto enjoyed territorial sovereignty can come to lose it has already been discussed in the prosecessionist argument from self-defense. This argument derives its strength in part from being the political analog of the common-law plea of necessity, as a justification for infringing property rights. As the example of a Jewish sanctuary state in 1939 shows, there are extreme circumstances in which the sanctity of property rights must give way.

To think otherwise is to make a fetish of property rights and to forget that their value and ultimate moral justification rest upon the contribution that respecting them makes to human freedom and well-being.[13] It is worth repeating, however, that in most cases of secession the stakes are not so high. Hence the prosecession argument from self-defense is of very limited applicability.

Whether considerations other than literal survival—such as the need to preserve a distinctive culture—can also void an existing valid claim to territorial sovereignty and generate a new valid claim on the part of a group is, as we have seen, much more controversial. And it should be emphasized that, as we noted in the discussion of the argument from cultural preservation, there are many other measures short of secession (including the establishment of special minority group rights within existing states) that can provide significant protections for minority cultures. So even if the need to preserve a culture can provide a justification for secession in the "no clear title either way" situation (as with parts of South Africa and of Quebec), it is much less convincing to hold that this need supplies a weighty enough reason for voiding a clear title and generating a new valid title on the part of the secessionists.

Given its complexity, it may be useful to summarize briefly the analysis of the territoriality issue provided thus far. Territorial sovereignty is an agency/trusteeship function carried out by the state on behalf of the people as a multigenerational community. It consists of control over borders and the administration of justice (including the protection of property rights) within the borders, and is not strictly speaking state ownership of the land within those borders.

A sound justification for secession has two territorial components: an argument to show that the state either never had or had but has lost territorial sovereignty over the seceding land, and an argument to show that the seceding group either has had or ought now to have territorial sovereignty. The strongest and simplest case for secession, the argument from rectificatory justice, establishes both components at once: By appealing to history, it shows that the state lacks territorial sovereignty over the seceding area because it unjustly expropriated the area from the seceding group, which has a valid claim to it.

Where no argument from rectificatory justice can be made out, establishing the territorial components of a sound justification for secession is more complex and difficult. It is not enough to show that the state lacks territorial sovereignty over the area in question; one must also show that the seceding group (rather than some third party, for instance) has a valid claim to territorial sovereignty. This can be done in either of two ways. First, it can be argued that territorial sovereignty has been *forfeited* because the people on behalf of whom the state acts failed to oppose the state's policy of discriminatory injustice against the seceding group. If secession is the only feasible measure for escaping this injustice, then this fact itself generates a valid claim to territory on the part of the secessionists. Second, it can be argued that the state's right of control over the territory is *overridden* by the necessity of survival for the seceding group, even if the state has perpetrated no positive injustices against it, if the group is the victim of a wrongful threat to its survival by another party, *and* if the state is failing to protect it (as in the example of Polish Jews). In some cases neither the state, the seceding group, nor any existing identifiable third party will have a clearly valid claim of territorial sovereignty over the seceding area. The weak and conflicting territorial claims cancel one another out, so to speak. In such situations the justification for secession must be decided by considerations other than those of territoriality.

VIII. Distributive Justice

The last antisecessionist argument to be considered raises profound and unresolved issues that lie at the core of the theory of distributive justice. More accurately, it forces us to face disturbing questions that are almost invariably passed over even in the most searching and sophisticated theorizing about justice. The most fundamental of these is: To whom are obligations of justice owed?[14]

The situation that forces us to take a stand on this question was mentioned briefly in Chapter 1: The haves are seeking to secede from the have-nots. The recent history of secessionist movements reveals at least two cases that seem to fit this description: The secession of Katanga from the Congo and that of Biafra from Nigeria. (The Slovene secessionist movement in Yugoslavia and the secessionist agitation of the Lombardy Party in Northern Italy may provide others.) In each instance the seceding group enjoys greater natural resources or a more developed, healthier economy, or both (and, in the Italian case, superior cuisine!).

The antisecessionist argument under consideration contends that secession under these circumstances is impermissible because unjust: In attempting to secede, the better off are shirking their obligations of distributive justice to aid the worse off. Once this characterization of the situation is granted, it is but a short step to the conclusion that secession may be resisted with force, since there is at least a strong presumption that force may be used, if necessary, to prevent injustice—in this case, the violation of the worse off's right to a portion of the wealth of the better off.

Notice that there is nothing to prevent successful secessionists from continuing to subsidize the well-being of those in the remainder state after separation has occurred. Of course, in many actual cases in which the better off wish to secede, their primary motivation for doing so will be to end the burdensome sharing of their wealth. The haves' motives for secession need not be so ungenerous, however. Some proponents of Northern Italian secession may be more concerned about what they perceive to be the inefficiency of the Italian government, especially the bureaucracy, and the squandering of the North's contribution to national revenues through poor administration and corruption than with the fact that there is a greater flow of tax revenue from the North to the rest of the country than vice versa. Thus better-off secessionists might simply wish to become politically independent in order to escape the shackles of bad government and to have more control over what they contribute to the welfare of others. They need not be seeking to secede simply in order to avoid any such contribution altogether.

Nevertheless, according to a familiar way of thinking about positive obligations (in this case, obligations to contribute to the welfare of those who are worse off), secession, if successful, would transform the moral scene. For it is often said that our positive obligations to our fellow citizens are much more substantial than those we have toward "strangers"—that is, toward those who are citizens of other states. On the most austere version of this view, the *only* positive obligations of justice we have are toward our fellow citizens. At most, the virtue of charity, not the dictates of justice, prompts us to contribute something to the welfare of those beyond our borders.

Moreover, obligations of charity (if they can be called obligations at all) are quite different from obligations of justice. The former are indeterminate in two ways: The better off have discretion as to how much they contribute (and what form it shall take) and discretion as to whom among the worse off they choose to aid. Further, it is often said that obligations of charity, unlike those of justice, ought not to be forced.

If this familiar way of thinking about the relationship between borders and positive obligations is granted, then the better off can unilaterally transform obligations of justice to their fellow citizens into mere obligations of charity simply by seceding, because doing so will convert fellow citizens into "strangers." The result will be that the better off no longer have determinate, much less enforceable, positive obligations to these individuals any more than to any other "strangers."

A less austere view of the relationship between citizenship and distributive justice yields similar though less extreme consequences. To this way of thinking, the better off do, as a matter of justice (not charity), owe *some* positive assistance to the worse off who are not their fellow citizens; but these obligations are *much less substantial* than those owed to fellow citizens. Even on this more moderate conception of obligations, secession by the better off constitutes a significant moral change: Simply by seceding, the better off can escape the more demanding obligations of distributive justice. In concrete terms the difference might be, say, that before secession the better off have an obligation of distributive justice to contribute 10 percent of their income to their worse-off fellow citizens and 5 percent to the worse off abroad, but after secession justice would require only that they contribute 5 percent to the worse off abroad (who would now include their former compatriots).

The point that these wholly arbitrary figures are designed to illustrate is that an effort by the postsecession better off to discharge their obligations of justice to worse-off strangers in an equitable way might well result in their making a much smaller contribution to their former fellow citizens than they did before secession. On the more moderate interpretation of the moral connections between citizenship and justice, secession does not relieve the better off of obligations of justice altogether, but it does reduce these obligations in general and shrinks the obligation to (former) fellow citizens markedly. The reason is obvious: Once the bonds of citizenship are severed, the worse off who were one's fellow citizens become indistinguishable (from the standpoint of justice) from all the rest of the worse off, and there is no reason why they should receive an especially large share when there are others who are equally or more needy. Thus the contribution that the haves make to their former fellow citizens after secession might be, say, only 1 percent on the moderate view (with the remaining 4 percent of the "justice budget" spread among other "stranger" groups).

The question is whether it is permissible to resist secession by the haves when secession is undertaken in order to reduce obligations to aid those who until secession were their fellow citizens, and to whom, until now, especially robust positive obligations of distributive justice were owed. Is it *unjust* for the better off to secede in order to relieve themselves of at least some of the burdens of distributive justice? If the more prosperous North of Italy tries to secede, would it be justifiable for the South to demand *as a matter of justice* that the North either abort the secession and remain a part of Italy or secede only on the condition that it will continue to support the South at a level of contribution comparable to that which it has hitherto provided?

To answer this question we have to dig deeper. We must ask *why* it is supposed to be the case that obligations of distributive justice among citizens are more demanding than those between citizens and strangers. And this question drives us to the core of distributive justice theory, to a watershed issue that divides competing theories into two radically different types: theories of *justice as reciprocity* and theories of *subject-centered justice*.

According to theories of justice as reciprocity, obligations of justice exist only among those who are *net contributors* to the cooperative surplus. The cooperative surplus is that portion of the total wealth in a society that exceeds the total amount that would be produced if each member produced independently, without cooperating with others. So the basic idea of justice as reciprocity is that justice is strictly a matter of mutual advantage in a very strong and special sense: We have *no* obligations toward those whose level of abilities or resources preclude them from making a positive contribution toward our well-being through cooperation.

If we accept the thesis of justice as reciprocity, then we have an answer—of sorts—to our quandary about the justice or injustice of secession by the haves. According to justice as reciprocity, distributive justice is a relationship among individuals who are contributors within a cooperative scheme, and assertions about what obligations a group has or does not have toward whom are intelligible *only* on the assumption that cooperation is ongoing. Hence justice as reciprocity cannot even in principle supply an answer to the question of whether *justice* requires *continuation* of a cooperative scheme or allows exit from it, as in the case of secession under consideration. For justice as reciprocity, questions about the justice of seceding to form a separate cooperative scheme are ill-formed—they fall outside the domain of justice.

It may be true that justice as reciprocity can recognize some transitional obligations of justice—obligations toward those who have been fellow contributors in the preexisting cooperative scheme during the process of excluding them from the scheme. But justice as reciprocity cannot support the view that justice requires one group to *continue* to include another group in the cooperative scheme when it is no longer to the former group's advantage to do so. So if our theory of distributive justice is of the reciprocity type, we cannot say that there is anything unjust about the better off seceding in order to escape the burdens of discharging obligations of distributive justice, so long as in seceding they form their own separate cooperative scheme and fulfill whatever transitional obligations they may have toward those from whom they disassociate themselves.

Notice just how radical justice as reciprocity is. That conception of the domain of justice cannot account for even what the familiar view about the relationship between citizenship and distributive justice assumes—namely, that we have especially robust obligations toward (all of) our fellow citizens. For not *all* of our fellow citizens are even potentially net contributors in the cooperative scheme. Some have irremediable disabilities that preclude this possibility. So according to justice as reciprocity we do not have obligations of justice at all, much less especially substantial ones, even to all of our fellow citizens, much less to "strangers."

In contrast, subject-centered theories of distributive justice hold that rights of distributive justice are not grounded solely in the individual's capacity to benefit others through cooperation; rather, they are grounded in other morally significant features of the individual herself—for example, in her capacity for moral agency, her ability to have her own conception of what is valuable, or, on some versions of this type of theory, simply her capacity for pleasure and pain. In justice as reciprocity, however, the individual's needs and capacities *as such* (apart from their role in benefiting others through cooperation) *count for nothing*. The difference in types of theories yields profound differences in practical implications: According to justice as reciprocity, severely disabled persons have no rights of distributive justice, whereas this is not the case on most theories of subject-centered justice.

It should also be clear at this point that the two types of theories of distributive justice can yield opposing answers to the question as to whether it is unjust for the haves to secede from the have-nots and then to justify not continuing to contribute to their welfare on the grounds that they are no longer fellow citizens. As we have just seen, according to justice as reciprocity, if secession terminates cooperation, then the obligations of distributive justice are thereby dissolved. So no injustice is done when the haves cease contributing after secession (so long as they discharge whatever transitional obligations they have).

For subject-centered justice, the matter is more complex. This view holds that whether one group owes obligations of justice to another group does not depend solely upon whether they remain in mutually advantageous cooperation with them. But different versions of subject-centered justice may count different features of persons as the basis for obligations and may also differ as to their accounts of the relative robustness of obligations as between different groups. All that can be said in general is that for any theory of the subject-centered sort, the mere fact of secession does not by itself entail the dissolution of obligations of distributive justice. Whether obligations of distributive justice persist after secession—and, if they do, how substantial they are—will depend upon the character of the particular subject-centered theory.

How one might go about deciding which type of theory is true, or, more modestly, which is more plausible, is a very difficult question that I have explored elsewhere.[15] Here I can note only that the harsh implications of justice as reciprocity—in particular, its conclusion that we, the better off, *owe nothing whatsoever* to either the severely disabled in our own society or to people of poor countries from whom we cannot benefit—make it unacceptable from the standpoint of most ethical traditions, whether religious or secular, since these include some duties of aid not based on our own benefit.

Consequently, at least in the court of world opinion, insofar as the latter is influenced by the common core of most ethical traditions, a group of better-off secessionists will probably find it very difficult to gain approval for their actions if they attempt to justify them by appealing to the view that we owe nothing to those with whom we do not choose to cooperate. It is not simply that justice as reciprocity is of little use from the standpoint of intersubjective moral justification (because it clashes so directly with the common core of values that are usually appealed to when groups try to justify their conduct before the court of world opinion). Even worse, no convincing argument has yet been made for why we should reject common-sense morality and adopt justice as reciprocity. In particular, although proponents of justice as reciprocity have attempted to show that this type of view alone is grounded in rationality, where rationality is understood as individual utility maximization, it seems that they have failed to do so thus far. It has not been shown that a rational individual will regard himself as having obligations of justice only to those with whom he engages in mutually beneficial cooperation. Accordingly, I will concentrate on the subject-centered type of view and its implications for secession by the haves.

If we assume that some version of the subject-centered type of theory is correct, then we can say this much, at least, about the case of secession by the haves: Whatever obligations of distributive justice toward fellow citizens have hitherto existed are not dissolved simply by seceding or by otherwise ceasing cooperation. However, if secession is justifiable on other grounds (and we have seen that there are several different sound justifications for secession under certain conditions), then secession by the haves, even where this results in their greatly reducing or even eliminating their contribution to their less fortunate former fellow citizens, need not involve any injustice.

The clearest case would be one in which the justification for secession is that the haves have suffered from discriminatory redistribution. In other words, their contribution to their worse-off fellow citizens has heretofore been exploitive. The state has forced them to contribute a share of their wealth that *exceeds* the demands of distributive justice. If the better off find that the only way to remedy this injustice is to secede, then they are justified in doing so.

Suppose that prior to secession the haves, as a result of discriminatory redistribution, were compelled to contribute 20 percent of their wealth to the have-nots who are their fellow citizens. Suppose that, according to whichever subject-centered theory we adopt, their actual obligation of distributive justice to their fellow citizens was only 5 percent. And suppose that in order to avoid further discriminatory redistribution, the haves secede. According to the familiar view that we owe more to our fellow citizens than to "strangers," the haves, after secession, may be justified in reducing their contribution to their worse-off former compatriots to *below* the 5 percent level. Depending upon the character of the subject-centered view we are assuming, they may have either a much smaller obligation to their former fellow citizens (who are now only one group of "strangers" among many) or no obligations of justice (as opposed to mere charity) at all. In this sort of case, at least, the mere fact that it is the haves who are seceding does not show that secession is unjust, and the fact that the haves will contribute less to the have-nots if they succeed in seceding does not show that it is justifiable to resist secession.

Matters are perhaps less transparent in the case where the haves' justification for seceding is not that they have suffered discriminatory redistribution or some other form of injustice. Consider the case in which the ground for secession is that the seceding group wishes to preserve its own distinctive cultural identity in more pristine form, or simply to enjoy undiluted prosperity and free itself from contributing to a less prosperous population in the rest of the country. *How* it came to be the better-off group may be highly relevant. If its greater prosperity is a result of unjust government preferment —if, for example, it has been the beneficiary rather than the victim of discriminatory redistribution—then its secession may be unjust, unless it pays appropriate compensation to the worse-off group it leaves behind.

This is far from a fanciful scenario. Suppose, for example, that the South of England, which is much more prosperous than the North, were to secede from the North and sever ties with Scotland as well. There is considerable evidence that for several centuries England, and in particular the powerful commercial interests in and around London, engaged in what is called internal colonialism, exploiting Scotland and the northern border region of England.[16] If this is true, then secession by the South would merely compound historical injustices. It would be comparable to a husband enriching himself at the expense of his wife and then divorcing her so as to avoid sharing his wealth with her, and without including compensation in the divorce settlement for his exploitation of her.

However, if there is no such history of injustice, if the greater prosperity of the seceding group is, as it were, untainted, and if all the other requirements for justified secession are met, it is difficult to see why secession by the haves could be considered an injustice simply on the grounds that it will lower the contribution of the haves to the have-nots. In other words, there may well be cases in which it is justifiable for the better off to secede simply in order to pursue their prosperity more effectively, unimpeded by the constraints that being in the same state with the worse off has imposed on them, without basing their justification for secession on any charge that they, the better off, have suffered injustice.

Nonetheless, as already noted, it does not follow that once secession has been accomplished the better off have *no* obligations to those they left behind. First, they will still have whatever obligations the better off in general have to the worse off, and these may include some positive obligations of justice. Second, the fact of long-term interdependence or, rather, the *reasonableness of reliance upon its continuation* on the part of the worse off, may also generate special, though limited, transitional positive obligations on the part of the better off. In principle, these transitional special obligations can be accommodated within a negotiated settlement. If so, they represent a condition on secession rather than an objection against it.

In practice, better-off secessionists will be likely to attempt to occupy the high moral ground by presenting their case as one in which they are seceding to avoid the injustice of discriminatory redistribution, whether or not discriminatory redistribution has actually occurred. "We are struggling to free ourselves from exploitation" is a considerably more stirring battle cry than "We are struggling to become even richer." It will be important, therefore, to deflate such self-serving rhetoric.

However, conflict over whether to accept the former characterization of the grounds for secession rather than the latter need not be simply a strategic exchange of rhetorical missiles. There may be a genuine moral issue here. Whether or not the contribution that the better off have been making to their worse-off fellow citizens is an instance of discriminatory redistribution depends upon whether it exceeds whatever they were required to contribute as a matter of distributive justice. But although there may be considerable agreement across a broad spectrum of ethical traditions and theories that the better off owe *something* to their worse-off fellow citizens (and also a good deal of agreement that whatever it is, it is more than what they owe to citizens of other nations), there is widespread disagreement *and theoretical uncertainty* as to *how much* they owe. In some cases the forced contribution of the better off to the welfare of their worse-off fellow citizens may be so extreme that on any but the most egalitarian theories of distributive justice it will be apparent that discriminatory redistribution is occurring. But in other instances this will not be so.

The problem is not simply that there are a number of competing theories that give incompatible answers to the question of how much the better off owe to the worse off, each with its steadfast adherents. In addition, at least some of the theories of distributive justice currently available may not be determinate enough to distinguish between distributive justice and discriminatory redistribution across the whole range of cases. The difficulty is that the principles of distributive justice they offer are often so abstract that it is difficult to determine their implications in concrete cases.

Quite apart from this problem of application, there is another consideration that should prompt some skepticism about the view that it is justifiable to forcibly resist secession by the haves on the grounds that doing so is necessary to prevent distributive injustice. If the requirements of distributive justice have such imperial authority, why should they not also justify one country *invading* another in order to force it to share its greater wealth with others, in the name of justice, especially since in many cases borders are largely morally arbitrary historical accidents? (Saddam Hussein has suggested that he was doing precisely this in his conquest of Kuwait.)

The quick response, of course, is that only obligations of distributive justice among fellow citizens have this authority, and that either there are no obligations of distributive justice to enforce among citizens of different nations or that whatever obligations exist among citizens of different nations are not so robust as to warrant enforcement. Yet this answer is perhaps not so satisfying in the end, despite the popularity of the familiar view about the privileged status of fellow citizens. For the leading theories of distributive justice—from utilitarianism to Rawlsian contractarianism —ultimately ground individuals' rights to distributive shares in characteristics that people have regardless of their citizenship. In utilitarian theories what ultimately counts is the capacity for pleasure and pain; in Rawlsian theories the capacity to be a chooser of ends, a moral agent with the capacity to form, revise, and pursue her own conception of the good. For such theories, restricting obligations of distributive justice to fellow citizens is sufficiently problematic to make it difficult to assert that the demands of distributive justice justify forcible suppression of secession by the better off, while at the same time denying that the demands of distributive justice justify invading a better-off state to redistribute some of its wealth to the worse off.

Suppose that we set aside the deep problem that we cannot know when redistribution is discriminatory unless we know what distributive justice requires. Suppose (or fantasize) that we know that justice mandates such and such a distribution of wealth in a particular society. Finally, suppose that the actual redistributive policy of the state in that society results in significant departures from that ideal pattern at a certain point in time, and in such a way that one group receives a greater share of social wealth than it would receive were the ideal pattern achieved. Can we conclude that the other group (or groups) are victims of discriminatory redistribution?

Before we could draw this conclusion two further questions would have to be answered. First, what is the proper time-frame for evaluating redistributive patterns? At one point in time or in the short run, a state's redistributive policy might look unjust, yet if a larger time-frame were utilized it might appear to be a perfectly just policy. Different theories of distributive justice may include different accounts of what the proper time-frame is. For example, Rawls's theory does not specify just distributions in terms of single "time-slices" but, rather, in terms of individuals' expectations of social goods over a lifetime.

A second, related question that must be answered before we can infer discriminatory redistribution from a discrepancy between what our favorite principle of justice requires and what various groups are actually getting at any particular time is this: To what extent, or under what conditions, does a government's need to make practical compromises excuse or defeat what would otherwise be valid charges of discriminatory redistribution?

Again an example will help. It has often been remarked that there has been a tendency in the African nations that emerged from colonial domination in the 1960s for the rulers to engage in massive redistribution of wealth from rural populations to urban populations. Typically the justification offered for these policies—which have often been branded unjust and discriminatory—is that they are necessary in order to maintain a strong enough base of support among the urban masses and the urban professional elite to keep the government in power long enough to ensure stability and economic development that will benefit all, including the rural population. (Similarly, Stalin attempted to justify the massive and brutal expropriation of foodstuffs from the Russian and Ukrainian peasantry on the grounds that it was needed to feed the urban populations that were building a better socialist society for all by contributing to the process of industrialization.)

It is no doubt true that in many cases (as with Stalin) such justifications are ideological ruses. Nonetheless, there is a serious moral issue here: To what extent is it permissible to compromise an ideal of distributive justice in the short run in order to ensure its realization in the end?[17] Remarkably, contemporary theorists of distributive justice have little to say about the problem of the proper limits on moral compromise.[18] My purpose, however, is not to engage these perplexing issues but only to emphasize that well-founded allegations of discriminatory redistribution, and hence a justified case for secession on grounds of discriminatory redistribution, require answering some very difficult questions, even if we assume agreement on what distributive justice ideally requires.

What are we to conclude about the antisecessionist argument from distributive justice, after this rather long but unavoidable excursion into the tangled core of the theory of distributive justice? The chief conclusions are these: First, if the haves can make a good case that they have been victims of discriminatory redistribution and that they can remedy this injustice only by secession, then the mere fact that their seceding may worsen even further the condition of the people they leave behind is not itself a decisive objection against secession. Second, even without making good a grievance that they have suffered injustice, the haves may be justified in seceding from the have-nots, and thereby lowering the welfare level of the latter, if they pay appropriate compensation for the have-nots' reasonable reliance on the continuation of a long-standing practice of support.

These conclusions complete our exploration of the moral case for and against secession. Without attempting to give a comprehensive summary of the results of the various arguments pro and con, this much can be said: There is a moral right to secede. It is a limited right, however, because some justifications for secession are sound and some are not, and because there are weighty moral considerations that can rebut the justification for secession in some cases and impose conditions on the process of secession in others. The nature of the scope and limits of the moral right to secede can be better ascertained by investigating how a constitutional right to secede might be framed. That task is taken up in the next chapter.

Notes

1. *Manchester Guardian Weekly*, August 19, 1990, p. 11.

2. Lea Brilmayer, "Secession and Self-Determination: A Territorialist Reinterpretation," *Yale Journal of International Law*, vol. 16, issue 1, January 1991, pp. 177–202.

3. See Ralph E. Boyer, *Survey of the Law of Property*, 3d ed. (St. Paul, Minn.: West Publishing Co., 1981), p. 236.

4. Lincoln's strongest arguments against secession and in favor of resisting it with force, however, did not appeal to the idea of self-defense as such. See the discussions of the strategic bargaining argument and the moral catastrophe argument later in this chapter.

5. See Wayne R. LaFave and Austin W. Scott, Jr., *Criminal Law*, 2d ed. (St. Paul, Minn.: West Publishing Co., 1986), Section 5.7.

6. Abraham Lincoln, address delivered at the dedication of the cemetery at Gettysburg, *Collected Works*, vol. VII, edited by Roy P. Basler, M. D. Pratt, and L. A. Dunlap (New Brunswick, N.J.: Rutgers University Press, November 19, 1863), p. 23.

7. Soft paternalism is paternalist intervention toward individuals, such as young children or the mentally ill, who are not capable of voluntary choice. Hard paternalism is interference with a person's voluntary (or competent) choice, allegedly for his or her own good. The argument under consideration contends that it is sometimes justifiable to resist the efforts of competent individuals to secede if they are seceding in order to establish a regime that will violate the rights of individuals, including those of their children or future generations, who did not competently choose to forfeit those rights, if free exit is not allowed from the rights-violating regime. Resisting the secessionists under these circumstances may be permissible even if the children of the secessionists support the secession, so long as they are not yet competent agents.

8. Ernest Gellner, *Nations and Nationalism* (Oxford: Blackwell, 1983), pp. 44–45.

9. Donald Horowitz, *Ethnic Groups in Conflict* (Berkeley: University of California Press, 1985), pp. 265–266. Michael Hechter, "The Dynamics of Secessionism," unpublished paper, Department of Sociology, University of Arizona, 1990.

10. Peter Aranson, "Calhoun's Constitutional Economics," forthcoming, *Journal of Constitutional Economics*, 1991.

11. Guido Calebresi and A. Douglas Malamed, "Property Rules, Liability Rules, and Inalienability: One View of the Cathedral," *Harvard Law Review*, vol. 85, no. 6, April 1972, pp. 108–128.

12. Leonard Thompson, *A History of South Africa* (New Haven, Conn.: Yale University Press, 1990), pp. 1–109.

13. For what may be the most comprehensive and balanced moral theory of property rights, see Stephen R. Munzer, *A Theory of Property* (Cambridge, U.K.: Cambridge University Press, 1990).

14. The discussion that follows draws on Allen Buchanan, "Justice as Reciprocity Versus Subject-Centered Justice," *Philosophy and Public Affairs*, vol. 19, no. 3, Summer 1990, pp. 227–252.

15. Ibid., pp. 250–252.

16. Michael Hechter, *Internal Colonialism: The Celtic Fringe in British National Development* (Berkeley: University of California Press, 1975), pp. 47–157, 311–316.

17. I am indebted to Dale Jamieson for making me aware of the importance of this issue.

18. I am indebted to Thomas Christiano for calling this to my attention.

4

A Constitutional Right to Secede

I. The Need for a Constitutional Theory of Secession

Preceding chapters clarified the concept of secession, identified different types of secession and conditions under which secession can be attempted, and offered a moral framework that provides substantial (though admittedly incomplete) guidance for resolving disputes about secession. But a moral framework without an appropriate institutional embodiment is merely a moral vision; and vision, though necessary for right action, is far from sufficient. This chapter begins building the bridge from vision to action, from theory to practice, by exploring how a right to secession might be included in one exceptionally powerful institution: the constitution of a modern state.

This is far from being a merely academic exercise. All indications are that we are entering an era of extraordinary constitutional activity. New constitutions are being developed in many quarters and old ones are being modified significantly, often in the context of struggles over secession. Eastern and Central European countries are drafting new constitutions or modifying old ones to accommodate their rising liberal and democratic aspirations, and some of these, such as Yugoslavia (and perhaps Czechoslovakia as well), face crises of secession. The U.S.S.R. itself is frantically enacting constitutional laws to provide structure for—and control over—secession movements in most of the fifteen republics. (Some of the republics themselves contain a number of distinct internal secessionist movements as well. One is reminded of George Will's remark that in the end Gorbachev may be the leader of the Duchy of Muscovy at most.)

Although the Soviet Constitution, as noted earlier, has long included a right to secede, until the current rash of secessionist activity it contained no provisions whatsoever as to how, for what reasons, or under what conditions secession might be undertaken.[1] This was almost certainly due to the fact that Soviet leaders never expected the right to be exercised—never intended to allow it to be exercised.

Other states facing secessionist movements in the future can profit from the Soviets' embarrassment by thinking proactively about constitutional provisions for secession. Chief among these is South Africa. Whether or not a right to secede ought to be included in a new constitution for that country is a difficult question. On the one hand, a realistic appreciation of the ethnic, racial, and ideological diversity of South Africa, along with a recognition that its borders are an artifact of historical accident and white domination, suggests that even a rather loose federal constitution may not suffice. On the other hand, for at least the last forty years the language of ethnicity, group rights, and pluralism has been employed to support a system that denies basic civil, political, and economic rights to the majority. (The most extreme instances of this are the Group Areas Acts, which legally prohibit blacks from working or living in certain areas, and the Black Homelands policy, which relegates blacks to economic and educational backwaters, while hindering their ability to work together for equal citizenship in the urban, First World economy of white South Africa—all in the name of protecting the "integrity of unique ethnic groups.") The anguished question is whether a history of *imposed* ethnic and racial separation in South Africa makes recognition of a *self-chosen* separation, through a constitutional right to secede, too risky.

This much is clear: The prospect of attempts at secession in a number of countries is significant, and developing strategies for coping with them if they occur is more than advisable. As we shall see, even if a constitution does not include a right to secede—indeed, especially if it does not include one—it may be necessary to utilize *other* constitutional devices for dealing with some of the problems of minorities that can lead to secession.

The case of Quebec raises the possibility that one strategy for avoiding secession, the adoption of a loose federal constitution, will not always suffice. The Canadian Federation is one of the most decentralized in the world, with individual provinces enjoying a high degree of autonomy over a wide range of affairs. Yet many Quebecois seek still greater independence, and the resources of the Federal Constitution appear increasingly incapable of accommodating their aspirations. So constitutional reform that replaces a centralized state with a federation does not by itself eliminate the problem of secession; nor does it make exploration of the possibility of a constitutional right to secede otiose. The most that can be said is that the transition from a highly unified state to a federation can address some of the problems that may lead to secession, to some degree.

The impending integration of Europe in 1992 makes this point even clearer. If the proposed political association is looser than a federation (even of the loose Swiss or Canadian varieties), we might call it a *con*federation to mark this difference of degree. It is important to understand that even for a form of union that allows such an extraordinary degree of independence for its members, a constitutional right of secession may still be desirable, if only as a lever for persuading dubious potential members to join. This is especially true (as was observed in Chapter 2 in the ease-of-entry argument) when the political association in question is of an experimental, untried nature. Under these conditions, commitment without advance acknowledgment of the option of exit may be less than prudent. Prior agreement on a right to secede may be the only solution. A constitutional right to secede overcomes the barrier to association that uncertainty raises by creating a satisfactory default position.

Lingering doubts may remain, however, about whether formal recognition of a right to secede may lead to unacceptable political fragmentation, if not outright anarchy. Our earlier response to this worry will become fully satisfactory only when we have seen in more detail what a constitutional right to secede might look like. So the experiment in constitutional design undertaken in this chapter is targeted toward two distinct audiences: those who worry that the idea of a right to secede is too explosive to legitimize, and those who are convinced that there is a right to secede but who see the need for a sensitive institutional embodiment of it.

II. A Framework for Constitutional Design

My purpose here is not to draft a model constitutional law of secession. Any reasonable attempt to do so would have to be limited to drafting a law of secession *for a particular constitution*, for at least two reasons. First, there is a requirement of internal constitutional consistency: A provision for secession would have to be substantively and procedurally compatible with the rest of the constitution. Second, just as different countries usually require different constitutions, they will also require different constitutional laws concerning secession, depending upon the particular facts about their current conditions, history, and moral-political traditions. So what I offer here is no do-it-yourself political divorce kit.[2]

What I do propose is a structured way of thinking about the issues that responsible drafters of a constitution that includes a right of secession ought to take into account and a sketch of alternative prototypes for such a right, along with some reflections on their comparative advantages and disadvantages. Because a right to secede is not the only alternative for dealing with conflicts of interest among groups within the state or between the state and a group within it, the comparison must be even broader: Whether there should be a constitutional right to secede depends in part upon what special advantages this right has *vis à vis* other constitutional provisions for coping with the same problems. In particular, it will be fruitful to contrast the constitutional right to secede with the right of group veto (whereby a constitutionally recognized group—say, a province, canton, or state within a federation—may unilaterally block the enactment of federal laws) and the right of nullification (which allows a constitutionally recognized group to void a federal law within that group's jurisdiction only).

From time to time, as we go about this relatively modest task, it may prove useful to employ in an informal way a certain thought experiment that some philosophers and philosophically minded economists have attempted to elevate into a rigorous technique for logically deriving constitutional principles.[3] I refer to the idea that we are to think of an ideal constitution as what would be chosen or agreed upon by rational parties to a hypothetical constitutional convention who are behind a "veil of ignorance"—that is, who are deprived of certain knowledge that might bias their deliberations and hence the constitutional rules they choose.[4]

For example, it has been suggested that when considering what sort of principles rational persons would choose we should exclude from their imagined deliberations any knowledge of their gender, race, social class, age, which generation they belong to, and even the content of their conception of the good, the concrete nature of their preferences and goals.

The usual explanation for including this informational constraint is that it is a device to help ensure *inter*personal impartiality or objectivity—fairness between different persons. Thus, if one does not know whether one is black or white, male or female, rich or poor, young or old, one cannot use that information to tailor principles to one's own special advantage. (For example, if one knew one was a white male, one might choose a set of principles that did not include a principle of equality of opportunity; or if one knew one were a member of the wealthiest class, one might choose a principle of distributive justice that guaranteed the inviolability of existing property rights.)

In the case of choosing constitutional principles, we should strive for interpersonal impartiality not only among members of the present generation of constitutionmakers but future generations as well. Hence a good constitution will not be too closely tied to the concrete needs and preferences of the present generation; it will be flexible enough and broad enough to allow for change.

Though some proponents of the veil-of-ignorance technique have failed to emphasize it, there is another, quite distinct rationale for its use: It helps ensure what might be called *intra*personal impartiality.[5] If a person does not utilize such concrete and particular information about himself in his deliberations, then his choice will not be influenced by transient or temporally parochial factors. For example, it is generally unwise for a young person to choose a college exclusively on the basis of her current, concrete interests, at the time of application, because her interests may change. This is but one instance of the fact that persons can, over time, revise even some of their more fundamental goals. Similarly, quite apart from the need to secure interpersonal impartiality (fairness among different persons or groups), it is important for constitutional principles and principles of political order generally to be able to accommodate changes in the individual's preferences and needs or those of his group.

This simple truth has significant implications for how we are to think about framing a constitutional right to secede. We should attempt to limit ourselves to arguments that proceed from the perspective of the citizen in general, rather than from that of either the secessionist or the antisecessionist exclusively. In other words, as ideal constitutionmakers, we should not assume that we will be part of a group that will wish to secede nor members of one that seeks to block secession. Instead, we must strive for the broader and longer view, thinking of the constitution as a document made to last and constructed to give due weight to all legitimate interests, not just of the present but of the future as well.

In earlier chapters we saw that there can be legitimate interests that favor secession (e.g., the interest in avoiding discriminatory redistribution, in reappropriating stolen territory, or in preserving a culture) and legitimate interests aligned against secession (e.g., the interest in the integrity of majority rule and in political stability). So there is a sense in which the perspective of the citizen in general must incorporate *both* points of view. Further, our deliberations must somehow take into account the possibility that we (or our children or grandchildren) may come to be secessionists or antisecessionists or both at different times. Hence it is appropriate that both the secessionist and antisecessionist perspectives be represented in the choice of constitutional principles, but that neither be exclusively represented.

In what follows, contrasting models of a constitutional right to secede will be sketched in bold relief. Then hybrid models utilizing elements drawn from each of the simpler and more extreme models will be articulated and evaluated from the standpoint of the moral reflections on secession developed in Chapters 2 and 3. Finally, the desirability of a constitutional right to secede will be compared with the desirability of the right of group veto and the right of nullification.

III. Two Pairs of Ideal Type Models for a Constitutional Right to Secede

The purpose of these models is simply to help structure the options for developing frameworks within which a constitutional right to secede might be formulated. I refer to the alternative models for a constitutional right as ideal types to indicate that they are logical extremes, patterns in bold relief, intended as *starting points, not recommendations*. It will soon become evident that features from each may be combined in any of several hybrid approaches.

A. The Substantive Model

In this ideal type, the connection between the morality of secession and the constitutional right is most direct. The constitutional right is to be formulated so as to specify all and only the sound moral justifications for seceding. Chief and least controversial among these would be that the group wishing to secede has been treated unjustly—its territorial sovereignty has been violated; or it has suffered discriminatory redistribution, or its members have been denied equality of opportunity, or their individual or states' rights have been violated; and forms of redress other than secession are not available. In this model, the applicability of one or more of the constitutionally recognized substantive justifications for secession is a necessary condition for exercising a constitutional right to secede.

B. The Procedural Model

According to this approach, a group wishing to secede need not establish that any substantive justification for seceding is applicable. Instead, only various constitutionally specified procedural requirements must be satisfied. For example, three-quarters of the eligible voters in the region must vote for secession and a waiting period of such and such length must pass.

Clearly, some procedural requirements are more plausible, morally speaking, than others. For example, recent Soviet legislation designed to specify that country's long-standing but contentless constitutional right to secede includes at least one provision that is inappropriate: A Soviet Republic may secede only if a strong majority of all the other republics and of the Politburo vote in favor of secession. If one of the chief reasons that a group seeks to secede is that it sees no other remedy for the injustice of discriminatory redistribution, as is so often the case in actual secession movements and seems to be the case with Lithuania, then this particular procedural requirement virtually ensures that they will not be allowed to secede. The same disregard for their interests that led to discriminatory redistribution in the first place is likely to result in a refusal to approve their bid for secession. The exploiters are not likely voluntarily to deprive themselves of their ill-gotten gains.

The substantive and procedural models embody presumptions about the legitimacy of secession or, more precisely, about where the burden of proof lies for establishing legitimacy. The substantive model expresses a presumption in favor of continued union and against secession: Secessionists must make a substantive case, showing that one of the approved justifications for dissolving the union applies. In that sense adoption of a substantive approach expresses a certain conservatism, an inclination not to risk tampering with the political *status quo*, at least so far as the existing boundaries of the state are concerned. The substantive approach assigns the burden of argument to the secessionists. They must show why they ought to be allowed to secede.

In contrast, the procedural model assumes the legitimacy of secession in principle, or at least embodies no presumption against its legitimacy. The procedural model does not require anyone to make a substantive case for secession; it places no burden of argument on the secessionists. Instead, it is as though the proceduralist merely says: If you wish to secede, you must first do this and this. This presumption may be construed as an expression of a less conservative attitude, due either to a lower estimate of the risks of disturbing the political *status quo* or to a conviction that the interests that secession can serve are of such importance that greater risks are worth taking.

If, as has just been suggested, the procedural model embodies a presumption in favor of secession, not requiring that a case be made for it, what could be the justification for having procedural requirements? In other words, if the assumption is that secession requires no justification, why impose procedural hurdles? Our earlier discussion of the rationale for surmountable obstacles to the exercise of a right to secede provides a first reason. In Chapter 3 we saw that even if we grant (as the procedural model does) that the interest in seceding is a legitimate interest requiring no justification, there can be opposing, equally legitimate interests—in particular, the interest in preserving the integrity of majority rule against strategic bargaining (and the interest in avoiding fragmentation that may increase dangers to national security by reducing the scale of the political unit below that required for adequate self-defense). There it was argued that what is needed is a way of balancing these interests, and that one way to accomplish this acrobatic feat is to adopt procedural constitutional hurdles that secessionist initiatives must clear (e.g., requiring a three-quarters majority in favor of secession among those within the area in question).

That argument can now be elaborated. Another approach to protecting the integrity of majority rule while allowing secession would be a constitutional law imposing *special exit costs* on secessionists—financial burdens over and above whatever is required by distributive justice in the political analog of the fair-property settlement in divorce. Thus, in addition to compensating the state (or the people whose agent it is supposed to be) for investments lost as a result of secession, the secessionists might also be required to pay an exit fee, a secession tax.

A special exit cost is a less familiar form of constitutional obstacle, but it can be viewed as simply another device for achieving the same end: a reasonable balancing of two important interests, one in majority rule, the other in secession. The purpose of using either or both of these devices is to reduce the bargaining force of the threat of secession, but to do so *without* rendering the right to secede impotent in practice. Only if the interest in preserving strict majority rule *always* outweighed the interest in secession would the need to avoid strategic bargaining (or to reduce the frequency of its use) support an outright denial of the right to secede. But to assume that the former interest always trumps the latter would be to overestimate the value of majority rule—to accord it virtually unconditional value.

Second, and quite apart from the need to constrain the use of the threat of secession in strategic bargaining, *all parties*, potential secessionists as well as those who may resist secession, will find it valuable to erect some obstacles to secession. As already argued, for reasons of both interpersonal and intrapersonal impartiality, parties to an ideal constitutional convention are to be conceived as not knowing whether they will turn out to be secessionists or unionists. However, it is crucial to understand that *both* groups or, more accurately, all citizens, as such, have an interest in making sure that secession will not be too easy. As the political sociologist Albert O. Hirschmann has noted, where *exit* from an association is virtually costless, there is little incentive to exercise the option of *voice*—the use of critical dialogue within the association to improve the quality of its performance.[6] It is in the interest of all citizens to avoid premature termination of criticism from within.

Similarly, parties to an ideal marriage contract (a two-person, domestic constitutional convention) might create obstacles to divorce (if existing obstacles were inadequate) in order to provide themselves with incentives to work through problems in the relationship rather than bolting at the first sign of crisis. In most if not all societies, substantial exit costs already exist in the case of marriage, in the form of financial loss for one or both parties, social stigma, potential harm to children (about whom both parties are presumed to care), or all of these. The deliberate creation of such incentive mechanisms as well as the act of utilizing exit costs provided by existing social and legal practices are instances of the more general phenomenon of *self-binding*, which we encountered earlier in the discussion of strategies that a group might use to preserve its cultural identity. (For example, a minority group might pass a law requiring that all its members use the group's own language in school and business.)

A third reason for including procedural requirements in a constitutional right to secede is to supply some test by which legitimate subjects for the right to secede can be identified and to determine when a legitimate group is actually committed to secession. Thus a constitutional right to secede in a federal system like that of Switzerland might include the requirement that three-quarters of the voters in a canton must vote in favor of secession before it can occur. The problem of designing constitutional procedures of this sort will be dealt with later in this chapter.

Once these three rationales for erecting hurdles to the exercise of a right to secede are appreciated, it becomes obvious that it is quite consistent to accept the presumption in favor of the legitimacy of secession that the absence of any substantive requirement expresses and yet require significant procedural hurdles. It may be appropriate to combine elements of the procedural and substantive approaches, requiring that secessionists not only provide a constitutionally approved substantive justification but also that they clear certain procedural hurdles. There is no inconsistency here, because the reason for insisting on procedural hurdles is quite independent of the fact that a successful substantive justification has established the legitimacy of the interest in seceding.

C. The Fault Model

This approach is a special version of the substantive model. It holds that secession is legitimate only if a substantive justification of a particular sort can be made out: The secessionists must be shown to have been treated *unjustly* by the state. We have already seen that the sort of injustice that often provokes and can sometimes justify secession is not limited to violations of individual rights. Valid grounds for secession can also include discriminatory redistribution, violations of so-called states' rights (the legitimate, constitutionally specified authority of political units within a state or federation), and violations of special minority group rights (e.g., language rights). Under the fault model, only those substantive justifications that involve injustice on the part of the state count as constitutional grounds for secession. The need to preserve cultural identity as such would not count as a legitimate justification for secession, nor would a group's desire to found an autonomous, small-scale democratic community.

D. The No-Fault Model

Any constitutional law of secession that exemplifies the procedural approach is *a fortiori* an instance of the no-fault model. Since the procedural approach requires no substantive justification at all, it also does not require the sort of substantive justification which establishes that the state has perpetrated injustice. However, a constitutional law on secession that was substantive rather than procedural might not require that the substantive justification be the special sort that establishes injustice by the state.

A constitution might recognize some "no-fault" substantive justifications but not others. For example, it might acknowledge the need to preserve cultural identity as a legitimate justification, while refusing to accord justificatory legitimacy to the desire to form a new type of democratic community. Yet recognizing the legitimacy of the need to preserve cultural identity as a justification for secession need not imply that anyone, including the state, is at fault for the precariousness of the group's cultural survival. This approach is called no-fault to emphasize that it does not require a *grievance* against the state. (Similarly, no-fault divorce requires no grievance against the other party. The analogy with no-fault versus fault divorce implied here is merely heuristic—it is an analogy, not an identity, and no assumption is made as to which is the preferable approach to divorce.)

It should be obvious that some of these approaches are mutually compatible. A constitutional law of secession might be of the no-fault, substantive type and yet include some procedural requirements. In other words, it would both require an approved substantive justification (though not require that it be of the injustice variety) and mandate certain procedures before secession was achieved. The possibility of such hybrids raises an interesting question: Are there certain combinations that are more appropriate than others?

Here the moral views on secession developed earlier offer substantial guidance. Recall that they included two highly relevant principles. The first is that among the sorts of injustices that can justify secession must be included not only violations of individual rights but also discriminatory redistribution. The second is that the moral justification for secession is not limited to injustice perpetrated by the state from which secession is desired; other reasons, such as the need of a group to preserve itself against threats to its survival by a third-party aggressor or the need to preserve its cultural identity, can, under certain highly constrained conditions, supply sound justifications for secession as well.

The first principle implies that it is morally arbitrary to restrict the constitutionally approved justifications for secession to violations of individual rights. The second implies that a pure substantive approach of the fault variety would also be morally defective because it would fail to recognize some sound moral justifications for secession. In other words, our earlier moral reflections on secession dictate that *if* a substantive approach to the constitutional right to secede is taken, the list of constitutionally approved substantive justifications for secession ought not to be restricted to grievances against the state.

Notice, however, that these moral principles do *not* dictate that a substantive approach be adopted. Although our moral position holds that some substantive justifications are *sufficient* for secession (at least when the conditions for a fair property settlement are satisfied), it does *not* imply that a sound substantive justification is *necessary*. A state may allow secession if it wishes, unless its doing so would violate the conditions of its trusteeship. So if the state wishes to take a purely procedural approach it may do so, so long as it does so in such a way as to ensure compensation to those in the remainder state when it is due, and so long as the process of secession is handled in such a way that morally unacceptable consequences to third parties are avoided. Nothing in the preceding moral arguments for or against secession implies that it is necessary to require a substantive justification from those who wish to secede. The use of appropriate procedural hurdles can adequately accommodate the legitimate interests that speak against secession. So although moral concerns do not dictate a substantive approach, they do indicate that if a substantive approach is used, the full range of sound moral justifications ought to be included.

The only duty the state has that might be thought to imply that secession as such ought to be resisted is its duty to be a good steward of the collective territory and resources of the people as an intergenerational community. But this duty applies only on the assumption that the state, or rather the people for whom it serves as steward or trustee, is (are) in fact the rightful owner(s) of the seceding territory. In many cases, as we have seen, this will not be so. Even when title to the territory is clear, however, fulfillment of the duty of stewardship may be consistent with allowing secession, because proper management of the collective property (and adequate protection of citizens' private property) may be compatible with transferring jurisdiction over the land to the secessionists in exchange for proper compensation.

Some still may not be convinced, however, that any reasons other than a grievance of state-perpetrated injustice provide a sound justification for secession. They may feel, for example, that the "mere" need to preserve cultural identity, even when all the additional conditions specified in Chapter 2 are met, is never sufficient.

Suppose for a moment that this rather conservative view is correct: that a constitutional right to secede should state that secession is legitimate only when the secessionists are the victims of injustice at the hands of the state. Relatively uncontroversial, common-sense moral judgment nonetheless places some constraints on the manner in which this sort of narrow substantive approach may be combined with procedural requirements. Fairness and sensitivity to the plight of the victims of injustice speak in favor of *minimizing* whatever procedural hurdles are added to a fault requirement of the special sort that requires the secessionists to establish that they have been treated unjustly. Where this special substantive justification applies, secession is a way, perhaps the only effective way, of remedying a serious injustice. Hence it is unfair to place further obstacles in the path of those who are seeking this last resort for freeing themselves from injustice. Onerous procedural obstacles merely compound the injustice, or at least make it harder for its victims to achieve justice under precisely those circumstances in which their only hope is to do so by their own efforts. It is the role of the state to ensure justice. When the state perpetrates injustice and refuses to desist from doing so, leaving the victims with secession as their only respite, whatever legitimate interest the state has in erecting constitutional obstacles to secession pales in comparison with the victims' interest in securing justice.

Conversely, if a no-fault model is adopted, it is easier to make a case for *higher* procedural hurdles, because there is no substantive requirement serving to screen out some bids for secession. In other words, the use of substantive criteria does some of the work that procedural hurdles do. So where there are no substantive requirements to constrain the exercise of the right to secede, the case for more significant procedural hurdles is correspondingly stronger. If substantive criteria are not used, as in the pure no-fault model, then the prospect of purely strategic or even frivolous invocations of the right to secede increases. Other things being equal, then, the more stringent the substantive criteria, the lower the procedural hurdles should be; and the less demanding the substantive criteria, the higher the procedural hurdles.

It follows that a demanding substantive criterion with no procedural requirements (or very undemanding ones), on the one hand, and a purely procedural secession law with demanding procedures, on the other, might be functionally equivalent. Secession might be just as easy (or as difficult) under the one approach as under the other.

Although a purely procedural approach is morally permissible, it might be thought that including a requirement of substantive justification is morally preferable because it more directly mirrors the moral facts about secession. Nevertheless, there is one important consideration that, under certain circumstances, can tip the balance in favor of a purely procedural right, with no requirement of substantive justification. It may be called the *biased referee argument*. The argument has two main premises. The first is that laws are not self-interpreting and that determining whether substantive standards for justification are met in a given case is usually more controversial, more dependent upon the exercise of judgment, than ascertaining whether procedural requirements are met. The second is that where there is room for controversy about the satisfaction of legal requirements there is also room for bias and that a minority seeking to secede is more likely to be the victim than the perpetrator of a biased judgment about whether the substantive standard has been met.

This argument in favor of exclusively procedural requirements is all but conclusive if one grants the further assumption that the arbiter of secession, the agent to decide whether the substantive criteria are met, is the more powerful of the two interested parties—namely, the state—*and* if it is also assumed that the state is a monolithic institution likely to be opposed to secession.[7] However, the edge of the biased referee argument is considerably dulled if the constitution provides that the judiciary (say, the Supreme Court) is to determine whether the substantive criteria for secession are met *and* if the judiciary is *in fact* sufficiently *independent* of state interests of the sort that are likely to oppose secession.

Now, whether the judiciary will be sufficiently independent to make reliance on potentially disputable substantive criteria for secession workable will vary, not only from country to country but also within the same country at different times in its history. At least when designing a constitutional right to secede for a country lacking an independent judiciary or one in which the continued independence of the judiciary in the foreseeable future is problematic, the safer course is to forswear substantive criteria altogether or, at a minimum, to utilize only those that are least controversial and hence least abusable.

An alternative response to the biased referee problem would be to include in the constitution a requirement that when disputes about the satisfaction of substantive criteria arise, the matter is to be submitted to arbitration by an international tribunal of some sort. No doubt many states will be reluctant to delegate such power to others. However, if international law comes to recognize systematically a right to secede and to develop appropriate institutional arrangements, this reluctance might be diminished.

IV. The Problem of Representation

The reflections on the morality of secession offered in Chapters 2 and 3 left a number of issues unresolved. Among these is what may be called the *problem of representation*. As indicated earlier in this chapter, two distinct problems fall under this heading. First, what sorts of groups are *prima facie* candidates for secession? In other words, are there conditions that a group must satisfy before it even has standing as the sort of group that might make a justified case for seceding? (Call this *the problem of legitimate status*.) Second, assuming that these conditions are satisfied, such that a legitimate group is identified, what further criteria must be satisfied if we are to say that the group chooses to secede? (Call this *the problem of authentic voice*.) For example, suppose that we believe Lithuania to be the sort of unit that can in principle make a justified case for secession—in other words, that Lithuanians, citizens of Lithuania, have legitimate status with regard to the possibility of secession. There is still the further question of how we are to ascertain whether the desire for secession voiced by some citizens of Lithuania should be taken to signal that Lithuania or, more accurately, the Lithuanian people choose to secede. If there is to be a constitutional right to secede, it will have to take a stand on both the issue of legitimate status and that of authentic voice. In a constitution for a federation, the most obvious way to answer the question of legitimate group status is to include in the constitutional rules concerning secession a stipulation that ascribes the right of secession to states in the federation (e.g., Soviet Republics, to which the Soviet Constitution ascribes the right to secede; or Canadian Provinces, or American States, or Swiss Cantons). In many real-world cases of secession, groups seeking to secede will already constitute a recognized political subunit within the state from which it strives to become independent, as with Lithuania, Serbia, or Quebec; and the same considerations that speak in favor of recognizing them as distinct units within a federation will help make the case for ascribing a right to secede to them, assuming that such a right is to be included in the constitution.

All of this makes a certain amount of sense, but only on the assumption that the current division into political subunits adequately captures all the groups that can have a legitimate interest in secession. If, on the contrary, the division into states or provinces or cantons leaves some important groups without a recognized political unit, then a constitutional right to secede that is ascribed only to those units will not suffice. Moreover, even if the current division of subunits now accords status to all important groups, that can change. This line of argument suggests that if a constitution includes a right to secede, it should also provide criteria or procedures whereby hitherto unrecognized groups can acquire legitimate status, standing as groups to whom the right to secede can be ascribed.

In other words, if the real question in disputes about secession is whether a particular group *ought* to be allowed to become independent from the state and exercise sovereignty over its own territory, then we cannot assume that only those groups to which the state *already* happens to accord a degree of independence are the only suitable candidates. At least from a moral point of view, there is no reason to assume that the right to secede can be properly ascribed only to groups that already have official political status as territorially based subunits.

If, for example, Lithuania, upon being annexed to the Soviet Union, had not been accorded the status of a republic but had been merged into the Latvian Soviet Republic, this would not diminish the moral force of the case for Lithuanian secession, because Lithuania was a sovereign nation at the time of annexation. In this type of case, the nature of the justification for secession—the charge of a historical violation of a state's territorial sovereignty—itself answers the question of legitimate status.

However, even if prior sovereignty is sufficient for legitimate status, it is not obviously necessary. The mere fact that a group has not achieved sovereignty in the past should not preclude it from being a legitimate candidate for being sovereign now.

It seems, therefore, that a constitution that includes a right to secede should also contain not only means for identifying which of the existing political subunits are suitable subjects for a right to secede but also a way of specifying how a group can come to have this status if it currently lacks it. The difficulty is that there seems to be no *general*, principled answer to the problem of legitimate group status. Any constitutional specification of what counts as a legitimate group will be arbitrary to a greater or lesser degree.

Nevertheless, there is one approach that, though far from fully satisfying, may be preferable to the alternatives. It proceeds on the assumption that legitimate status regarding secession is *derivative* upon constitutional status *for other purposes*. Now, in a well-designed constitution, the highest-level subunits in the system (states or provinces or cantons in a federation) will be those units that should enjoy the greatest degree of independence —the ones that already most closely approximate the conditions for being recognized as sovereign political units. But if this is so, then the rationale for recognizing a unit as being among the highest-level units recognized by the constitution will also be a rationale for according it status as a unit to whom the right to secede can be ascribed, *if* the constitution is to include a right to secede.

In other words, there is no need for a separate solution to the problem of legitimate status regarding secession. The rationale for the constitutional recognition of highest-level subunits itself already contains the answer to the problem of legitimate status if the constitution is well designed.

In contrast, if the existing list of highest-level subunits is inadequate —if some group has a good case for being added to the list—then the same sorts of familiar arguments to show that the list should be expanded will also provide reasons for ascribing a right to secede to those additional groups, if there is to be a constitutional right to secede. So the solution to the problem of legitimate status piggy-backs on the solution to a more familiar problem of constitutional design, that of selecting appropriate highest-level political subunits. If secession is the limiting case of independence (full sovereignty), and if a sound constitutional system provides a hierarchical system of political subunits arranged according to different degrees of independence, then the right to secede from the entire system should be accorded (and only accorded) to the highest-level subunits.

Hence, to make a case for having legitimate status with regard to secession in a system that recognizes a right of secession, a group must simply show that it ought to be recognized as one of the highest-level political units in the system. If it succeeds in doing so, it should also be recognized as a unit to whom the right to secede can be ascribed. (It is another matter altogether, of course, as to whether it can also make the case that it satisfies the constitutional criteria [procedural and/or substantive] for successfully exercising the right, and hence, that it ought to be allowed to secede.) This is not to say that the problem of identifying legitimate groups for purposes of secession is anything less than forbidding; rather, the point is that it is not a *new* problem, if we adopt the piggy-back approach.

Of course, the problem of legitimate status is not confined to the case in which the constitution recognizes a right to secede. I have argued that there is a moral right to secede (even where there is no constitutional right), and so the question arises as to which groups are the sorts of entities that can have this right.

It appears that any proposal for a general set of substantive and nontrivial criteria for picking out all and only those groups to which a right to secede can properly be ascribed is doomed to failure. (One could say that the right to secede may be ascribed to groups that have the right to form their own completely independent, that is, fully sovereign, political units—but this would be utterly trivial and circular.) The moral theory of secession advanced here attempts to offer no such general criterion. Instead, it holds that a proper account of the various justifications for secession determines which groups have the right: namely, those that satisfy the conditions for justification. On this view, then, the notion of legitimate status is derivative upon that of a sound justification for seceding. There is no independent concept of legitimate status.

The problem of authentic voice is, if anything, more vexing than that of legitimate status. Even if we have properly identified a legitimate group to which to ascribe the right to secede, there will still be a degree of ineliminable arbitrariness in any proposal for what counts as the authentic voice of the group. Should a two-thirds majority in favor of secession suffice? Or is three-quarters necessary?

Note that the problem of authentic voice is more acute if the system from which a group wishes to secede is one that has prevented the members of the group from selecting representatives to voice their desire for independence. For example, when Turkey forcibly annexes part of Kurdistan or Armenia and then refuses to recognize Kurds or Armenians as having legitimate political standing and prevents this group from developing mechanisms of representation for its members' preferences, Turkey then cannot justifiably dismiss Kurdish and Armenian demands for secession on the grounds that those who voice them have no legitimate standing to represent those people. In some cases a free referendum will allow direct knowledge of the group's preferences, and this will be especially appropriate where no legitimate mechanisms for representation exist.

However, the referendum approach has its own problems. In some actual cases of secession, deciding the issue simply on the basis of the results of a referendum would merely compound historical injustices. For example, as Mr. Gorbachev is fond of pointing out, approximately 48 percent of the population of Latvia is non-Latvian. Those of a suspicious bent of mind will infer that there is more than a coincidental connection between this fact about the demography of Latvia and Gorbachev's insistence that a two-thirds (66.6 percent) majority should be required for secession. What he fails to mention is that the vast majority of this 48 percent are Russians, most of whom are, or are children or grandchildren of, persons who were moved into Latvia as colonists to secure Soviet control over the area after it was forcibly annexed in 1940.

This type of situation is all too common. In many cases secession is an attempt to gain independence from a state (in the Soviet case, an empire) that unjustly annexed the territory in question, and annexation is often followed by *colonization*. If the question is whether the group that was wronged ought to be allowed to reclaim its sovereignty, then neither the colonists nor their descendants have any legitimate voice in that decision. They should be disqualified from voting in the referendum. Whether those non-Latvians who played no part in the original injustice should be compensated for their losses if they are expelled from the newly independent Latvia, or whether a condition of permitting secession should be that all who are currently Latvian citizens (Russians included) are accorded full citizenship rights after secession, is a separate matter.

Deciding who is a "true" Latvian and who is a Russian Latvian may, however, turn out to be difficult. (Genotyping from blood samples would enable the distinction to be made in a relatively accurate and objective way—if it is correct to assume that Latvians are a distinct biologically related group and if those administering the tests or reporting their results could be trusted. Because *other* genetic information would also be attainable from the same blood sample, there are serious issues of privacy that raise questions about the propriety of this approach.)

Even where there is no danger of a tainted referendum, the problem of deciding how strong a majority in favor of secession should be required still remains. There is no magic figure, whether it be two-thirds, three-quarters, or seven-eighths. The most that can be said is this: The higher this particular procedural hurdle is, the lower should be the other hurdles, other things being equal. Without minimizing the problem of arbitrariness, it is useful to remind ourselves that the same problem arises in any area in which majority rule is used—from the enactment of particular laws, to constitutional amendments, to the initial ratification of constitutions.

V. A Right to Secede Versus Other Constitutional Rights for Groups

In Chapter 1 I noted that in addition to a right to secede there are at least two constitutional rights that can help overcome reluctance to enter new and untried forms of political association by limiting the commitment of those who might otherwise not enter them: the group veto right and the right of nullification. The former is the right of a group to veto legislation; the latter is the right of a group to void a law in (only) its jurisdiction. Each of these latter rights can serve other purposes as well. Like the right to secede they can serve to protect minorities in a number of ways. They can be exercised in order to *prevent* certain injustices from being perpetrated against a minority. For example, if a piece of tax legislation would constitute discriminatory redistribution against a member state in a federation, the group veto allows the potential victims to block that legislation. If the law can achieve its unjust distributive effects only by taking tax money from people in a certain area, then the right of nullification allows them to void the offending tax law in their area. So secession is only one way of responding to such injustices.

Moreover, even when no injustice is at issue, nullification and veto can be valuable tools for protecting groups' interests. For example, if an ethnic group possessed the right of group veto, it could block attempts to make another group's language the official language of the country. These three constitutional rights may be contrasted with another way of limiting commitment to collective decisions in a political association and of responding to abuses of government power: the right to revolution. This right is generally conceived of as a purely moral right, not a constitutional right. One reason for this is obvious: The decision to revolt is tantamount to a rejection of the constitutional approach to conflicts, an admission that political processes are beyond redemption.

Each of the three constitutional rights has this advantage over the extraconstitutional, purely moral right to revolution: In principle, each can be exercised without utterly rejecting the authority of the government and without forsaking politics for naked force. Yet if each of these three constitutional rights can, under certain circumstances, serve the same functions of limiting commitment and protecting minorities, what is there to recommend the right to secede as opposed to either of the other two? Whether or not an ideal constitution would include a right to secede depends upon the comparative advantage or disadvantage of including that right rather than either or both of the other two rights. How are we to decide where the comparative advantage lies?

What is needed is a thorough investigation of the comparative advantages and disadvantages of these alternative constitutional devices. This in turn requires the development of a set of criteria for assessing the preferability of one device over the other. Here I will only begin that process. My purpose is not to argue that a good constitution must include a right to secede but simply to make a strong case for taking secession seriously as a reasonable constitutional alternative and to offer guidance for formulating a right to secede if that option is taken.

What makes the process of assessment complex, as we shall presently see, is that we get *opposite rankings* of the three constitutional rights, depending upon which perspective we adopt—that of potential exercisers of the right or that of those who may oppose its exercise. The chief factors that determine the relative preferability of each right from the standpoint of the potential exerciser of that right are (1) *the independence-effect* (the degree of independence or control that its successful exercise would bring to the exerciser) and (2) *the exercise-difficulty* (the product of the cost of exercising the right and the probability that an attempt to exercise it will not be successful). From the perspective of those who may resist exercise of the right, the chief factors determining relative preferability can be lumped together under the heading of (3) *the disruption-effects* (the negative effects that the exercise of the rights respectively has on the political *status quo*). The meaning of these criteria will become clearer as we employ them in the comparative evaluation of the right to secede, the right of group veto, and the right of nullification.

First consider criterion (3), disruption-effects. The second device, nullification, is in principle the least disruptive and secession the most, with group veto occupying an intermediate position. Nullification is like a minor stroke that deprives a person of partial control over only one limb—voiding a law only in the area that exercises the right. Group veto paralyzes the whole political organism, though only with regard to the legislation over which the veto is exercised. Secession is like the total loss of a limb.

So, according to the criterion of minimizing disruption-effects —that is, the state's interest in avoiding interference with its ordinary operations —we get this ordering of preferences among the three constitutional rights:

1. the right of nullification,
2. the right of group veto, and
3. the right to secede.

The opposite order of preference emerges if we shift to the perspective of the potential exerciser of the right *and* view these rights simply from the standpoint of their strategic bargaining value (threat advantage). This is so because the strategic bargaining value of the right (i.e., of having the right in the constitution) to those who can bargain with the threat of exercising it is directly proportional to the cost that the successful exercise of the right would impose on those against whom the threat is advanced, and this, on our simplified model, is equivalent to the disruption-effects. So, according to the criterion of strategic bargaining value, we have this ordering:

1. the right to secede,
2. the right of group veto, and
3. the right of nullification.

However, it is crucial to notice that this ranking holds only *ceteris paribus*. The strategic value of each of the three rights will vary, depending upon the *height of the constitutional hurdles* placed in the path of its exercise. For example, the difficulty of exercising each of these rights can be increased by requiring stronger majorities (say, three-quarters rather than a simple majority) in favor of secession within the relevant group. So even though the strategic value of the right to secede *in itself* is greater than the strategic value of a right of group veto and of nullification *in themselves*, which right has the greatest strategic value, *all things considered*, will depend upon the character of their respective constitutional embodiments and in particular upon the height of the procedural hurdles. It will also depend upon the *narrowness of the list of approved substantive justifications*. This relationship can be captured, albeit rather crudely, by the following formula: The strategic bargaining value of having a right in the constitution (for a potential exerciser of that right) equals the disruption-effects of the exercise of the right minus the exercise-difficulty of that right, and this in turn equals the height of the procedural obstacles to its exercise plus the narrowness of the substantive criteria for its exercise.

Consider now the other criterion of preference that emerges from the perspective of the potential exercisers of the rights: the independence-effect. The right to secede, if successfully exercised, achieves the highest degree of independence and in so doing provides a group with the strongest assurance that it can escape whatever deleterious effects that continued membership in the larger association may have on its own welfare and freedom. Successful exercise of the group veto right achieves more independence and control than nullification, but less than secession. So on this criterion we have the following ordering:

1. the right to secede,
2. the right of group veto, and
3. the right of nullification.

To summarize: From the perspective of those who may exercise the rights in question, there are two main criteria of preference for ranking the right to secede relative to the right of group veto and the right of nullification: the independence that successful exercise of the right would bring for those who exercise it and the strategic bargaining value of having the right in the constitution. These two criteria yield the same ordering, on the assumption that strategic bargaining value is a function of the state's incentive to avoid the disruptive effects of increased independence on its operations. For the same reason, the perspective of the state, insofar as it is concerned with minimizing disruption and hence independence, yields precisely the opposite ordering, with nullification most preferable, secession least preferable,[8] and group veto in between.

It is important to note, however, that under certain conditions, other factors may be overriding, leading to different preference orderings on balance. For example, even though secession would produce greater independence, exercise of a right of nullification might be more attractive to a group if it would allow that group to preserve the benefits of continued membership in the state while avoiding some of the costs. Thus a group might prefer to nullify certain laws requiring it to contribute, say, to national defense and take a free ride on the contributions of others, rather than to secede and be faced with the cost of maintaining its own defenses.[9] Clearly, the danger of free-riding would have to be taken into account in determining which sorts of laws a right of nullification should and should not apply to.

Now, because the proper perspective for ideal constitutional design requires interpersonal (and intrapersonal) impartiality, both the perspective of unionists and that of secessionists must somehow be incorporated into the thought experiment of a choice of constitutional principles by parties to an ideal constitutional convention. The party to the ideal constitutional convention, bereft of information about where she stands on any actual issue of conflict of interests, must adopt both perspectives, viewing herself both as a potential member of a discontented minority bent on greater independence and as a potential member of the majority concerned chiefly with maintaining the political *status quo*, including federal legislative power and territorial integrity. How are we to choose among these constitutional alternatives if the two legitimate perspectives rank them oppositely?

If there were some reasonable way for such a party to assign different *weights* to criteria that lead to opposite orderings of the desirability of the three constitutional rights, then one perspective could be said to dominate and a single ranking of the three constitutional rights would emerge. For example, if it were known that the dangers of disrupting the body politic were so great that an impartial citizen would weigh them more heavily than the need to provide relatively easy exit for a discontented group, then it would be possible to make plausible arguments in favor of, say, including a group veto right and/or a right of nullification in the constitution, while forgoing inclusion of the more potentially disruptive and hence more dangerous right of secession. But such information about risks is highly contingent—it varies between countries and over time with respect to the same country.[10] *How* great the risk of including a right to secession is will depend upon the current conditions, history, and political culture of the state in question.

What this means is that ideal constitutional theory can at best help us to isolate the factors that ought to be taken into account in deciding among these alternative rights. It cannot tell us that every constitution ought or ought not to include a right to secede, much less exactly what that right should look like.

Instead, the exploration of ideal constitution theory begun here, when taken together with the moral views on secession developed in the first three chapters, can at most establish that a right to secede is one morally legitimate constitutional alternative and place some constraints on the shape of a constitutional right to secede if this alternative is to be utilized. There is no general answer to the question: Ought a constitution to include a right to secede?

At this point, the world of political reality rescues ideal theory from radical indeterminacy. It is a fact of current life that secession movements are under way, with more to come. It is also a fact that there is growing support for including some sort of right to secede in a number of constitutions. The arguments in this book help bolster and clarify the attractiveness of a constitutional right to secede by articulating the moral concerns that can justify secession and by showing how they provide a structure for choosing among alternative models for delineating the scope and limits of a constitutional right to secede. If, as I believe, current political events have irrevocably placed the right to secede on the agendas for constitutional reform, then the fact that some if not all of the ends such a right can serve could also be achieved by the alternative rights of group veto and/or nullification (when combined with special substantive minority group rights) does not limit the usefulness of our analysis of secession as much as might first appear to be the case. Even if in theory there are satisfactory (or even superior) alternatives to a right to secede, it is important to know that a right to secede is one way to address important moral concerns, especially if it is one that is salient in our current political world. At the same time, I will have accomplished a major goal of this investigation if the admittedly incomplete comparative assessment of these three constitutional alternatives at least expands the list of options under serious consideration, leading, perhaps, to a reconsideration of current political agendas regarding secession.

Once various restrictions on the right to secede are clearly recognized, and once we abandon the conceptually cramping and politically dangerous assumption that discontent groups must choose between achieving complete sovereignty and being recognized only as cultural or ethnic groups without any degree of political autonomy, we will see secession as only one alternative among many. We will realize that there is a range of possible degrees and forms of political independence, and that secession is only the most extreme alternative, not the only one.

Notes

1. *Constitution (Fundamental Law) of the Union of Soviet Socialist Republics* (Moscow: Novosti Press Agency Publishing House, 1977), p. 56, Article 72: "Each Union Republic shall retain the right freely to secede from the U.S.S.R."

2. In the United States, do-it-yourself "divorce kits" and "will kits" can be purchased and used by individuals who cannot afford or do not wish to employ lawyers.

3. James M. Buchanan and Gordon Tullock, *The Calculus of Consent* (Ann Arbor: University of Michigan Press, 1971); John Rawls, *A Theory of Justice* (Cambridge, Mass.: Harvard University Press, 1971).

4. Rawls, *A Theory of Justice*, pp. 17–22, 136–142.

5. Allen Buchanan, "Revisability and Rational Choice," *Canadian Journal of Philosophy*, vol. 5, November 1975, pp. 395–408.

6. Albert O. Hirschman, *Exit, Voice, and Loyalty* (Cambridge, Mass.: Harvard University Press, 1970), pp. 33–43.

7. John C. Calhoun, *A Disquisition on Government*, edited by C. Gordon Post (New York: Liberal Arts Press, 1953), pp. 7–10.

8. This assumes that the loss of territory (through secession) and, to a lesser extent, the loss of legislative power (through nullification or group veto), will be viewed very negatively by the state and those who support it. But, of course, there can be other ways in which the state may suffer disruption of its functions. In some cases, keeping a violently discontent minority within the state may be more disruptive than allowing it to secede. For this reason, it is important to note that in the comparative analysis undertaken here 'disruption-effects' is being used in a rather specific sense to refer primarily to the loss of state territory and/or diminutions of the state's legislative power through nullification or group veto.

Even though secession might be less disruptive, all things considered, than the continued presence within the state of an extremely discontented group, it is worth noting that states almost without exception disparately seek to prevent any losses of territory, whether through secession by groups within or through annexation by other states. The fact that states are almost always willing to incur great costs to avoid loss of territory suggests that this sort of disruption-effect is especially serious, or at least is perceived to be especially serious, by the state and its supporters. If this is so, then it makes sense to give prominence to this sort of disruption in an analysis of the pros and cons of a constitutional right to secede. Nevertheless, as our comments on the future of South Africa in Chapter 5 will suggest, in some cases ethnic conflict may become so severe that secession is, all things considered, the least disruptive alternative, even from the standpoint of the state and its zeal to preserve territory. I am indebted to Pat Fitzgerald for the observation that there are many ways in which intergroup conflict can be disruptive to the state and that under certain conditions secession may not be the most disruptive alternative.

9. I am indebted to Paul Heyne for this point.

10. This contingency is a problem quite distinct from another one—that different persons have different attitudes toward risk: Some are risk-averse, some are risk-neutral, and some even prefer risk.

5

Conclusions

I. An Overview of the Moral and Constitutional Theory of Secession

Traversing the twisting course of critical dialogue between voices speaking in favor of and against secession, we have concluded that there is a moral right to secede, though a highly qualified one. To say that there is a (qualified) moral right to secede is to say that those to whom the right is ascribed ought (under certain conditions) to be allowed to secede, without interference from others, and that others have a weighty obligation not to interfere. It is also to imply that there are considerations in favor of secession (again, under certain circumstances) that are of such great moral weight that such a strong bar to interference with secession is justified. Thus this assertion of a moral right, like all others, is not an assertion that a peculiar sort of ghostly entity, a right, exists (a thing that goes "ought" in the night, so to speak). Rather, the assertion that there is a moral right to secession should be understood as a kind of shorthand for the longer, yet quite unmysterious and this-worldly claim that there are sound moral reasons, and reasons enough, for not interfering with secession (under those conditions), even if interfering would serve other interests. A further implication is that the case against interfering is so strong that certain sorts of countervailing reasons, such as the fact that interfering would produce greater utility overall, that normally can count as conclusive reasons for interfering in other contexts, do not suffice to justify interference here.

According to this way of understanding what it is to say that there is a right, assertions of right are essentially *conclusory* and hence *argumentative*. An assertion of right is a conclusion about what the moral priorities are. At the same time, because it is a conclusion, it is an admission that it is appropriate to demand support for this conclusion, reasons why such priority ought to be recognized. And it is vital to recognize that there is a plurality of different kinds of considerations that can count as moral reasons to support a conclusion of this sort and that the conclusion that an assertion of a right expresses will usually be an all-things-considered judgment, the result of a balancing of conflicting considerations.

For this reason no attempt was made to begin the investigation with an assertion of a right to secede or with a single more fundamental principle from which a right to secede is supposed to be derived. The former approach would overlook the fact that assertions of right are conclusory, the latter that the conclusions in question must be supported by a number of different moral considerations, at least some of which cannot be conveniently formulated in crisp principles, much less in a single principle.

Now there may be some who view this understanding of what it is to assert a right to be so deflationary that they prefer to eliminate talk about rights entirely and replace it with more modest claims about what the moral priorities are. I have no fundamental objection to this sentiment, though I believe that both for reasons of convenience and because talk about rights has certain advantages in motivating people to act, it is sometimes preferable to keep rights-talk (while keeping it in line by avoiding implications about ghostly entities). So I would not protest too loudly if those who abhor the notion of a right wish to translate my first thesis into the claim that, at least under certain circumstances, there are such exceptionally weighty reasons in favor of not interfering with secession that considerations that normally would justify interference, such as the promotion of overall utility, do not suffice; or that the interest in seceding ought to be accorded a certain privileged status; or that we ought to recognize the choice to secede as having an especially powerful moral authority and act accordingly; or, more simply, that (under certain conditions) certain reasons that secessionists offer to justify their actions ought to be regarded as sufficient reasons, and certain reasons for opposing their actions that normally would count as sufficient reasons for interfering with others' actions ought not to be regarded as sufficient in these cases.

In addition to asserting that there is a moral right to secede and trying to formulate clearly the chief considerations this support that essentially conclusory statement, I have also offered an account of the scope and limits of that right. Its main outlines may be summarized here (though with some danger of sliding over the nuances of the more detailed discussions in Chapters 1, 2, and 3). (1) The state's refusal to cease serious injustices it is perpetrating against the seceding group can justify secession as well as revolution. However, since secession involves the taking of territory and resources and goods within it, the justifiability of secession on grounds of injustice may depend upon whether the secessionists compensate innocent third parties for the losses they suffer as a result of the taking of the territory. (2) Among the types of state-perpetrated injustices that can justify secession are not only the violations of basic individual civil and political rights that orthodox liberal political philosophy recognizes as legitimate grounds for revolution but also the injustice of discriminatory redistribution, the state's exploitation of one group to benefit others. (And the charge of discriminatory redistribution, whether that label is used or not, is almost always one of the chief complaints of secessionists in the real world.) (3) Under certain highly circumscribed and extreme conditions, reasons other than the grievance of state-perpetrated injustice can justify secession. These include the need to preserve a group's culture and the necessity of a group's defending itself against threats to the literal survival of its members by third-party aggressors when the group's own state is not protecting it. (Even if one insists on construing the latter as a case of injustice by the state on the grounds that the state has an obligation of justice to protect all its citizens, the case of secession to preserve a culture does not fit under the heading of secession on grounds of injustice.) (4) In order for the need to preserve the group's culture to justify secession, the following conditions must be satisfied. (a) The culture in question must really be threatened —at the very least its prospects of demise in the near future must be significantly greater than the risks that all cultures face. (b) Less drastic ways of preserving the culture than secession (e.g., special minority group rights, a looser federalism, constitutional rights of nullification or group veto) must be unavailable or inadequate. (c) The culture in question must meet minimal standards of moral decency (the cultures of the Nazis or the Khmer Rouge do not warrant preservation, through secession or any other way). (d) The seceding group is not seeking independence in order to establish an illiberal state, that is, one that violates basic individual rights *and* from which free exit is denied to those who do not wish to subject themselves to these conditions. (e) Neither the state nor any third party has a valid claim to the seceding territory. (Of course, secession in order to preserve a culture is permissible if both parties consent to it, and this may in fact occur in one important contemporary case, that of Quebec, regardless of whether all of the conditions listed above are satisfied.)

The fifth condition (e) is especially significant. It rests upon an important principle: If the state (or, rather, the people whose agent it is) has a valid title to the territory, then only the most weighty reasons, namely, a grievance of state-perpetrated injustice or the necessity of self-defense against threats to the literal survival of the members of the group, can justify secession. On the other hand, if the state's title to at least some of the seceding territory is dubious (as I believe it is in the case of Quebec), then the need to preserve a culture can be reason enough to justify secession (at least if the other four conditions are met).

This principle is intended to capture and articulate clearly what I take to be a widespread and reasonable common-sense moral judgment about the relative moral gravity of grievances of injustice. It reflects the belief that although the need to preserve a culture (or even, perhaps, to form a new kind of political association such as a small-scale, direct participatory democracy) may be of sufficient moral weight to generate a valid claim to territory for which there is no clear, preexisting title (the "no clear title either way" situation), it is not substantial enough to extinguish a valid preexisting claim on the part of the state.

The approach to the territoriality issues advocated in this volume makes certain assumptions about the status of property rights in general, as well as about the nature of territorial sovereignty. Most importantly, it assumes that neither ordinary property rights nor territorial sovereignty are moral bedrock and that consequently neither is sacrosanct.

In part this is simply the application to the case of property rights of the general thesis noted above that assertions of rights are conclusory. Whether or not a state's or a people's claim to a piece of land ought to be given the special protection and high priority that we associate with rights will depend upon a number of different moral considerations. Situations can change. New developments, such as the people's failure to prevent its agent, the state, from treating some citizens unjustly or the failure to protect some citizens from genocidal assault from without, can void previously valid title and in effect generate a new title on the part of those whose only succor depends upon having control over their own territory.

To say that a group has a right to a piece of territory is, on this view of the nature of rights, to say that it is morally permissible for them to exercise certain forms of control over it, that others have a very weighty obligation not to interfere with this control, and that failure to honor this obligation constitutes a serious wrong, a grievance against the group that has the right. Granted that rights-statements are conclusory, it is also to imply that there are adequate moral grounds for according the group this protected freedom to control the territory.

Thus to say that under certain conditions a group's need to protect itself from unjust threats to the existence of its members or to escape the continued perpetration of injustices against it by the state can *generate* a valid claim or right to territory on the part of the group is simply to say that circumstances have come into existence which supply adequate moral grounds for according the group this protected freedom to control the territory. In other words, even if it were the case until now that the group did not have a right to the territory, a sound moral case can now be made for concluding that it is permissible for the group to exercise control over the territory and that others have a very weighty obligation to respect its efforts to do so.

In principle, then, there is nothing mysterious about the idea that special circumstances can generate a valid claim or right where none existed before. It can become permissible for a group or individual to exercise control over something when it was not permissible in the past, and others can become obligated not to interfere when they had no such obligation in the past. Property rights broadly construed, including the right of territorial sovereignty (which, properly speaking, is a right of jurisdiction), can be adjusted and even overturned by changes in the morally relevant circumstances.

Throughout this investigation, the importance of the territorial issue has been emphasized. I have argued, however, that although the territoriality thesis is correct, the historical grievance version of it is not. The former simply states that any sound justification for secession must include a valid claim to the seceding territory on the part of the group that wishes to secede. The latter insists that to establish a valid claim to it the secessionists must show that the territory in question was rightfully theirs but was unjustly taken from them in the past (as with the Soviet seizure of the Baltic states in 1940).

There are two reasons for rejecting the historical grievance version—that is, for denying that a historical grievance about stolen territory is a *necessary* condition for justified secession. First, the historical grievance thesis fails to recognize that other forms of injustice besides an unjust taking in the past, including discriminatory redistribution and the current violations of the basic individual rights that have long been recognized as grounds for revolution, can justify secession. Moreover, the grievance of discriminatory redistribution is not only one of the most common grounds for seceding, it is the chief ground in some of the actual cases in which there is a strong consensus that secession was justified (e.g., the secession of the American Colonies from the British North American Empire). Second, and perhaps somewhat more controversially, the historical grievance version of the territoriality thesis also fails to recognize that under certain conditions both the right of self-defense and the need to preserve a culture can justify secession, in the absence of any historical grievance concerning territory.

Assuming that there is a (qualified) moral right to secede, is there a good case for a constitutional right to secede? Or should we think of the right to secede, like the right to revolution, as an extraconstitutional, purely moral right, to be appealed to as a last resort, when political and constitutional resources have proved inadequate?

I have argued that this question admits of no general answer, for two distinct reasons. First, in some countries secession never becomes a serious issue, either because their populations are highly homogeneous or because there are other ways for disparate groups to get what they feel they need or deserve. For example, regardless of how strong one thinks the prosecession arguments canvassed in this book are, and no matter how convinced one is that there is a moral right to secede, it might be silly to agitate for amending the Swedish Constitution to include a right to secede. (Yet this might not have been the case less than one hundred years ago, when Sweden included Norway, which seceded peacefully.) In brief, if the state isn't likely to be broken, there's no need to establish a rule for how to break it up. There is no principle of morality or of constitutional law which requires that all moral rights be constitutionally embodied. Second, there are alternatives to a constitutional right to secede that can, under certain circumstances, respond adequately, and perhaps with less risk, to the problems that a constitutiona right to secede is intended to solve. Chief among these are special minority group rights (e.g., language rights or other special rights, such as collective property rights, designed to protect a minority culture) and constitutional rights of nullification and group veto. I have sketched a list of factors (including what I have called disruption-effects, exercise-difficulty, and strategic bargaining value), along with a set of simple formulae expressing relations among them, that are of some use in determining the relative advantages and disadvantages of these various legal and constitutional devices for coping with problems of conflicting group interests.

However, I have also attempted to make clear the fact that there are severe limits to abstract constitutional design. Whether a constitutional right to secede is preferable to some combination of the other options will depend upon how we *weigh* the conflicting factors, and what weights are appropriate will depend in part on highly contingent facts about the actual risks associated with the alternatives—and these will vary from case to case. Nonetheless, I hope to have provided at least the major elements of an analytic framework for the comparative evaluation of proposals for a constitutional right to secede.

Quite apart from how we would answer the threshold question as to whether to have a constitutional right to secede if we were free to set political agendas by untrammeled philosophical reasoning, there is the question of *how* a right to secede ought to be framed, assuming that (as in the Soviet Union) there is to be one. Here the moral thinking about secession developed in Chapters 2 and 3 provides some guidance for evaluating alternative proposals for various combinations of the substantive, procedural, fault, and no-fault ideal types of constitutional laws on secession developed in Chapter 4.

The use of substantive requirements reflects a presumption in favor of the political *status quo* and places a burden of justification on would-be secessionists. Exclusive reliance on procedural requirements in effect presumes the legitimacy of the interest in secession, specifying only how it is to be satisfied. In principle, purely substantive and purely procedural approaches can be functionally equivalent in this sense: They can make secession just as easy or just as difficult and can enhance or reduce the ability to use the threat of secession as a strategic bargaining tool, depending on how narrow or wide the substantive requirements are and how high or low the procedural hurdles are.

However, some combinations of procedure and substance are morally preferable to others: For example, if only grievances of state-perpetrated injustice were allowed as valid justifications for secession, it would be inappropriate to increase the difficulty of successfully exercising the right to secede even further by imposing especially onerous procedural requirements as well. Several other conclusions were also advanced in the discussion of constitutional design. The morality of secession does not require that a constitutional right to secede (if there is to be one) include any substantive justification requirement. But if substantive justification requirements are to be included in a constitutional right to secede, there is a strong moral case for including also the full range of sound moral justifications, not just, say, historical territorial grievances. And, finally, a strong argument for using a purely procedural approach is that doing so minimizes the problem of the biased referee by avoiding the danger that a group will have to rely upon the very political apparatus from which it desires to sever itself to determine whether inherently disputable substantive requirements for severance are satisfied.

II. Applying the Theory

Although no attempt has been made here to offer a simple moral report card on past, existing, or expected secession movements, the normative theses about secession advanced in this work have been illustrated by and applied to a number of such cases. It will be helpful to tie together several conclusions that emerged as the analysis unfolded concerning four especially interesting cases: the American Southern secession, the secession of the Baltic Republics from the Soviet Union, the possibility of secession in South Africa, and the much more likely secession of Quebec from Canada.

I have argued that the strongest case for American Southern secession was one based on the grievance of discriminatory redistribution. A cautionary remark is in order, however: Whether the South was in fact a victim of discriminatory redistribution cannot be decisively determined simply by noting that there was a net revenue drain from South to North. At most, this quantitative fact establishes a presumption that there is discrimination or counts as some evidence of discrimination. Whether it in fact constitutes an injustice depends on whether the redistributive pattern in question is morally arbitrary, and that, in turn, depends upon what distributive justice requires. For example, if distributive justice requires a net transfer of resources from the better-off citizens in one region to the worse-off citizens in another, then the fact that there is a net drain of revenue from the former to the latter does not show that the better off are victims of discriminatory redistribution.

It is worth noting, however, that during the period in question the United States was not a welfare state in any significant sense. So if, as the data cited earlier indicate, there was a net revenue transfer from the South to the North, it could not be explained as the appropriate result of a just welfare system to which the country was then committed. Further, by most reasonable measures, it was the South that was the worse-off region.

It should also be emphasized that the argument for the justification of Southern secession on grounds of discriminatory redistribution is entirely independent of the resolution of what was taken to be the crucial issue during the debate that preceded the South's bid for independence. Many, perhaps most, participants in that debate believed that the secession was justified if (and only if) the political units that entered the Union in 1787 were sovereign states at that time. It was assumed that if the states were sovereign, then each could unilaterally withdraw from the "compact" into which they had each freely entered, whenever it wished, for whatever reason. Consequently, much ink and vituperous oral argument were expended on attempts to show that the states were sovereign at the time of union and that the U.S. Constitution was such a compact.

The analysis presented here shows that it was a mistake to assume that secession could be justified only under these conditions. Establishing that the Southern states were previously sovereign is no more necessary than showing that the American Colonies were sovereign at the time they began the struggle for independence from Britain. In both instances a case for secession can be made on the grounds of one type of grievance of injustice: discriminatory redistribution. Nor would showing that the states were sovereign at the time of entry into the Union be *sufficient* to justify Southern secession. Whether a previously sovereign political unit may with justification secede will depend upon a number of factors, including the terms of the agreement itself, whether its doing so would unjustly expose the remainder state to lethal threats by third-party aggressors, and whether the secessionists make a good-faith effort to render whatever compensation is due to the citizens of the remainder state. (In particular, it is worth noting that even if it were assumed that the states were each fully sovereign at the time the "compact" of union was made, this would not show that any of them had a right to withdraw from the union *unilaterally* and *unconditionally*. In general, contractual obligations are not so easily dissolved; and the American Constitution contains nothing to override the assumption that in entering the Union the states were genuinely binding themselves.)

But in the case of Southern secession there was another moral factor that defeated what might have otherwise been a sound justification for secession: the fact that the South was fighting to preserve slavery. Recall that the investigation of the morality of secession in Chapters 2 and 3 concluded that it is justifiable to resist secession if secession is undertaken to form a state that will systematically subject minorities within it to grave injustices while barring their exit from it. This condition for justified opposition to secession was fully and clearly met in the case of Southern secession. Even if discriminatory redistribution was a reason for secession, there can be no doubt that a chief goal of Southern independence was the preservation of slavery.

Application of the views on the morality of secession developed in this book to contemporary cases also yields substantive results. Secessionist movements in the Baltic states enjoy the strongest and clearest justifications: The most obvious ground for severing from the Soviet Union in each of these cases is that of rectificatory justice. Latvia, Estonia, and Lithuania were all sovereign states at the time of Soviet conquest, and each had as clear a title to territorial sovereignty as one is likely to find, none apparently being guilty of having unjustly taken their territories from identifiable groups that could still be said to have a legitimate claim on it.[1]

However, even if they are relatively unproblematic from the standpoint of what I have called the moral statute-of-limitations problem concerning territorial sovereignty (the fact that if one goes back far enough there are bloodstains on almost every deed to a state territory), the Baltics do illustrate another moral complexity of secession: the problem of antisecessionist minorities. In Lithuania approximately 80 percent of the population is Lithuanian, 20 percent is non-Lithuanian; of the latter, moreover, most are Russians.

Recall, as I argued in Chapter 3, that those non-Lithuanians who oppose secession should at most receive some limited compensation for their losses (or perhaps be offered not only emigration but dual citizenship or some special resident-alien status in Lithuania), but that those who are Soviet colonists or their descendants ought not to have a voice in the decision whether to secede.

In Latvia the situation is more perplexing. There only 52 percent of the population is Latvian, and 48 percent non-Latvian (including chiefly Russians, Byelorussians, and Ukrainians). Yet even here what counts, ultimately, is not simply the numbers but also how the people of the various groups got there. Colonists who came in the wake of an unjust conquest do not have the same moral standing in determining the fate of a region as does the indigenous population.

If, as seems likely, there are significant numbers of non-Latvians in Latvia who do not fit the description of colonists and who do have a legitimate interest in determining the political status of that country, then it is imperative that they be given an appropriate voice in the decisions. Although there can be no one, uniquely preferable solution to the problem of minorities, it should be emphasized that the single most important response to this problem is the one that Latvia is in fact apparently making: guaranteeing full, equal citizenship rights, equal protection under the law, equality of opportunity, and the freedom to emigrate to all members of the population, regardless of nationality or ethnic group membership.[2]

The case of South Africa is especially difficult. As noted at the outset of this inquiry, the current borders of South Africa are an artifact of conquest, and as a consequence that country is deeply pluralistic, both ethnically and racially. This fact raises the question as to whether a postapartheid unitary state is possible or, if possible, desirable. So it is natural to ask, as well, whether a new constitution for that country, which De Klerk's white government now acknowledges is a necessity, should include a right to secede or whether the problems of pluralism can be addressed in some less radical manner. It was also noted that some who are actively engaged in the struggle for justice in South Africa understandably fear that even public discussion of the possibility of secession is dangerous, playing into the hands of the divide-and-conquer strategy that the forces of racial oppression in South Africa have used with such ruthless skill and utter moral cynicism for decades.

A second, at least equally serious reason against putting the idea of a constitutional right to secede on the immediate or midterm political agenda in South Africa is the fact that the various racial and ethnic groups are no longer sufficiently concentrated in discrete geographical areas to make territorially based independent groups feasible. Assuming that the main impetus for secession would come from racial or tribal groups, the fact that they are no longer localized means that secession would require massive shifts of populations across the country. Moreover, the uneven distribution of natural resources in the country ensures that any attempt to parcel out territory by consensus or any other reasonably fair, nonviolent means is virtually impossible.

The issue of whether the possibility of secession should play a significant role in the political transformation of South Africa is made all the more difficult both by the rapid changes occurring there and by the tremendous uncertainty as to where they are leading. Virtually any substantive prediction in this regard would signal insensitivity, ignorance, or arrogance. At most I feel reasonably confident in venturing the following conclusion: The dangers of divisiveness resulting from incorporation of a right to secede in a new constitution for South Africa are so great, and the obstacles to a just, consensual division of territory among legitimate groups are so formidable, that at least for the present the more responsible course is to strive for a constitution that provides a single set of basic civil and political rights, equal protection under the law, and equality of opportunity for all, with special provisions for substantive special group rights (e.g., language rights) where necessary. Whether or not a right to secede ought to be or may be included in a second (or third) generation of constitutional changes is another matter.

The analysis offered here strengthens the argument that injecting the issue of secession into the core of the political debate at present is dangerously divisive, by making it clear that there are a number of potentially less divisive alternatives for coping with the problems of pluralism. These include a variety of special group rights, the right of nullification, and the right of group veto.

This proposal is provisional, however. If the current political violence between Zulus and Xhosas (and others who support the African National Congress) continues to escalate, creation of a separate Zulu state might prove to be the only way to contain divisions among blacks that threaten the black liberation movement itself and that may provoke a white backlash that could undo recent progress toward constitutional reform. It is to be hoped, however, that Zulu aspirations for political power can be accommodated in a loose federalism in which that group is accorded some special status. However, if non-Zulus are unwilling to adopt constitutional measures that would add further power to the numerical superiority that Zulus already enjoy, the only possibility for a peaceful solution may be Zulu secession.

The case of Quebec is an especially controversial and intriguing one for a theory of secession. It is no doubt true that in the past Francophone Canadians suffered ethnic discrimination of various sorts. It is much more problematic to hold that those Francophone Canadians *who live in Quebec* are *now* victims of ethnic discrimination. (It may be true that Francophones in *other* parts of Canada suffer some forms of ethnic discrimination, but it is hard to see how independence for those living in Quebec would remedy that problem, if it exists.) For this reason I deemed it more fruitful to use the case of Quebec to explore the question of whether the need to preserve a culture can justify secession, even in the absence of injustices. If, however, one believes that Francophone Canadians in Quebec are still suffering some forms of injustice, then one can understand my discussion as exploring the issue of whether the need to preserve a culture provides an additional sound argument for secession.

The discussion of the argument from cultural preservation in Chapter 2 yielded no neat answer to that question. But it did show that if the need to preserve a culture is to provide a sound justification for secession, several specific conditions must be satisfied. I also argued that the satisfaction of at least two of these conditions is quite controversial in the case of Quebec—the first being the requirement that the culture really is in peril, and the second being that no morally acceptable and politically feasible alternatives to secession would provide adequate protection for the culture. Whether these conditions are satisfied is an empirical matter.

Hence one very salutary result of the analysis in this book is that it focuses attention on the right questions and makes clear what kinds of questions they are. Equally clear is that the constitutional alternatives to secession explored in Chapter 4 have not received the attention they deserve in the debate over secession by Quebec.

I acknowledged at the outset that the moral reflections and speculations on constitutional design presented in this book are only the beginning of a full-blown normative theory of secession, and that ideally the normative theory must be complemented by an adequate positive or explanatory theory of secession. I shall now end this beginning by clarifying a point that was only hinted at in my earlier uses of the analogy between political and domestic secession—that is, divorce. Ultimately, the quest for theoretical understanding cannot rest content with a political theory of secession. For in the end it must be recognized that political secession is only one instance of the more general phenomenon of separation and union—the emergence from and merging into relationships with the other. This is the oldest, most disturbing and profound, yet most necessary, human drama. There are few meaningful events in a human life that are not encompassed in its acts. An adequate political theory of secession would be the application to the special case of the state of a much more general theory, if we could attain it.

Notes

1. See V. Stanley Vardys and Romuald J. Misiunas, eds., *The Baltic States in Peace and War, 1917–1945* (University Park: Pennsylvania State University Press, 1978); Romuald J. Misiunas and Rein Taagepera, *The Baltic States: Years of Dependence, 1940–1980* (Berkeley: University of California Press, 1983).

2. Remarks by Prime Minister of Latvia delivered to National Press Club, Washington, D.C., July 23, 1990, Cable News Network.

References

Ackerman, Bruce. 1980. *Social Justice and the Liberal State*. New Haven, Conn.: Yale University Press.

Adams, James Truslow. 1927. *New England in the Republic, 1776–1850*. Vol. III, *The History of New England*. Boston: Little, Brown.

Aranson, Peter. Forthcoming. "Calhoun's Constitutional Economics." *Journal of Constitutional Economics*.

Arneson, Richard. 1990. "Primary Goods Reconsidered." *Nous* 24:437–438.

Barry, Brian, and Russell Hardin, eds. 1983. *Rational Man and Irrational Society?* Beverly Hills, Calif.: Sage Publications.

Bedau, Hugo, ed. 1969. *Civil Disobedience: Theory and Practice*. New York: Western Publishing Co.

Beran, Harry. 1987. *The Consent Theory of Political Obligation*. New York: Croom Helm.

Bledsoe, Albert Taylor. 1866. *Is Jeff Davis a Traitor?* New York: Innis and Co.

Boyer, Ralph E. 1981. *Survey of the Law of Property*, 3d ed. St. Paul, Minn.: West Publishing Co.

Braudel, Fernand. 1972. *The Mediterranean and the Mediterranean World in the Age of Philip II*. Vol. 1. translated by Sian Reynolds. New York: Harper and Row.

Brilmayer, Lea. 1991. "Secession and Self-Determination: A Territorialist Reinterpretation." *Yale Journal of International Law*, vol. 16, no. 1, January 1991, pp. 177–202.

———. 1989. "Consent, Contract, and Territory." *Minnesota Law Review* 74:6–10.

Buchanan, Allen. 1990. "Justice as Reciprocity Versus Subject-Centered Justice." *Philosophy and Public Affairs*, 19:227–252.

———. 1989. "Assessing the Communitarian Critique of Liberalism." *Ethics* 99:852–882.

———. 1985. *Ethics, Efficiency, and the Market*. Totowa, N.J.: Rowman and Allanheld.

————. 1984. "What's So Special About Rights?" *Social Philosophy and Policy* 2:61–83.

————. 1981. "Deriving Welfare Rights from Libertarian Rights." In P. G. Brown, C. Johnson and P. Vernier, eds., *Income Support*. Totowa, N.J.: Rowman and Allanheld.

————. 1975. "Revisability and Rational Choice." *Canadian Journal of Philosophy*. 5:395–408.

Buchanan, Allen, and Dan W. Brock. 1989. *Deciding for Others: The Ethics of Surrogate Decisionmaking*. Cambridge: Cambridge University Press.

Buchanan, James M., and Gordon Tullock. 1971. *The Calculus of Consent*. Ann Arbor: University of Michigan Press.

Buchheit, Lee C. 1978. *Secession: The Legitimacy of Self-Determination*. New Haven, Conn.: Yale University Press.

Calhoun, John C. 1953. *A Disquisition on Government*, edited by C. Gordon Post. New York: Liberal Arts Press.

Cohen, G. A. 1978. "Robert Nozick and Wilt Chamberlain: How Patterns Preserve Liberty." In J. Arthur and W. H. Shaw, eds., *Justice and Economic Distribution*. Englewood Cliffs, N.J.: Prentice-Hall.

Constitution (Fundamental Law) of the Union of Soviet Socialist Republics. 1977. Moscow: Novosti Press Agency Publishing House.

Dworkin, Ronald. 1977. *Taking Rights Seriously*. Cambridge, Mass.: Harvard University Press.

Feinberg, Joel. 1990. "In Defense of Moral Rights." The Romanell Lectures (one of three unpublished lectures).

————. 1986. *Harm to Self*. Vol. 3, *The Moral Limits of the Criminal Law*. New York: Oxford University Press.

————. 1984. *Harm to Others*. Vol. 1, *The Moral Limits of the Criminal Law*. New York: Oxford University Press.

————. 1979. "Civil Disobedience in the Modern World." *Humanities in Society* 2:37–59.

Foote, Shelby. 1974. *The Civil War: A Narrative*. Vol. III, *Red River to Appomatox*. New York: Random House.

Galston, William A. 1989. "Pluralism and Social Unity." *Ethics* 99:717–726.

Gellner, Ernest. 1983. *Nations and Nationalism*. Oxford: Blackwell.

Gerard-Libois, Jules. 1966. *Katanga Secession*, translated by Rebecca Young. Madison: University of Wisconsin Press.

Gorbachev, Mikail. 1990. Quoted in *New York Times International*, June 4, 1990, p. A13.

Gray, John. 1986. *Liberalism*. Minneapolis: University of Minnesota Press.

Hechter, Michael. 1990. "The Dynamics of Secessionism." Unpublished paper, Department of Sociology, University of Arizona, 1990.

————. 1975. *Internal Colonialism: The Celtic Fringe in British National Development, 1536-1966*. Berkeley: University of California Press.

Hirschman, Albert O. 1970. *Exit, Voice, and Loyalty*. Cambridge, Mass.: Harvard University Press.

Horowitz, Donald. 1985. *Ethnic Groups in Conflict*. Berkeley: University of California Press.

Hume, David. 1978. *A Treatise of Human Nature*, 2d ed., edited by L.A. Selby-Bigge. Oxford: Oxford University Press.

Jacobs, Jane. 1984. *Cities and the Wealth of Nations: Principles of Economic Life*. New York: Random House.

Kendall, Frances, and Leon Louw. 1987. *After Apartheid: The Solution for South Africa*. San Francisco: ICS Press.

Kymlicka, Will. 1989. *Liberalism, Community, and Culture*. Oxford: Oxford University Press.

————. 1989. "Liberalism, Individualism and Liberal Neutrality." *Ethics* 99:883-905.

LaFave, Wayne R., and Austin W. Scott, Jr. 1986. *Criminal Law*, 2d ed. St. Paul, Minn.: West Publishing Co.

Lincoln, Abraham. 1989. *Speeches and Writings 1832-1858*, edited by Don E. Fehrenbacker. New York: Library of America.

————. 1989. *Speeches and Writings 1859-1865*, edited by Don E. Fehrenbacker. New York: Library of America.

Locke, John. 1982. *Second Treatise of Government*, edited by Richard H. Cox. Arlington Heights: Harlan Davidson.

Malamed, A. Douglas, and Guido Calebresi. 1972. "One View of the Cathedral." *Harvard Law Review*.

Mason, E. S., R. Dorfman, and S. A. Marglin. 1972. *Conflict In East Pakistan: Background and Prospects*. Cited in Subrata Roy Chowdbury. 1975. *The Genesis of Bangladesh*. New York: Asia Publishing House.

McPherson, James M. 1988. *The Battle Cry of Freedom*. Oxford: Oxford University Press.

Mill, John Stuart. 1975. *On Representative Government*. In *John Stuart Mill: Three Essays*, with an introduction by Richard Wollheim. Oxford: Oxford University Press.

————. 1959. *On Liberty*. New York: Bobbs-Merrill.

Misiunas, Romuald J., and Rein Taagepera. 1983. *The Baltic States: Years of Dependence, 1940-1980*. Berkeley: University of California Press.

Munzer, Stephen, R. 1990. *A Theory of Property*. Cambridge: Cambridge University Press.

Nowak, John E., Ronald D. Rotunda, and J. Nelson Young. 1986. *Constitutional Law*, 3d ed. St. Paul, Minn.: West Publishing Co.

Nozick, Robert. 1974. *Anarchy, State, and Utopia*. New York: Basic Books.

Nwanko, Arthur, and Samuel Ifejika. 1970. *The Making of a Nation: Biafra*. London: C. Hurst and Co.

Rawls, John. 1990. "Justice as Fairness: A Briefer Restatement." Unpublished manuscript, Department of Philosophy, Harvard University.

————. 1971. *A Theory of Justice*. Cambridge, Mass.: Harvard University Press.

Raz, Joseph. 1986. *The Morality of Freedom*. Oxford: Oxford University Press.

Roback, Jennifer. 1990. Unpublished manuscript, George Mason University.

Sandel, Michael. 1984. Introduction, in *Liberalism and Its Critics*, edited by Michael Sandel. New York: New York University Press.

Simmons, John. 1979. *Political Obligation*. Princeton, N.J.: Princeton University Press.

Thompson, Leonard. 1990. *A History of South Africa*. New Haven, Conn.: Yale University Press.

Thoreau, Henry David. 1967. "Civil Disobedience." In *The Variorum Civil Disobedience*, annotated by Walter Harding. New York: Twayne Publishers, Inc.

Vardys, V. Stanley, and Romuald J. Misiunas. 1978. *The Baltic States in Peace and War, 1917–1945*. University Park: Pennsylvania State University Press.

Von Humbolt, Wilhelm. 1969. *The Limits of State Action*, edited by J. W. Burrow. Cambridge: Cambridge University Press.

Williams, Robert A., Jr. 1990. *The American Indian in Western Legal Thought*. Oxford: Oxford University Press.

————. 1990. "Encounters on the Frontiers of International Human Rights Law: Redefining the Terms of Indigenous Peoples' Survival in the World." *Duke Law Review*. Forthcoming.

Woodward, C. Vann. 1974. *The Strange Career of Jim Crow*. 3d rev. ed. New York: Oxford University Press.

About the Book and Author

This important study, the first book-length treatment of an increasingly crucial topic, treats the moral issues of secession at two levels. At the practical level, Professor Buchanan develops a coherent theory of the conditions under which secession is morally justifiable. He then applies it to historical and contemporary examples, including the U.S. Civil War and more recent revents in Bangladesh, Katanga and Biafra, the Baltic states, South Africa, and Quebec. This is the first systematic account of the conditions and terms that justify secession from a political union.

But Buchanan also locates this account of the right to secede in the broader context of contemporary political thought, introducing readers to influential accounts of political society, such as contractarianism and communitarianism, and showing how the possibility of secession fits into a more complete understanding of political community and political obligation.

At both levels this is an important book. It will interest not only political and social theorists but any reader concerned with one of the most momentous issues of our day: the future of troubled political federations and other states under conditions of ethnic and cultural pluralism.

Allen Buchanan is professor of philosophy at the University of Arizona, Tucson. He is the author of numerous articles in political philosophy and bioethics, and of the following books: *Marx and Justice: The Radical Critique of Liberalism* (1982), *Ethics, Efficiency, and the Market* (1985), and (with Dan W. Brock) *Deciding for Others: The Ethics of Surrogate Decisionmaking* (1989). In 1982 Professor Buchanan served as staff philosopher for the President's Commission on Medical Ethics.

Index